GAME ON

GAME ON

Why College Admission
Is Rigged
and How to
Beat the System

SUSAN F. PATERNO

ST. MARTIN'S PRESS
New York

First published in the United States by St. Martin's Press,
an imprint of St. Martin's Publishing Group

GAME ON. Copyright © 2021 by Susan F. Paterno.
All rights reserved. Printed in the United States of America.
For information, address St. Martin's Publishing Group,
120 Broadway, New York, NY 10271.

www.stmartins.com

Design by Donna Sinisgalli Noetzel

Library of Congress Cataloging-in-Publication Data

Names: Paterno, Susan F., author.
Title: Game on : why college admission is rigged and how to beat the system /
    Susan F. Paterno.
Description: First edition. | New York : St. Martin's Press, 2021. | Includes index.
Identifiers: LCCN 2020057567 | ISBN 9781250622648 (hardcover) |
    ISBN 9781250622655 (ebook)
Subjects: LCSH: Universities and colleges—United States—Admission. |
    College costs—United States. | College choice—United States.
Classification: LCC LB2351.2 .P375 2021 | DDC 378.1/610973—dc23
LC record available at https://lccn.loc.gov/2020057567

Our books may be purchased in bulk for promotional,
educational, or business use. Please contact your local bookseller
or the Macmillan Corporate and Premium Sales Department
at 1-800-221-7945, extension 5442, or by email at
MacmillanSpecialMarkets@macmillan.com.

First Edition: 2021

10 9 8 7 6 5 4 3 2 1

To my sons and daughters, who graciously allowed
me to Boswell their lives. And to their dad, Robert,
on whose constant intercession I rely for help.
I'm blessed to be among the lucky few writers
married to a brilliant editor.

Contents

Note to Readers

The material in this publication is intended to provide general guidelines and is for informational purposes only. Although this publication is designed to offer current, accurate, and clear information, the subjects covered involve rapidly changing policies, processes, and laws. The publication is sold with the understanding that neither the author nor the publisher is engaged in rendering professional services. Readers should not regard this publication as a substitute for legal, investment, or other professional advice and, if professional advice or other expert assistance is required, the services of a competent professional should be sought.

The publisher makes no representations or warranties to readers or users with respect to the accuracy or completeness of the contents in this publication, makes no warranties of merchantability or fitness for a particular purpose, and specifically disclaims any responsibility for any liability, loss, or risk (financial, personal, or otherwise) that may be claimed or incurred as a consequence, directly or indirectly, of the use and/or application of any of this material.

Reference in this publication to products, websites, and other potential sources of additional information does not mean that the publisher endorses such products or the information or recommendations in such sources.

Introduction

This book came out of my journey through the college admissions industrial complex, a pilgrimage I've taken with four children over two decades. I've experienced the changes I document, stumbling as the landscape became darker and more disorienting. Desperation drove me to dial Rick Singer in 2016, three years before he was arrested for masterminding the largest criminal conspiracy ever to influence undergraduate admissions. Thankfully, he never called back. Celebrities Felicity Huffman and Lori Loughlin, now convicted felons, probably wish Singer hadn't returned their calls either.

If anyone could, I should have seen the traps. I've been a professional journalist since the 1980s and a college professor for nearly three decades. For six years, I was on my university's faculty admissions committee sorting through hundreds of applicants. But even that didn't prepare me for the torturous slog that has come to characterize modern college admissions.

I want families to learn from my mistakes, to help them avoid sleazy consultants like Singer, to give them crucial information to stay ahead of the changes and make the college search less opaque, frustrating, and frightening. I'd cheered two sons as they graduated from the University of California in the early 2000s, and a daughter as she'd opened acceptances from Harvard and Yale a decade later. But by the time our last child started public high school in 2013, college admissions had escalated into a high-stakes game of emotional and financial survival.

I learned the truth at a 2015 workshop for parents with kids in high school called "Reducing Test Anxiety." It quickly became a fear fest, with statistics to prove that students needed the highest possible test scores and grades to get the scholarships they'd need to make college affordable. Leaving the classroom, I bumped into one of the guidance counselors and sarcastically suggested that she rename the workshop "Ratcheting Up Fear about Paying for College." She smiled. "Oh, did you like it?"

Before that night, I had no clear understanding of the connection between grades, test scores, and financial aid. That workshop taught me how colleges use financial aid to recruit the best-prepped and highest-achieving students. That was not how I remembered my own journey to college. When I graduated debt-free from Occidental College in 1980, tuition was $5,000. It's now close to $53,000 plus nearly $18,000 for room, board, and expenses—more than $70,000 a year, unaffordable for my husband and me, two teachers.

My husband paid his way through the University of Colorado in the 1970s as a cook in the dining hall, then as a caregiver for the sons of a faculty member. We had been married a few years by 1996, when my oldest stepson applied to the University of California, Berkeley, stress-free. It cost us $12,000 a year for room, board, and tuition. Three years later, his younger brother applied to the University of Santa Cruz, also stress-free. It cost $15,000 a year. Hassle-free government loans made it easy for us to borrow $160,000 to pay for both. That was our first big mistake.

By the time our third child started talking about college in 2008, we were in a precarious financial situation. We'd fallen into what Andrew Ferguson, author of the book *Crazy U*, calls the "bottom quintile of the lower upper-middle class," highly educated but unable to afford private colleges without loans or significant tuition discounts. She told us she wanted to go east for college, maybe to Middlebury, Bowdoin, Amherst, Wesleyan, Carleton, or Williams. Her first choice was Swarthmore.

"Swarthmore?" I asked, puzzled, vaguely remembering the name from the Mamas and the Papas' pop hit "Creeque Alley." I had no clue it was one of the best colleges in the nation. "Why do you want to go to Swarthmore?"

The intellectual fervor! The honors program! The small classes! The research opportunities!

"OK," I said. "Apply to *Swarth*more," I said.

"It's '*Swath*more,'" she said, correcting me. "No *r*."

Her journey to college was befuddling, like her childhood obsession with the soundtrack to the musical *Carousel*. We nicknamed her Boo, after Buddha, an old soul trapped in a toddler's body. Before preschool one day she pronounced, "No gold is worth your love." She quoted Eleanor Roosevelt to chase away a third-grade bully and exhausted us with intellectual pursuits. In fourth grade, we spent hours in thrift shops looking for the perfect Eva Perón Halloween costume. She'd planned and executed every birthday party and family vacation on meager budgets since she was ten.

In ninth grade, she began researching colleges as though she were writing a doctoral thesis, and obsessively reading the *New York Times* college admissions blog *The Choice*. By tenth grade she'd expanded her college list to include Harvard and Yale, an alarming development given the single-digit acceptance rates. It seemed a prescription for disappointment. "At least she's not interested in Stanford," I told a friend the next day at lunch.

My friend had spent years compulsively plotting her son's admission to a top-tier liberal arts college. I wanted to know her thoughts about my plan to convince Boo to apply to Occidental. "She's a legacy. She'll get in."

"You're not seriously going to let her go *there*?" She sniffed. "A second-tier college?"

"Occidental? Second tier? Says who?"

She scoffed. "Clearly you haven't seen the latest *U.S. News* rankings. Have you hired a coach yet?"

"We're still paying off college loans for the boys. So, no."

"Look at the rankings," she said. "And be careful what you wish for."

As Boo's senior year approached, I was both anxious and conflicted. I considered myself the mom equivalent of Garfield, the orange tabby who prioritized food and sleep over work. College admissions was bringing out the Tiger Mom stereotype. Though I hated myself for it, I called a private admissions consultant. No hourly services available, she said, only high-priced packages. The consultant agreed to accept Boo as a "senior-year emergency" for $7,500. Each consultant I called said the same, some dismissively telling me I was remiss in waiting until senior year. Good parents hire coaches in middle school, one said. "Good luck."

We urged Boo to make an appointment as quickly as possible with her school guidance counselor. It was early September, plenty of time, I figured, for them to pick target schools and organize applications.

A week passed, and no appointment. Two weeks passed. I was getting worried. By the time Boo's guidance counselor responded with a November appointment, we were in pitched battles about the number of applications to submit. I had applied to three colleges, was accepted to two, was wait-listed at the other. Boo wanted to apply to eighteen. She had friends applying to twenty and more, submissions that each required a half dozen unique essays, often with supplemental portfolios that involved massive work.

I appealed to her counselor for an earlier appointment to sort out the mess. She lectured me about letting Boo take ownership of the process. It's a common and tone-deaf mandate high school counselors give families. Asking a teenager to independently manage more than a dozen college applications is like handing the controls to a pilot who learned to fly on a video game, then demanding she land the plane successfully.

I took my friend's advice and hired a professional, a local child psychologist who had DIYed one daughter to Oberlin and another to Harvard. We paid $65 an hour for eight sessions. She didn't promise much beyond helping her meet deadlines, but that was good enough for Swarthmore, I figured. When it was over, we'd paid a little more than $2,000 for her to apply: $470 to the College Board to take five AP tests; another $150 to the College Board to take the SAT and send scores; another $150 to the College Board to take five Subject Tests; $150 to a coach who did nothing but advise Boo to take the ACT; $62.50 to take the ACT; $520 to the therapist/coach; and $660 in application fees.

From January to March, we waited. The first rejection arrived in a slim envelope: Swarthmore. I held the letter to a window to make out the words, regretting every Garfield mom decision I'd ever made. I recalled wistfully the Mother's Day card Boo gave me, "Treasure the one who lightens the burden of anyone else." Holding the letter to the light, I decided to hide it without telling anyone. That's when her eleven-year-old sister walked into the room.

"What are you doing?" she asked.

I begged her to keep the secret. "With you it'll be different," I promised.

"You're right," she said. "Because if I have to go through what she just did, I'm not going to college."

Boo's little sister, Stevie, had developed the perplexing habit of challenging every parenting decision by demanding, "What evidence do you have to support your opinion? I need facts." We'd nicknamed her Punky, after the pint-size, punk-inspired, precocious progenitor of "girl power" Punky Brewster. She was warm and bright, with a wicked sense of humor. In middle school, she stumbled on "pusillanimous" in a book and pranked friends and family by throwing it into every conversation. She gave me Grumpy Cat slippers for Christmas, a homemade "Garfield Mom" candle for my birthday, and a T-shirt for Mother's Day that reads "Assume Nothing."

When she started ninth grade, I received emails from her guidance counselor urging parents to start prepping children for the SAT and ACT right away.

"As in now?" I asked.

"Never too early to start thinking about it!"

I didn't care where Stevie went to college. I only wanted to make sure we could afford it. Harvard and Yale had accepted Boo, and both offered financial aid that made tuition less than what it would have cost for her to go to the University of California. She chose Harvard, which is where I called her to beg for help with Stevie's applications.

"I'll help," Boo said. "But it's a lot harder to get into college now than it was when I was applying. Plus, you know Stevie. She goes her own way."

"I don't care," I said. "Just tell me what I have to do."

Her first order: Find a math tutor.

As so many parents know, math is nothing like it was for us. Math classes were turned upside down in the last decade with a new pedagogy called the "flipped classroom." In the flipped classroom, students struggle through new material at home and are expected to ask questions in class the next day about what they don't understand. For students who don't understand what they don't understand, math classes became punishing lessons in futility. Teachers without adequate training and with forty students each period pushed students through difficult concepts with no time to linger before moving to the next lesson.

Stragglers had to figure it out alone or ask their parents to hire tutors. An entire industry of tutoring companies had sprung up to service desperate parents like me—Wyzant, TutorNerds, Varsity Tutors, and Cardinal Education all competed for my attention and money. Though Stevie needed a tutor, we just couldn't afford one. We were spending $800 a month to pay back student loans for our sons; $1,550 a month for Harvard tuition; $1,800 a month for health insurance; an $1,800-a-month mortgage; $200-a-month car payments; $555 mandatory monthly fees to the public charter school; plus utilities, food, insurance, property taxes, and medical bills not covered by insurance. We'd refinanced the house twice. Even with two professional salaries we had about $50 per week left for discretionary spending—if we stopped takeout, Starbucks, and cable. I called Boo in Boston.

"How do I find a math tutor for $25 an hour?"

"I don't know. Google it?"

The next day I was in a Lyft to the airport for a business trip. In chatting with the driver, the conversation turned to my tutor search.

"I'm a tutor," he said cheerily.

His name was David, and he charged $175 an hour for in-person tutoring in Los Angeles and $85 an hour for online sessions with affluent clients in Texas and on the East Coast. "These parents are so intense," he said. "Their kid gets a 1550 on the SAT and the parents pay for more sessions so they can get a 1600." He called the SAT and ACT "a great deception. They're not a measure of college readiness.

They're a measure of how well you understand the design of the exam."

The test sellers pitch propaganda to high school teachers, administrators, and parents. "Everybody regurgitates the lies because they can't unearth the truth." He commiserated with me about finding a good, affordable tutor. Tutoring and test prep, he said, "is a universe unto itself, and parents don't know about it until they're sucked into it."

"If you're making such good money," I asked, "why do you drive for Lyft?"

"To relax."

Sophomore year was transforming my once-cheery Stevie into a gloomy, dejected, depressed cog in the public school machine. It was too late in the year to transfer to an easier math class, the principal said. He offered suffering and failure as options. I appealed to the guidance counselor. She suggested hiring a private tutor but had none to recommend. "Maybe ask her teacher?"

A compassionate and patient man, her teacher was so devoted to his students that he arrived at 6:30 a.m. every day to help them. Because Stevie took the bus forty-five minutes each way, she arrived on campus after his sessions ended. Getting to school early required my husband to leave the house at 5:45 a.m., fight commuter traffic, drop her at 6:30 a.m., then rush home to start work by 8 a.m.

A sidebar on my heroic husband. He had no fear of waking growling teenagers at 6 a.m. He served hot breakfasts and made sack lunches, writing dad jokes on paper napkins. He enforced the family's eight-hours-of-sleep rule and showed no sympathy when they begged for more time to finish homework. He supported, but didn't endorse, my college admissions strategies. He often responded to my plans with an eye roll. "You're amazing," he'd say, and not in a good way.

Somehow, he convinced Stevie to get up at 5:15 a.m. I watched the Honda's taillights fade as they headed to school in darkness. She arrived at 6:30 a.m. and found a line ten kids deep waiting for help. By the time the first-period bell rang, she hadn't reached the front.

We had to find a tutor. But where? And how? I waded through online profiles, looking for the cheapest tutors with the best reviews. I hired one from Varsity, one from Wyzant, and one out of a booth at Panera. My husband found two more at the high school where he teaches, and a friend referred another.

Each failed after a week or two. Stevie blasted through them with the efficiency of Murphy Brown firing incompetent assistants, a half dozen in quick succession, leaving us deeply frustrated about paying for nothing.

"What's wrong with them? Can't you find one you like?"

Two had a cursory grasp of the concepts, she said. One was faking it. Three were just mean. She was right, of course.

By then, the College of William & Mary had emerged as a front-runner. A public university in Virginia, William & Mary is adjacent to Colonial Williamsburg, where we'd spent a fun family vacation. It had a 35 percent acceptance rate, hardly an Ivy League stretch.

I called Boo. "Does she really need to take AP calculus for William & Mary?"

"She does if you want her to get a merit scholarship," she said. "Otherwise you'll have to pay something like $70,000 for out-of-state tuition and room and board."

I plunged back into the shadowy swap meet of smarmy sellers. Wandering lost among the merchants, I encountered one repugnant vendor after another. Excellent tutors exist, but how to find them? I channeled my inner Garfield mom to find peace in giving up. I read *The Gift of Failure, The Blessing of a Skinned Knee, The Blessing of a B Minus,* and *How to Raise an Adult: Break Free of the Overparenting Trap and Prepare Your Kid for Success.* All were interesting but aimed at wealthy families able to pay full tuition, not parents at or below the bottom quintile of the lower upper-middle class struggling to avoid debt. Since colleges give top applicants the best discounts, high math scores correlate with lower tuition and less debt. I had to keep going. I asked counselors, teachers, and parents for tutor referrals. Each one was too expensive or incompetent.

I despaired of ever finding anyone. Then Greg floated into our lives, like Mary Poppins but in shorts, flip-flops, and a tank top. No one remembers who referred Greg or how I got his phone number. When he called back, I discovered he was in our price range. He accepted very few students, he warned, and never traveled more than five miles from his house. He lived a block from my parents. I begged him to meet us there the next day.

Greg arrived with no books or supplies, just an amiable, low-key, unflappable personality. He was a fitness instructor with a degree from the University of California, Berkeley, and an abiding passion for math. His fees were so much lower than other tutors that I asked him why he did it. He liked seeing students learn to love math as much as he did, he said.

Stevie took to Greg immediately. For the next three years, Greg restored order to chaos. "I would never have made it through high school without Greg," she said. "He was more like a therapist than a math tutor. I felt so stupid in math class, but Greg never made it seem like it was my fault. He made me feel valid. His enthusiasm never died. He never stopped being excited about math, about being excited to solve the next problem. The few times we couldn't solve a problem, he'd say, 'Yep, math can be frustrating!' and we'd move on."

By the end of junior year, she'd regained her confidence. Her grades were well within the range for excellent colleges. But were they good enough to get into a college that charged only what families can afford to pay?

I googled "schools that meet full financial need with no loans" and found only ten, all with tiny acceptance rates: Amherst (13 percent), Bowdoin (14 percent), Brown (9 percent), Columbia (6 percent), Harvard (5 percent), MIT (7 percent), Pomona (8 percent), Princeton (6 percent), Stanford (5 percent), and Swarthmore (12 percent).

We seemed to be playing roulette on a wheel with three choices: Golden Ticket, Tears, or Bankruptcy.

I spent the next hour on Amazon researching admissions guides. I settled on two books written by a coach named Rick Singer— yes, that one. Each slim volume had "50 Secrets"—time-intensive tasks that required starting in middle school to complete by senior year. The book pitched an admissions consulting company called The Key. The Key promised to identify Stevie's strengths, unlock her potential, choose the right college, and position her for admission. It was a local number, so I called and left a voicemail. No response. I called a week later. No response.

As Boo packed for graduate school in England, she suggested we hire someone to keep track of Stevie's applications.

"Hire someone? Aren't you doing it? For free?"

"I can't force her to meet deadlines from Cambridge," she said.

"But she refuses to let me hire anyone to help her!"

"Then you and Dad will have to do it, I guess."

"Oh, *hell no*," I said, remembering Boo's applications covering the dining room table, so many stacks of papers and files and books and articles that we had to eat on the floor the first half of her senior year. "I have to figure out a way to hire someone secretly."

"You do you, Mom."

Since Stevie still refused to work with an admissions coach, I went back to Singer's *Getting In: Personal Brands*, fifty chapters of inscrutable, contradictory, and belated advice. Chapter 34: "Build a Team." (Too late.) Chapter 41: "Don't Relax." (Duh.) Chapter 42:

"Make a New Plan." (Seriously? Make a new plan? In chapter 42 out of 50?)

I made a new plan. Motivated by the fear of impending bankruptcy, I decided to hire someone secretly and then somehow convince Stevie to use him. The least expensive was Collegewise, a chain with nearby offices. The company charged $4,200 for unlimited counseling, a budget breaker, but I gave it a go.

Managing director Paul Kanarek, the public face of the company, joined Collegewise in 2015, after starting the Princeton Review's California franchise in 1983, a spinoff of the East Coast admissions company. Kanarek had expanded the local branch to multiple cities and centers, sustaining double-digit growth for a quarter of a century before selling the Princeton Review to Bain Capital in a $60 million corporate restructuring.

In his Collegewise bio, Kanarek describes himself as a reckless teenager with an academic record so poor, "his mother would be the first to tell you that there wasn't the remotest chance of his launching a career in education." Not a ringing endorsement, but the website claimed consultants had Ivy League degrees and experience in admissions.

I called and reached Lauren. Lauren talked in rapid-fire responses that sounded simultaneously bored and peeved. "What are your credentials?" I asked. "How do you individualize programs for students? How will you find a counselor who can hit it off with my quirky daughter? Where do you get up-to-date information about what colleges want in applicants? If I buy the unlimited package, how hard is it to get an appointment?"

She gave blanket promises. If we hired Collegewise, the company would find the "right-fit" counselor. She admitted that counselor would probably be her, since she had a caseload below the required forty students. Face-to-face meetings would be tough, she added. "I'm booked for the rest of the week. But I can see her Friday for thirty minutes between 4 and 5 p.m. Or I can talk to her on the phone."

I pondered how to explain to her that I'd need to hire her secretly, and that my daughter would not be joining us.

"What if I come without my daughter?"

"We only meet with kids, not parents."

"But her high school goes from 8 a.m. to 5 p.m. Since she's so busy, maybe we can make an exception? And I can come alone?"

"No."

The next day, I asked Stevie, "Will you meet with Lauren? For just thirty minutes?"

"No."

"Will you talk to her on the phone?"

"No."

I called Boo in England. "Now what?"

"She'll be fine. Relax."

"But she has to be branded and packaged! Who's going to do that?"

Boo agreed to look at her applications and reminded me of Stevie's strong track record. "She's smart. She can figure it out."

I pivoted. "What do you think of my new plan? I'll hire an online coach and pretend to be Stevie. I'll get the information, give it to you, and you tell her it was your idea."

"That's so unnecessary. She'll be fine."

"If I hire the online coach without telling her, I'll have the information she needs even if she doesn't want to use it."

I could tell Boo was alarmed. "You do you, Mom."

I found Bill, a fresh-faced online coach with a sweet disposition and credentials I liked. He had graduated from Wake Forest University and worked for Kenyon College, an excellent liberal arts school Stevie was interested in attending. He charged only $599 for six months of unlimited online counseling.

Over the next few months, Stevie's strategies to thwart me made the Tiger Mom's defiant daughter Lulu look like an amateur. She blocked every one of my parries with a defiant toss of her head. I finally quit my relationship with Bill at the beginning of November after he tried to sell me on the Xanax of binding early admission.

"Apply early decision to Pomona College," Bill said. "It's a great school and she has an excellent chance of getting in." Her aunt, uncle, and cousin are alumni and donors, he said, "so she's a legacy. The early decision acceptance rate is 25 percent, three times higher than the rate for regular decision."

"But if they accept her," I said, "she'll have to unconditionally agree to attend. And we'll have to take whatever bargain-basement financial aid they offer. We can't afford $70,000 if they stiff us. Besides, she really doesn't want to go to Pomona."

He pushed. "But she has a great chance of being accepted. Look at the other schools on her list. All risky. With Pomona, by December 10, she'll be in, and the stress and anxiety will be over."

"Thanks," I said. "She'll think about it."

I called Boo in a panic. "I'm stuck. How do I get out of this?"

"I've gone over her applications and she has a great shot," she said. "Just relax."

"How?"

"Stop talking to these people. She'll be fine."

Stevie never applied early to Pomona and wouldn't let me read her applications. I asked what topic she'd chosen for her personal statement. Contradicting all advice I'd ever heard, she told me she'd written about a word.

"A word?" I was horrified. "*What* word?"

"Pusillanimous."

By the end of November, I needed Valium. By Christmas, when Boo returned from Cambridge on break, I needed Ativan. By the time Stevie submitted her last application at midnight on New Year's

Eve, hunched over the laptop next to her sister, we heard fireworks exploding nearby. It was over.

In March, after Boo had returned to Cambridge, Stevie was accepted to Harvard, Williams, and seven other colleges. Her safety, American University, with a 40 percent acceptance rate, rejected her. Why? Who knows?

College admissions is, like parenting, mysterious and baffling. Do the job poorly and we get Rick Singer. But how to do it right? Having somehow survived my final journey through the college admissions industrial complex, I returned with a secret: No one sells a legal magic formula to open the gates to dream colleges. Most companies in the unregulated and grossly overpriced admissions marketplace are ineffective and often useless. We keep them in business largely because, as Hamlet discovered, demons and con artists know how to exploit our weaknesses.

I called Boo to thank her for being Glinda the Good Witch to my hapless Dorothy. "With you and your sister out of house, I have a new project," I said.

"Oh no, what is it now?"

"I'm writing a book to help families find great, affordable colleges."

A great idea, she said, her tone suggesting this was just another of my wacky plans. "You do you, Mom."

1

The Culling

How Applying to College Became Brutal

If anyone seemed headed to the Ivy League, it was Dayo Adetu. Dayo was a scholar and athlete at Sidwell Friends, the Harvard of Washington, D.C.'s private schools, now a $46,490-a-year hyperselective college prep that has educated the children of four US presidents.

Dayo scored in the 96th percentile on the SAT, was ranked thirty-seventh nationally in track-and-field, earned a B average in the high school's most demanding courses, and was one of a few African Americans at an academically rigorous Ivy League feeder. To ensure student success, Sidwell provides a dizzying array of counseling services unavailable to 99 percent of America's high school students.

Counselors meet regularly and individually with students and parents. They arrange tutors, an in-house specialist to help with SAT prep, and a "learning support coordinator" to assist with accommodations for standardized testing. In return, Sidwell demands far more from students than most high schools in America and rewards parents with the highest-quality coaches to guide their children to college. Its handbook reassures families that counselors "will stay in touch with admissions officers, making sure they have all the necessary documents required to 'read' students correctly," so admissions officers see "their particular strengths coming through loud and clear."

Dayo started Sidwell in kindergarten. By senior year she had won a National Achievement Scholarship and was an Advanced Placement Scholar, a National Merit Commended Student, and the only African American girl in her tenth-grade accelerated math class.

As captain of Sidwell's track-and-field team, she met with coaches from Princeton, Columbia, and Brown. Princeton's athletics department sent her a letter of support, and Columbia's coaches placed her on a preferred list. Her senior year, she took rigorous classes, competed in track meets, visited colleges, and worked with her counselors to complete a dozen elite college applications.

She applied to Yale, Harvard, Princeton, Columbia, Cornell, the University of Pennsylvania, MIT, Caltech, Johns Hopkins, the University of Virginia, and McGill. She thought she had what it took to get in—she was an underrepresented student of color with good grades and an award-winning athlete. Comparing her to others in her class, her counselor rated Dayo "excellent," one level below the highest possible rank, reserved for a rare few. She described Dayo as "self-reliant, responsible, and determined." Her history teacher also gave Dayo an overall "excellent" rating, and described her as "outstanding" in four categories: intellectual promise, work habits, motivation, and integrity. He called her "reflective, thoughtful, intellectual, insightful, and well-rounded."

Not so long ago, an impressive record of achievement like hers would have guaranteed admission to almost every college on her list. For Dayo, though, it wasn't enough. Of 126 students in her class, she was the only one who didn't receive at least one unqualified offer of admission. Hard work, academic demands, exhausting schedules, financial sacrifices, worry, uncertainty, doubt, anxiety, and depression brought her a dozen rejection letters. Her family sued Sidwell, insisting school officials had discriminated and retaliated against Dayo, sabotaging her chances of getting into the colleges she wanted to attend.

The saga of Dayo Adetu illuminates the myth of the perfect fit. Students long for a Hogwarts Sorting Hat. What they get is a brutal culling. Anyone inside the turbulent world of college admissions has heard anguished parents tell similar stories, though probably not as extreme. Applying to elite colleges is the equivalent of a years-long death march to an unknowable destination, accompanied by deep despair and occasional shreds of hope.

It makes sense that the decision is so fraught. A degree is the best way to boost income, family stability, and health over a lifetime. Americans without degrees say they feel more pain, drink more, and die more often from "deaths of despair," according to a report by the Kaiser Family Foundation. Two-thirds of all jobs will require education beyond high school in the coming decade, a Georgetown University study reports. And apart from maybe a house, a college degree is the largest expense most Americans incur in a lifetime.

Once based on financial need, scholarships and grants are increasingly going to highly prepped, high-scoring applicants with the best grades in the hardest classes, regardless of family income. Receiving an acceptance letter from a selective college, or graduating with little or no debt, requires navigating an immense and daunting global marketplace that has grown exponentially in just two decades. Given the current crisis in college funding, it's no surprise that hiring admissions consultants is commonplace.

Teens with their sights set on selective schools walk a lonely road paved with fear, crowded with hordes of sellers hawking contradictory advice and competing for the billions of dollars families spend to get their kids into "dream colleges."

Unregulated and increasingly digital, this bizarre bazaar is rife with unpredictable prices, no rules beyond maximizing profit, and scams that target families at all income levels. Vendors range from mom-and-pop entrepreneurs to billion-dollar corporations. Many share similar marketing strategies. They prey on the uncertainty families feel about their children's futures, reinforcing the confusion that surrounds college admissions. Stoking parents' deepest fears for their children, they then exploit them by selling the same message: You will fail without us.

As elite degrees become more coveted and less available, even wealthy families face never-before-seen barriers they have no idea how to overcome. The crisis stems largely from America's misplaced obsession with top-ranked colleges.

Fewer than 4 percent of applicants attend the most selective colleges—those with admission rates under 20 percent—and fewer than 1 percent enroll in Ivy League schools, MIT, and Stanford. The national media keep a laser focus on elite colleges—often on journalists' own alma maters and their aspirations for their own children. In a frantic search for affordable degrees, families unwilling or unable to buy into the admissions marketplace are forced to participate anyway. They pay thousands of dollars for high-stakes admissions tests. They pay for the prep required to score well, to send results to colleges for applications, scholarships, and financial aid. They pay transcript fees and for travel to required auditions or to "demonstrate interest" and curry favor with colleges for tuition discounts.

In slick ads and media marketing pitches, colleges hint at qualifications students need to get accepted. Too often, though, especially at the most selective colleges, the criteria are kept deliberately mysterious, confounding students trying to parse the precise measures they must meet for admission. Those seemingly unsolvable riddles have produced a Hydra-like admissions industrial complex claiming to sell certainty.

Getting into college is not the same as paying for it, as the nation's $1.5 trillion in student debt attests. Only a few dozen colleges nationwide promise to charge what families can afford—all elite schools, with billion-dollar endowments and generous aid. They also routinely reject 90 percent or more of their applicants, admitting more students with family incomes in the top 1 percent than in the bottom 60 percent.

Money and fear drive admissions at every income level, contributing to the crippling anxiety so many teens feel about getting into college. While rates of depression, anxiety, and substance abuse are highest among affluent teens, the vast majority of high school students grapple with the fear that earning a degree is a dream beyond their grasp. That worry is real. Those born in 1980 to the highest-income families were several times more likely to earn degrees than middle- and moderate-income Americans, a 2018 study in the journal *Demography* reported. More than half who start college drop out within six years, and only 33 percent of Americans ages twenty-five and older hold a bachelor's degree. Students report unprecedented angst, academic pressure, and rejections from dream colleges, crushing them emotionally and financially. How did it come to this?

The Birth of College: Expansion and Exclusion

Applying to college today means wading through a maze of unfamiliar jargon and acronyms. It begins with registering for the AP, SAT, ACT, the Common App, the FAFSA, the CSS Profile. It continues with personal statements and supplemental essays; assembling arts portfolios and athletics profiles; facing endless digital delays and frustrating broken links; and challenging, punishing, continual deadlines. The journey from high school to college has changed drastically since the Puritans founded Harvard, America's first college, in 1636.

Higher education's objective was clear then: educate the nation's spiritual and scholarly leaders. By the mid-eighteenth century, America's colleges had grown to ten institutions that admitted a few wealthy white men, trained them in religion and classics, and sent them off to become ministers, lawyers, and teachers.

Abraham Lincoln believed that to prosper, the nation needed citizens educated in science and the liberal arts. On education he wrote, "I can only say that I view it as the most important subject which we as a people can be engaged in."

Intended for white men, higher education was expanded under the 1862 Morrill Act to establish and subsidize at least one public university in every state to teach agriculture, science, military tactics, mechanics, engineering, and classics. Land grants funded sixty-nine colleges, including Cornell, the Massachusetts Institute of Technology, and the University of Wisconsin–Madison. The act was amended late in the century to include money for several of what became historically Black colleges and universities.

Small, private liberal arts colleges were established to help men transition from rural farms to complex urban careers. Barred from higher education by law and custom, women and people of color had few educational options outside of churches and seminaries.

Those barriers began to fall during the progressive late nineteenth century, when high school became compulsory and women started prying open the college gates. Women championed a new commitment to egalitarianism and social reform. Progressives saw education as a key to equality, even as legal discrimination continued. Large-scale migrations of Southern Blacks to Northern cities after World War I, and after the Great Depression, sent millions into urban areas seeking opportunity. The Great Migration provoked an intense debate among intellectuals about how to best educate the new urban masses. Out of that debate was born the archetype for modern college admissions, a plan conceived and implemented by Harvard's James Bryant Conant.

The Tyranny of the Test

James Bryant Conant was a prominent scientist, political figure, and educational leader. As president of Harvard in 1933, Conant embraced a notion, gaining currency at the time, that admission to higher education should be based on merit, not rank or class. He wanted to admit men with intellectual promise from all walks of life rather than simply doing what Harvard and the Ivy League had always done: accept privileged students from northeastern prep schools based on an essay exam.

With the assistant dean of faculty, Henry Chauncey, Conant adapted an instrument called the Scholastic Aptitude Test to determine admission to Harvard. Pioneered in the 1920s by eugenicist Carl Brigham, the SAT allegedly predicted success in higher education based on native intelligence.

Conant and Chauncey used a version of the SAT to award scholarships at Harvard throughout the 1930s, hoping to replace the existing elite prep-school boys' club with a technocracy based on merit rather than on heritage, wealth, or social status. They waged a ten-year campaign to streamline admissions, consolidating IQ and essay admissions testing into the Educational Testing Service, known as ETS.

After resigning from Harvard, Chauncey went to Princeton to direct the ETS in 1946. The ETS was the first to develop and administer widespread admissions testing for members of the College Board, now numbering more than six thousand colleges and universities.

The SAT was intended to be a great equalizer, a test to identify the best and the brightest. In fact, elite universities continued to use quotas to admit all but white Christian men, a barrier of bigotry for women, students of color, and Jews.

Quotas, for example, kept Stanley Kaplan, the Jewish son of a Brooklyn plumber, out of medical school. Kaplan graduated at the top of his City College class. But, after filling ethnic quotas, all five of the city's medical schools rejected him. In 1938, as Chauncey and Conant were launching the SAT, Kaplan decided to start a for-profit tutoring company to prepare students for high-stakes admissions testing.

Kaplan reverse engineered the test, then coached students to beat it. He spent hours debriefing test takers to create practice sessions based on the test's questions and answers. He drilled students on test-taking strategies and alerted them to penalties assessed for guessing. "Acquiring test-taking skills is the same as learning to play the piano or ride a bicycle," Kaplan wrote in *Test Pilot: How I Broke Testing Barriers for Millions of Students and Caused a Sonic Boom in the Business of Education.* "It requires practice, practice, practice. Repetition breeds familiarity. Familiarity breeds confidence."

Kaplan's timing was fortuitous. Within a decade, the SAT had become the college admissions gatekeeper for millions of high school applicants. The number of Americans applying to four-year colleges after World War II boomed. Within two decades, lawmakers had passed the 1964 Civil Rights Act; the 1965 Higher Education Act; and Title IX, the 1972 Education Amendments giving women access to federal financial aid. The number of college applicants grew to record highs.

The College Board insisted the SAT was an intelligence test that couldn't be gamed. But Kaplan proved otherwise. The strategies Kaplan taught produced significant score gains, as much as 100 points, he said, a claim the College Board and the Educational Testing Service attacked. The myth-busting Kaplan became a self-described "thorn in the side" of the test makers, a reluctant nemesis. He believed in the

SAT, but not as an intelligence test. The SAT tested acquired knowledge, not innate intellect, he said, and he could teach students how to beat it. Pitting the College Board against Kaplan, the federal government investigated "and declared us the winner," Kaplan wrote in his autobiography. Coaching, in fact, improved students' scores an average of 50 points, the government concluded in 1979.

Kaplan's business exploded, triggering a multibillion-dollar industry that became rife with cheating and corruption. Within a few years, hundreds of businesses flooded the market—from $1,000-an-hour entrepreneurs to multimillion-dollar companies like the Princeton Review, Varsity Tutors, and Kaplan Inc., a corporation worth $1.5 billion. Paying for test prep helped monied students improve scores and gain wealth advantages now standard in college admissions.

Rankings, Reagan, and Retailing

The triumph of high-stakes admissions testing provided a lucrative business opportunity for a dying newsweekly. Using admitted students' test scores as a main gauge of institutional quality, *U.S. News & World Report* created "Best Colleges," an annual college-rankings guide.

Rankings turned the choice of a college from an educational matter to a high-stakes economic and social transaction, the *New York Times* reported in 1997. College rankings became profitable beyond its creators' wildest dreams, helping *U.S. News* morph from a newsweekly to an advertising and marketing juggernaut.

The rise of rankings inflamed convulsive changes that led to the current state of hypercompetitive admissions. From World War II to 1980, it was widely accepted that young people were entitled to affordable, decent, quality higher education, said Richard Freeland, former Massachusetts commissioner of higher education. Then came Ronald Reagan. Reagan began dismantling Great Society programs that promoted social and racial equality, rebranding them as "entitlements." Need-based financial aid became "one of those entitlements that we created in the 1970s that was excessive," Reagan's budget director David Stockman told Congress in 1981. "We could probably cut it a lot more."

Free-market lawmakers reduced middle-class tuition subsidies, shifting more costs to students and their families. Legal, social, cultural, governmental, economic, technological, and demographic shifts in the 1980s and 1990s created a bewildering perfect storm that continues to batter higher education today. "People started viewing public higher education not as a social obligation to the youth of the country, but as a benefit," Freeland said. "The whole equation flipped."

Private colleges restructured and adopted market-driven practices that drove up tuition. Administrators hired enrollment managers to attract as many applicants as possible—partly due to pressure to improve rankings, but also to keep seats filled. By rejecting a higher percentage of students, colleges improved their rank, which, in turn, intensified competition and ensured the enrollment needed to meet revenue goals.

Airline deregulation produced cheap fares that allowed students to apply to colleges far from home and visit campuses to demonstrate interest to admissions officers. The growing number of high school graduates and college-eligible students broke records. Low supply and high demand forced students to compete more intensely for admission to selective public universities and the few private colleges that asked families to pay only what they could afford.

Colleges used the ease and power of the Internet to market themselves to far more students than they had ever reached before. Slickly packaged brochures and websites featured alluring photos of ivy-covered, redbrick, gold-leafed, and whitewashed nineteenth-century architecture. No longer did students submit paper forms through the mail. Digital technology permitted them to submit a limitless number of applications using the Web-based portal for the Common

Application. With one Common App form, students could apply to 20 of the more than 900 member colleges. It requires students' personal information, including parental employment, education, extracurricular activities, and essays with 650-word limits.

The Common App went from routing a few thousand applications a year in the late 1970s to processing more than four million in 2019. For families new to college applications, however, the Common App can be a confusing rabbit hole, requiring documents that can take up to a month to collect.

Big Tuitions, Big Discounts

The Common App's multimillion-dollar transformation parallels the rise of an academic arms race. Using data analysis, algorithms, and financial aid optimization software, enrollment managers boosted application numbers and then recruited the highest-achieving students with steep discounts, triggering a precipitous increase in tuition.

College tuition rose faster than inflation, partly due to administrative bloat. The number of administrators grew 60 percent, ten times the rate of growth of tenured faculty members between 1993 and 2009, according to a Bloomberg study. Critics attacked the new business model—and its reliance on profit-motivated partnerships with private corporations—as intellectually bankrupt.

Higher education was fast becoming a corporate-sponsored training program for student-customers. Liberal arts colleges and universities transformed from protectors of shared culture into multinational corporations "driven by market forces, more interested in profit margin than in thought," argued Oxford scholar Bill Readings in *The University in Ruins*. And the customers just kept coming.

Priced out of private colleges, highly qualified middle-class students fled to public universities. To lure back academic superstars—students who raise a school's rankings—private colleges dangled "merit scholarships," slashing tuition for even the wealthiest applicants. Colleges use merit aid "to get students in the doors," said Stephen Burd, an analyst with the policy think tank New America. "And if they can get wealthier students, that's even better."

Administrators had a perverse motivation to tolerate numbers-driven admissions. Hold out the possibility of merit aid, and more students apply. The more applicants, the more students a college rejects. The more rejected students, the lower the acceptance rate. The lower the acceptance rate, the better the ranking.

The more prestigious and exclusive that Americans think a college is, the more they're willing to spend whatever it takes to attend. Students now routinely apply to a dozen or more colleges, stoking the fires of selectivity. Some counselors encourage—and sometimes require—students to file dozens of applications, a scattershot approach that costs thousands of dollars in fees alone.

Buying Advantage

James Bryant Conant's dream of establishing a new, meritocratic elite based on intelligence rather than inherited wealth created, over time, the very inequality he had hoped to eliminate. To find right-fit colleges, misguided counselors urge families to book the equivalent of the nineteenth-century grand tour. Rival private jet companies have forged successful partnerships with elite consultants, charging hundreds of thousands of dollars for all-inclusive packages that provide wealthy students appointments with campus power brokers to curry favor with admissions officers. For everybody else, if they can afford campus visits at all, the grand tour to college is a stressful road trip in a cramped car with a surly teenager complaining about shared bathrooms in barely affordable budget motels.

Elite admissions is now an extreme sport, inspiring fraud, cheating, and disreputable merchants selling dubious products. The worst offender, criminal mastermind Rick Singer, found an eager market in the uberrich willing to buy his too-good-to-be-true side-door-guaranteeing admission to elite colleges. Capitalizing on a wildly profitable niche, Singer helped funnel millions of dollars in bribes to coaches and university officials.

Singer's arrest—along with dozens of celebrities, financiers, and titans of industry—put a blinding spotlight on the current crisis in college admissions. As villainous as Singer is, he's a distraction, a bit player in the Wild West of a multibillion-dollar college admissions industrial complex. Con artists worldwide have been plying the same trade for at least a decade. Ten years ago, Gerald and Lily Chow paid more than $2 million to admissions consultant Mark Zimny after he promised he'd help usher their sons into elite American universities, including Harvard. When the Chows became suspicious about Zimny, they sued him and his company, IvyAdmit. The Chows discovered that some of the payments they'd made to Zimny to "grease the admission wheels," as he'd promised, went to his personal bank account instead.

More recently a media-dubbed Tiger Mom enrolled her daughter in Manhattan-based Ivy Coach's premium plan—at a cost of $1.5 million. Though her daughter was admitted to an Ivy League college, the mother paid only half the fee. Ivy Coach sued, defending its costs without irony: "Parents appreciate that it is worth investing to help their children earn admission to an outstanding school, when they'd otherwise earn admission to only a pretty good school." (Ivy Coach dropped the lawsuit.)

Even bribes are more common than anyone suspects, according to former admissions officer Hillary Reinsberg. In a BuzzFeed essay, Reinsberg describes parents offering her cash, fancy dinners, and better jobs in exchange for getting their kids admitted to the selective college where she worked. For the right price, corrupt teachers and therapists will write bogus letters to give kids more time on standardized tests, crooked SAT proctors will allow flagrant cheating, and coaches will take kickbacks and bribes to put unqualified kids on recruited-athlete lists.

The Failure of Free-Market Lawmakers

Americans now owe $1.5 trillion in student debt, creating a public backlash against higher education. Fear of being barred from the door to prosperity has bred simmering resentment. Exploiting that resentment, Donald Trump deflected blame and attacked universities as breeding grounds for monied elites like him. Ironically, billionaire Trump led an army of multimillionaires to destroy the ladder that once allowed Americans to climb out of poverty. He halted loan relief, eliminated safeguards to prevent abusive and illegal lending practices, and tried to cut tuition subsidies to needy students, policies his successor, Joe Biden, has promised to reverse.

While tuition costs climb, need-based financial aid has declined by triple digits and funding for public higher education in some states has decreased 50 percent since 2008. Fierce competition has fueled public anger. Families look at universities as "gatekeepers to success in society," said Tulane University president Mike Fitts. "They can't feel like they're shut out and their kids are shut out."

For the first time, the federal government is taxing academia and rewriting the Higher Education Act to make college more expensive and less affordable. Trump-supporting Republicans want to limit the amount students can borrow but refuse to increase funding for need-based financial aid.

Reducing subsidized loans pushes students into the arms of

private lenders and restricts low- and middle-income students from accessing funds they need to pursue degrees. Lucrative jobs that once required no more than high school diplomas are long gone thanks to globalization, automation, and the decline in manufacturing. "We're creating a permanent underclass in America based on education," said Brit Kirwan, former chancellor of the University of Maryland. "That's something we've never had before."

The academic arms race has given the private sector unprecedented business opportunities, spawning an economy with profit motivations that have little to do with equal access to a better life. "Republicans [want to] starve the public sector in order to 'open' higher education for business" by raising prices and increasing college debt, said Sara Goldrick-Rab, founding director of the Hope Center for College. "And most of the public appears to be unaware."

The Winning Formula

Given the odds stacked against them, how can families win the Hunger Games of higher ed? By making the rules work in their favor.

First, it's a numbers game.

Too many students apply only to elite or selective colleges with acceptance rates in the single digits or low teens, without realizing how little chance they have of being accepted. The first obstacle is overcoming the academic index score. Colleges with the highest barriers to entry require applicants to meet certain academic benchmarks to get to the first competitive decision-making round. To quickly review applications, many evaluators calculate student grades and test scores into a single number.

Nearly all colleges and universities publish the average test scores and grades for admitted students. At Columbia, Harvard, Princeton, and Yale, for example, 75 percent of accepted students score between 1470 and 1490 out of 1600 on the SAT or between 31 and 33 out of 36 on the ACT. Those same schools report average admitted students' grade point averages between 3.9 for Princeton and 4.2 for Harvard.

Second, hooks help the wealthy.

Students admitted to elite colleges with middling grades and test scores usually have "hooks," or unknown, unstated advantages. Applicants with hooks—children of alumni and faculty, athletic recruits, celebrities, donors, families with the potential to do massive fundraising—enjoy special privileges everyone else yearns to have.

Ivy League hopefuls without hooks need to be superstars to stand out in a crowded field of stellar applicants. They need to excel in academics—math, science, humanities—and score in the top 1 to 2 percent on high-stakes admissions tests. They need to curate publicly recognized and award-winning accomplishments, as artists or writers or scientists or humanitarians or linguists or environmentalists or filmmakers or public servants or nationally ranked athletes. But even that isn't enough. They also have to convince elite colleges that they'll go on to great achievement in life.

Third, elite colleges expect applicants to have a fervent support team of education professionals cheerleading for them.

Lackluster backing from high school administrators, counselors, and teachers puts even students with the highest academic index score in the elite college reject pile. While struggling for an

A over an A– or an A– over a B+ might seem petty, Ivy League aspirants need the highest scores and the most laudatory letters of recommendation possible. At the best prep and suburban high schools, students compete fiercely for the few slots elite colleges give them.

The highest-achieving students from low-ranked high schools often do better in college admissions than middle-ranked students at top-ranked preps. Why? Top-ranked high schools produce hyper-competitive superstars battling to win recommendations from the same few teachers and counselors. At lower-ranked schools, super-stars stand out, attract the attention of influential counselors, and land the flattering letters admissions officers expect.

Fourth, the process is so secretive that colleges can reject students with impunity and no explanation.

Private—and some public—colleges and universities use holistic criteria to evaluate candidates based on intangibles beyond grades and test scores. Colleges define the subjective qualities they seek in students using their financial, social, cultural, and political goals. Those priorities, rarely made public, change annually.

So many applicants have perfect or near-perfect grades and scores that the Ivy League can fill their classes with just those kids, the academic equivalents of LeBron James and Michael Jordan. Cracking the code to elite college admissions is an unsolvable puzzle. Rules are hidden in bromides, decisions made behind locked doors. Secrecy makes it impossible for students to trace why seemingly qualified applicants are rejected and seemingly unqualified ones are accepted. Pinpointing why elite colleges accept or reject students is like finding a kitten on a volcano at night with a flashlight. It's possible, but unlikely.

The best admissions hedge is money. Money buys consultants

with the experience and knowledge to position students in a way to attract attention. Consultants in wealthy cities like Washington, D.C., advertise $350-an-hour rates and $20,000 packages that exclude extras that, as one advertised, "provide reminders, check-ins and scheduling to keep students and parents on task."

The next best approach is building a fail-safe brand. That's what Cassandra Hsiao did. Like Dayo, she applied only to elite colleges. Unlike Dayo, she was accepted to every one of them, twenty-two total, including all eight Ivies. She was one of five students nationwide in 2017 to join what one news organization dubbed "the nation's most exclusive college club." After being accepted to Harvard early, she read the email twice, through tears, she said. "I just couldn't believe it."

Cassandra graduated from a public high school in Santa Ana, the urban heart of Orange County, California. Unassuming and genuine, Cassandra is bubbly and friendly, as comfortable talking about celebrities as she is gushing about how much she loves Martin McDonagh's dark and bleak play *The Pillowman*. She wanted the best grades and scores she could earn, a value she learned from her parents. "My mom raised us with this idea of excellence versus perfection. She raised us to be inwardly focused, to run your own race and to reach for excellence."

She prepped herself for the ACT (took it twice after studying for twelve weeks, scored 35 out of 36) and the SAT (took it once after studying for four weeks, scored 1540, in the 99th percentile); won myriad honors, including a $2,500 National Merit Scholarship; and had the highest grades in her senior class. Her sophomore year, crucial for Ivy League contenders, was brutal. Besides calculus, she took AP World History, honors Spanish, honors literature, honors chemistry, and a leadership class. She remembers "a lot of tears that year."

Both her parents have degrees from foreign universities, and her dad has an advanced degree in engineering from Iowa State University. Cassandra was born in Malaysia; spoke Chinese and English as a child; and "bounced around" Taiwan, Malaysia, and the United States before her family moved to Southern California in 2004.

Disenchanted with the local elementary school, her parents home-schooled her for fifth and sixth grades. Her mother helped land her first internship, for a youth magazine as a celebrity reporter, at age eleven. Her parents drove her hundreds of miles around Los Angeles and Orange Counties so she could interview stars, even after she transferred to a public middle school an hour away from home. Online you'll see her with a microphone interviewing Hollywood's biggest stars, preternaturally sophisticated and polished.

Over time, she appears first as a little girl in floppy hats; then as a teenager wearing signature hair bows; finally as a woman, hand on hip, confidently commanding the red carpet. That evolution required enormous family investment and sleep deprivation. Despite a punishing curriculum that included after-school creative writing classes, Cassandra was one of fifteen in a class of four hundred to graduate with a 4.5 or better grade point average.

"Everyone is good at something, everyone is so talented and deserving," she said, a feeling "that can also be crushing. Because it can also feel like everyone is better and smarter and more talented than I am."

Her family never hired tutors or admissions consultants. They never felt she needed them. Plus, she confided, "it's just so expensive." Besides keeping her on deadline, helping with logistics, and driving—sometimes four or more hours a day—her parents relegated academics, test prep, and college applications to her. Cassandra invested hours in researching colleges online, crafting a branded message that matched her story and her interests to each college's strengths.

She applied to so many colleges for one reason, she said. "Because I'm Asian. For Asians, getting into the Ivy League is like winning the lottery. You never know what's going to happen. A standard Asian has to score higher on tests to be seen as qualified. If you're Asian, you never know if you're going to get in with the same qualifications and test scores and interests as everybody else who gets in."

The Journey's End

Cassandra and Dayo eventually reached their destinations, each taking different paths to where they are today. Cassandra used one Ivy League's financial aid offer to negotiate reduced tuition at another campus. Once she had the deal she wanted, she filmed a YouTube video featuring herself in cap and gown, thanking God, her parents, family, friends, teachers, mentors. "I know a lot of you have been asking, 'Where have I decided to go?' Well . . . the answer is . . . *this*!" She throws open her gown, revealing a blue Yale T-shirt, as background music plays "Bulldog! Bulldog! Bow-wow-wow!" The summer after high school, Cassandra and a friend with a near-perfect ACT score started a new business. They marketed themselves as test prep and college coaches, two new cogs in the swelling admissions economy.

Dayo's journey to college was far more agonizing, a painful trial that tarnished the reputation of one of America's most prominent prep schools and illuminated the opaque ordeal so many families endure. Dayo thought she had what it takes to succeed. Then she ran into reality.

Sidwell educates a significant number of children from powerful political families, and its alumni include Chelsea Clinton and Malia and Sasha Obama. At Sidwell, parents expect counselors and administrators to advocate for their children and help them get into selective colleges. Elite schools have rewarded Sidwell by accepting an astounding number of its graduates. In the nine years before Dayo's graduation, nearly five hundred Sidwell students—about half its graduates—were accepted to the colleges Dayo hoped to attend.

Enrolling in a prestigious high school, taking the hardest classes available, doing what she thought was expected, representing the diversity that top colleges promote—all of it wasn't enough to survive the elite college culling. Though Spelman was likely to accept her, Dayo withdrew her application. In the end, she was left with no outright acceptances. The experience took a deep psychological toll, the Adetus said in their lawsuit. Dayo suffered from "severe, substantial emotional injuries as a result of [Sidwell's] conduct," alleged a psychiatrist report filed in the case. "The malicious, deliberate and outrageous behavior of the staff at Sidwell Friends School created an overwhelmingly damaging emotional experience for Dayo. This trauma has affected all areas of her life, and it is my professional opinion that this protracted traumatic experience puts her at risk of worsening anxiety and depression."

Her father, Titilayo Adetu, said he felt Sidwell did nothing to promote Dayo at one of her top-choice colleges, the University of Pennsylvania. "If you keep quiet to a school like the University of Pennsylvania, where there are thousands of other well-qualified students, why would they take her?" he asked in his deposition. "Why would they even consider her?"

To counter the family's complaints, Sidwell retained Rick Singer as an expert witness. At the time, Singer sold himself to Sidwell as a legitimate $300-an-hour college admissions expert. With no formal training or professional accreditations, he boasted that he had helped tens of thousands of students get into college even as he was secretly masterminding the largest undergraduate admissions fraud in American history. In his report for Sidwell, Singer diminished Dayo's academic and athletic achievements and her "lackluster personal brand."

At a less competitive school, Singer said in his report, "Dayo might have stood out more prominently, but at Sidwell, she was merely average." He belittled her accomplishments, criticized her for the way she wrote about her experiences as an African American. Dayo failed "to illuminate a greater understanding of her culture," Singer said. "There is nothing to suggest she has overcome obstacles or grown as a person in a way that would appeal to a university official looking for reasons to overlook her academic performance. Dayo has done almost nothing to set herself apart from the crowd."

Sidwell put it more bluntly. Dayo was nowhere near an "academically competitive candidate" for the elite colleges she wanted to attend, the school had previously alleged. In the final analysis, Sidwell said, Dayo was "unwilling to take responsibility for her studies and for her own academic results."

The courts sided with Sidwell. The Adetu family failed to prove that the school put Dayo at a disadvantage, an appeals court concluded. The Adetus then tried but failed to persuade the US Supreme Court to take the case. Shunted aside, Dayo nevertheless persisted. The year after graduating from Sidwell, she took online courses through a local university. She reapplied to college and was accepted to Williams, the nation's highest-ranking liberal arts college, and the University of Pennsylvania, an Ivy League that had rejected her as a Sidwell senior.

Dayo graduated from Penn with a bioengineering degree and planned to continue her graduate studies in Philadelphia. She is thriving, she wrote on Facebook. "It has been a long, transformative and rewarding period in my life. I am grateful for everything I've learned and forever grateful for the amazing people I have met."

2

Chasing Ghosts

The Fear of Failure

Higher education made it possible for my family to live the American dream. My parents grew up in Brooklyn, the first in their families to graduate from college. My brother, sister, and I did better, earning graduate degrees from UCLA, USC, and Northwestern. My siblings and I sent five kids to elite colleges, two to Harvard. But the story of those three generations is far more complicated than it seems. My family's success has less to do with merit than it does with timing, luck, genetics, and how America doles out scarce educational resources.

My parents enrolled in Brooklyn College, the poor man's Harvard, in 1938, less than a decade after it opened. It was free, the first New York City public liberal arts college to accept women. An Italian immigrant, my mother took classes with groundbreaking psychologist Abraham Maslow, met Eleanor Roosevelt, and earned a biology degree. After college she worked as a laboratory physiologist at City College, a job once reserved for men like my dad who had gone to fight in World War II.

The postwar period was a financial windfall for my parents' generation. Ninety percent of them—particularly white men and the women they married—earned more than their parents. After the war, men reclaimed their jobs from women, who, like my mother, retreated with them to the suburbs to create the baby-boom generation. My mom raised three babies while my dad worked for Liberty Mutual until the Korean War, where he served as a Marine Corps colonel. In 1962, an aerospace company recruited him to move to Orange County, California.

My family's move coincided with Governor Pat Brown's "California Idea," a model of higher education copied nationwide. Brown promised state residents high-quality degrees free of charge. California public colleges offered a path to the middle class, a road traveled largely by white men who earned almost twice as many degrees as women in 1969.

By the 1970s, John F. Kennedy's mandate to "take affirmative action" to treat job applicants "without regard to their race, creed, color, or national origin" was extended to women and college admissions. Gates that had been closed to all but white men opened wide. My high school championed the American dream in its 1976 yearbook, bursting in red, white, and blue and emblazoned with the hoary slogan "1776: A Dream of Freedom, 1976: Freedom to Dream." My all-white classmates had reason to cheer. Their families benefited more from the American dream than any others in the nation's history.

After World War II, the government subsidized degrees for millions, prioritizing higher education as an investment in the nation's economic future. A degree was the ticket to good-paying careers, social stability, and a healthy life. In the next two generations, however, the US went from being one of the most egalitarian nations in the world to one of the least, according to the Brookings Institution. It became a country where few children rise above the circumstances of their birth—especially if they grew up middle-class.

That transformation began in earnest in 1981, when President Ronald Reagan started pulling up the drawbridge to higher education. Reagan appealed to free-market and social conservatives preaching individual rather than government solutions to public problems.

Cuts to government tuition subsidies, combined with rising costs, restricted access to affordable degrees. Tuition at private colleges has increased 800 percent since 1980. At public universities tuition has climbed 230 percent since 1988, while government spending per student has declined 5 percent. A degree now costs more in the United States than in almost every other developed nation.

Political rhetoric that embraced individualism, independence, and freedom to choose allowed affluent, college-educated children of the World War II generation to prosper while national wealth inequities grew. The newly rich joined forces with the old elite touting the virtues of America's meritocracy. Anyone who works hard, they insisted, had an equal chance to succeed. In fact, the rich got richer at a much faster pace, widening the gulf between the wealthy and everyone else working hard to catch up.

Americans with limited education saw their earnings plunge while wealthy parents were pouring time and money into preparing their children for college. Economists Garey Ramey and Valerie A. Ramey called the escalation of early childhood investment "the rug rat race."

In "No Rich Child Left Behind," Stanford's Sean Reardon paints a frightening picture of America's growing academic inequality. Before 1980, affluent students had little advantage over those from the middle class in academic performance. "Over the last few decades these differences in educational success between high- and lower-income students have grown substantially. . . . Just as the incomes of the affluent have grown much more rapidly than those of the middle class, so, too, have most of the gains in educational success accrued to the children of the rich."

Even for the rich, educational success is far more important than it used to be, he said. The rich have more money than they used to, and they use it differently. "High-income families are increasingly focusing their resources—their money, time and knowledge of what it takes to be successful in school—on their children's cognitive development and educational success," Reardon said. Though middle-class and poor families are also increasing the time and money spent on their children, "they are not doing so as quickly or as deeply as the rich."

Disregarding all evidence to the contrary, Americans stubbornly cling to the Horatio Alger fable, believing that anyone who works hard enough has equal opportunity to earn wealth, power, status, influence—and an acceptance letter to Harvard. The myth makes elite colleges alluring to strivers, and the fear of rejection even worse than the striving.

America's obsession with elite colleges masks deeper systemic problems in higher education. Getting into college is not the obstacle. Paying for it is. A dwindling number of public universities and a few elites charge families only what they can afford to pay. The rest push loans, encouraging students to take on crippling debt to pay for overpriced degrees with little traction in the marketplace.

Hundreds of thousands in the class of 2021 will leave college with an average of more than $30,000 in debt, hindering them from getting married, buying houses, affording children. Their parents will carry an additional average of more than $35,000 in loans, with a national total of $1.5 trillion. The language of individual merit has shaped higher education policy for four decades, rhetoric that hides inequalities based on wealth and race.

Competition for high-quality affordable degrees is a cutthroat contest that leaves parents exhausted and teenagers wracked with anxiety—all before a single tuition bill is paid. After decades of declining public aid, tepid economic growth, and surging income inequality, Americans are frustrated and fearful. The rich fear losing status. The middle class fear falling behind. The poor fear staying trapped in poverty.

In 2015, Donald Trump declared, "The American dream is dead." Can colleges revive it?

The Great Society and the War on Poverty in the 1960s gave Americans a hand up so they could live the dream. Thanks to expanding support for higher education, many Americans did. Government tuition assistance in the 1970s allowed a generation of working- and middle-class students to rise above their inherited social class. Affirmative action gave women and students of color access to higher education that white men took for granted. Free or near-free public colleges flourished.

Parents willing to scrimp and save could give their children debt-free degrees. That was the gift America gave my family. Though my father's income wildly fluctuated—he endured five aerospace layoffs in less than a decade—my siblings and I have degrees from private colleges.

By the time I graduated from high school in 1976, my dad had died, but government support and my mother's salary as a public school teacher allowed me to attend Occidental College. At Occidental, I met Barack Obama, another middle-class kid on scholarship, in a political philosophy class. He transferred to Columbia University, received a Harvard law degree, and was elected US president in 2008. I graduated debt-free, earned an advanced degree from Northwestern University, and returned to Orange County in 1982 as a reporter to cover the rise of Ronald Reagan.

Reagan redefined the government's "hand up" to lift all Americans to mean "handouts" to the lazy and ignorant. "Government is not the solution to our problem," Reagan said in his 1981 inaugural address. "Government is the problem." Republicans rebranded affirmative action as "racial preference" and "reverse discrimination" that punished whites. Social programs became "entitlements," "big government," "the welfare state," and "death taxes."

Helping students finance degrees was no longer a government priority, Reagan's budget director David Stockman told members of Congress in 1981. "I do not accept the notion that the federal government has an obligation to fund generous grants to anybody that wants to go to college. . . . If people want to go to college bad enough, then there is opportunity and responsibility on their part to finance their way through the best they can."

Under Reagan, the gates to affordable degrees started slamming shut, putting private college out of reach for high-achieving boys like Mike Pompeo. In 1986, I visited Wayne and Dorothy Pompeo in their modest Santa Ana home to talk to them about their decision to send their son Mike to West Point. The next week, I traveled to the academy to interview Donald Trump's future secretary of state for the *Orange County Register*, where I worked as a reporter.

Pompeo's forebears, like my family's, had immigrated from Italy. Our fathers both worked in military and aerospace. My family moved to a wealthier part of Santa Ana with better schools than the working-class neighborhood where Mike Pompeo grew up. He attended a high school the government had subsidized to allow students to compete with more affluent schools like my own.

By the time he graduated in 1982, average college costs had more than doubled, to $1,200 for the University of California and $9,000 for private colleges. Pompeo's siblings attended public university, but his parents wanted more for Mike. "We wanted the best for Michael," Dorothy said. "But we really couldn't afford a private college." Though Wayne struggled to stay on the edge of the middle class, Dorothy told me she fully expected Mike would one day become president. "We knocked ourselves out for our kids. The kids come first. Our house is falling apart, but we always put material things after our kids."

Mike chose West Point partly because it was free, he said, but also because "I liked the idea that it was an elite place. And it was still fair. Everyone starts out even no matter how much money you have, or what kind of prestigious family you come from." Though his parents split the party ticket, Pompeo is a lifelong Republican, bred in the axis of the Reagan youth movement. He was part of the crowd cheering Reagan's call to "Make America Great Again" by cutting taxes that subsidized student aid and dismantling regulations and reforms that had provided their parents with a stepping-stone to the middle class.

Pompeo used his West Point and Harvard Law degrees to hoist himself into the ranks of the elites he had longed to join. He became an associate in one of the nation's leading white-collar criminal defense firms and an evangelical Christian. He moved to Kansas, divorced his small-town wife, and married Susan Justice Mostrous, a former Wichita State homecoming queen, adopting her son from her second marriage.

Following an undistinguished career in private industry, Pompeo was elected to Congress in 2011 with help from the libertarian Koch brothers. Trump appointed him CIA director in 2017 and secretary of state in 2018. Pompeo remains a "Let's Make America Great Again" stalwart. One of his few public statements on higher education focused on attracting legal immigrants to US universities, "folks from Europe, folks from Asia," he told students at Emporia State University. He promised "a robust immigration system where we can bring the most creative minds from all across the world who want to come to America, to participate in the American Dream."

Leon Chua is the sort of highly educated immigrant Mike Pompeo would welcome. Ethnic Chinese, Chua has an undergraduate degree from a university in the Philippines. His Chinese wife also has a degree earned in the Philippines, summa cum laude in chemical engineering. Chua immigrated to the United States in 1961 with a scholarship to do graduate work at MIT. His daughter Amy, the eponymous Tiger Mom, was born in Champaign, Illinois, in 1962, where Leon was earning his doctorate at the University of Illinois. The Chuas arrived in the United States a few years before the federal government began abolishing immigration quotas for Asians.

In the following two decades, low-skilled Asian immigrants came to the US in historic numbers. In the 1990s, new federal laws attracted highly skilled workers to the technology industry. A second wave of well-educated immigrants from Korea, Japan, India, and China began arriving. Motivated to succeed, they raised their children with the same pull-yourself-up-by-the-bootstraps philosophy my parents taught me.

That was Amy Chua's upbringing. When Amy was eight, Leon accepted a faculty appointment at UC Berkeley, one of the nation's highest-ranked public universities. Chua went to public high school, graduated with honors, and started Harvard in 1980, four years after the college first accepted women. After finishing Harvard Law, Chua joined the faculty at Yale Law School. In 2011 she published a book, her third, on the virtues of Chinese parenting. Her *Wall Street Journal* manifesto, "Why Chinese Mothers are Superior," became the bestselling *Battle Hymn of the Tiger Mother*.

Capturing the striving that has come to characterize elite college admissions, Chua cloaked it in Asian superiority. Chua's book broadly paints Asians as handmaids to wealth, power, achievement, status, and influence, willing to abuse their children to climb the ladder to success, rank, and status.

Her own wealth and pedigree gave her daughters advantages so extreme it makes her Tiger Mom shtick seem bizarre and a little pathetic. She and husband Jed Rubenfeld (Juilliard School, Princeton,

Harvard Law) are both Ivy League graduates and Yale Law School professors. It's hard to imagine applicants more advantaged than Chua's daughters. As children of Harvard graduates, both are legacies, a preference that gives the offspring of alumni advantages so well documented researchers have dubbed the practice "affirmative action for the rich."

Though few families have Chua's deep-pocketed resources, her book presumes all parents are equally able to adopt the strict, expensive child-rearing she used to usher her children into Harvard. Chua quickly became a media megaphone for the Asian model minority, a cliché that hides a darker reality and a divided community. Inequality among Asian Americans has doubled since 1970, a Pew study found. Two-thirds of all Asian Americans have annual incomes of less than $100,000, and 16 percent—nearly three million—live near or in poverty. Asians have displaced Blacks as the most economically divided group. That message is lost on most Americans, who see little difference between poor and highly educated Asians, lumping them into Crazy Rich Asian and Tiger Mom stereotypes.

When Asians began outperforming whites on high-stakes admissions tests, parents gathered in high school auditoriums from Boston to Palo Alto to complain. Tiger Moms produced math whizzes, musical geniuses, and high-scoring robots with perfect grades, they said, but they also encouraged academic pressure and competition that led to suicide and jeopardized their children's emotional health. Those stereotypes became trickle-down racism.

High school senior Michelle Zhang wrote for Silicon Valley's newsweekly about the shame she felt as a high-achieving Asian. "Someone told me to my face, 'You're *too* good at everything. *You're* the reason I'm not getting into a good college. *You're* the reason why everyone else here is so stressed out.'"

Though Chua's daughters had every conceivable boost needed to win the admissions sweepstakes, she describes inflicting her children with college prep so extreme and expensive it seems to have induced a sort of Stockholm syndrome. The *New York Post* featured Lulu Chua-Rubenfeld strutting the Harvard campus perfectly decked out in designer duds. "I was raised by a Tiger Mom—and it worked!" After graduating in 2018, Lulu revealed in *Slate* how she felt about being known as the "Tiger Cub." "I love it. I love the whole thing," she said. "My mom and I are increasingly similar. . . . I've really absorbed a lot of her values."

Compare the Tiger Cub's advantages to the raw deal America handed Norman Coulter. Coulter should have been a poster child for the American dream. But by the time he was ready for college, the gates to affordable degrees were slamming shut. The tuition subsidies that helped Obama and me through private college were no longer available to Coulter.

Federal and private loans were fast replacing student grants. Grants declined 25 percent between 1980 and 1985 alone. Tuition was rising far faster than family income—increasing threefold at public and private colleges between 1980 and 2000. Colleges were encouraging low- and middle-income families like the Coulters to borrow far more money than they could repay.

Coulter was raised by a single mom with a high school diploma and big dreams. As a young woman, Denice Collins moved to Los Angeles to find opportunities denied African Americans in her native Arkansas. She earned a certificate to drive school buses, working hard after separating from Norman's dad to support him and his sister, Norman said. He remembers growing up in a neighborhood defined by its restrictions. Penned in by freeways, geography, and segregationist redistricting, the part of South Central Los Angeles they lived in had no major grocery stores, and had dangerous parks and underfunded schools. In 1984, the Coulters heard about a program that made it possible for South Central students to attend wealthier schools in the San Fernando Valley, where enrollment was declining. The Coulters applied. Norman was accepted.

He was eight, riding a city bus three hours every day to an overwhelmingly white, affluent neighborhood in Woodland Hills, a suburb bordering the Santa Monica mountains. He was glad, he said, to leave behind the gangs, knifings, shootings, and killings in his neighborhood. He read far above his grade level, played every after-school sport offered, and starred as the Cowardly Lion in *The Wizard of Oz*.

When he was about to start high school, his family moved to West Covina, twenty miles east of downtown in the San Gabriel Valley. Coulter enrolled in West Covina High, a middle-class school that was far more ethnically diverse than South Central or Woodland Hills. He thrived.

He earned perfect grades, starred on the basketball team, and decided to join the military. Unlike Mike Pompeo, Coulter wasn't guided to West Point; no one even mentioned it. "I should have been at West Point. But I didn't know how to do that. I didn't know to ask." In his senior year, a Chapman University coach recruited him. Thinking he'd been accepted, Coulter was surprised when the coach called in April to ask about his missing application. "I didn't know what to do or how to apply for scholarships. I had to figure it out on my own."

Coulter was seventeen when he and his mother drove from Los Angeles to Chapman to discuss financial aid. The university reduced Coulter's tuition by half and persuaded him to take out loans to cover the balance, he said. Sitting in the financial aid office, wracked with doubts about debt, he remembers telling his mother, "We can't afford this. This doesn't make sense." He'd be happy playing basketball at community college or joining the Army or Marines, he said. But she insisted. She wanted the best for him. That meant going to Chapman.

Norman enrolled, but planned to transfer to the University of Nevada his second year and try for a basketball scholarship. At Chapman his first year, his classes were so small he had personal relationships with most of his professors, many of whom invited him to their homes for dinner. He attended parties with trustees whose names were on buildings. He feared that abandoning the academic network he was building at Chapman for a basketball scholarship at a public school would hurt his future career opportunities. "I wagered on staying, hoping my education would somehow pay me back, and went into gross debt."

Decades later, he said, he still wonders why financial aid officers persuaded him to borrow so much money. "They saw we couldn't afford it. They saw our tax returns. I'm from a single-parent home. My mom drives a school bus for a living. They come back and say, 'This is your financial aid award.' Even the language is whack. They call it an award. This is an *award*? What's the award? That you won indebtedness and financial servitude for the rest of your life? I signed up because my mom said I should. I enlisted in a different kind of bondage."

Though Coulter lacked the pedigree that helped get Chua to Harvard and the connections that sent Pompeo to West Point, he is one of the most impressive students I've met. He distinguished himself at Chapman with original thinking and a dogged work ethic I rarely see in students. He excelled as the campus newspaper's opinions editor, played varsity basketball, and graduated with honors. In the four years he was at Chapman, the university raised tuition and room and board nearly 25 percent, forcing him to borrow almost $20,000 a year to cover the gap. Though he loved much about the university, in retrospect he sees another side. "Chapman was selling a product. All the while, I'm a human debit card and they're swiping me."

After graduating with an English degree, he borrowed more money to finance an advanced degree in theology to pursue a career in the ministry. Unable to repay his loans on what he was earning, he returned to school in 2007 for a teaching credential. No matter how hard he works, he can't earn enough to get out of debt, a common predicament for Americans like Coulter who came of age in the 1990s.

Now in his forties, Coulter has been paying off $100,000 in student loans for more than twenty years. Those payments, along with rent, swallow 50 percent of his public school teacher's salary every month. He and his wife are raising a blended family with three girls and a boy. The debt he holds makes it impossible for him to buy a house, take a vacation, or save for his kids' college. For Coulter, the American dream is at best deferred, he said. "Debt is the newest form of acceptable slavery."

The decade after Coulter left Chapman, degrees became even more unaffordable. Tuition at colleges and universities nationwide continued to skyrocket, while need-based financial aid waned. *U.S. News's* "Best Colleges" incentivized schools to boost their selectivity rankings by awarding the best-prepped, highest-achieving students—usually the wealthiest—discounts regardless of family income. Families fixating on rankings led to supercharged competition for elite colleges.

Affluent parents bought advantage in the college admissions industrial complex, spending tens of thousands of dollars on consultants, coaches, tutors, test prep, airplane tickets, rental cars, and hotels to visit colleges and curry favor with admissions officers. Unscrupulous merchants sold products to help students cheat on tests, plagiarize essays, fake transcripts, and forge letters of recommendation.

So much about applying to college has changed and so little of it makes sense. The bewildering, scary, anxiety-provoking race to the top has become fiercely cutthroat in ways unimaginable to baby boomers, a competition marked by misunderstandings, fear of the unknown, and race-baiting. Conservatives attacked affirmative action because it aimed to help students like Norman Coulter. California and Texas banned race as a consideration in public college admissions, and other states followed.

While lawmakers cut funding, public colleges and universities struggled to meet growing demand. Rather than provide grants, the federal government made it easier for students to finance degrees with money borrowed from private lenders, enriching bankers but indenturing an entire generation. The rising stakes stoked fear. And fear brought out the worst in parents.

Private consultants took advantage of the angst and confusion, channeling that fear into profits. Though most sell legal advantage, a few, like Rick Singer, peddled fraud and bribery. Singer's crimes, so unprecedented, had incited "national fear," a federal prosecutor said, shaking trust in higher education as the public realized the system was rigged to advantage the wealthy.

Singer set up shop in a multimillion-dollar mansion in Newport Beach, California, in 2011, calling his company "The Key" to helping wealthy parents get their unqualified children into elite colleges. He catered to families living in the nation's wealthiest enclaves, "the California dreamscapes of a Nancy Myers movie," as one writer described his adopted hometown.

Newport Beach was the perfect proving ground for Singer's rogue operation. Blond and athletic, Singer spoke the language of privilege in a town of yacht clubs and plastic surgery. He moved easily along the Gold Coast in neighborhoods where 95 percent are white or Asian, where Ferraris and Maseratis roar down the Pacific Coast Highway, where the local dealership stocks a Mercedes-Benz S-Class AMG for $263,395 and shoppers can buy a Tesla at the Fashion Island shopping mall while enjoying sweeping views of the Pacific.

Singer knew how to monetize striving. He recruited uberwealthy parents, promising to break open the locked gates to elite colleges. His clients included Douglas Hodge, a pillar of society and the former CEO of PIMCO, a billion-dollar Newport Beach financial company. With a net worth of $45 million, Hodge sat on the board of his children's private high school, Sage Hill, the toniest on the Gold Coast. Hodge paid Singer $850,000 over a decade to build bogus profiles for his five children and bribe coaches, counselors, and tutors. Off the kids went: two to USC, two to Georgetown, and one, he hoped, to Loyola Marymount. Hodge pled guilty in 2020 and was sentenced to nine months in prison and a $750,000 fine.

Another Sage trustee, Michelle Janavs, paid Singer $100,000 to help her two daughters cheat on the ACT and another $200,000 to have one of her daughters admitted to USC as a beach volleyball recruit. Heir to the Hot Pockets snacks fortune, Janavs also pled guilty and was sentenced to five months in prison and a $250,000 fine. Singer's name "came up continuously," Shellee Howard, a Corona del Mar college consultant, told a local reporter. "Parents would ask me, 'Can you guarantee my kid will get into the school he wants, like Mr. Singer?' He was making a guarantee he could get their kid in their first choice. I said, 'I can't. That isn't how it works.'"

The illusion of Newport Beach perfection distracted everyone from recognizing the fear that gave rise to Singer and the darkness enveloping sixteen-year-old Patrick Turner. Though Patrick lived only a few miles from Singer, he didn't know him. But he did know what desperate feels like. Sweet, honest Patrick, a mop of wavy hair framing ruddy cheeks, left his childhood bedroom on a cool and cloudy January morning in 2018. He arrived alone at dawn at a baseball diamond where he'd spent countless happy hours playing with friends, teammates, and family. He never wanted it to come to this, he wrote in a note he left behind. But he felt he had no choice. He walked to center field and died by suicide.

After Patrick's death, his parents, John and Kim Turner, showed his letters to reporters, dispatches that read like reports from summer camp, full of longing, naivete, and fear. He wrote of never fitting into the competitive world closing in on him, of realizing he'd never achieve the kind of perfection he believed his high school demanded. Nobody at school seemed to care about the kids like him, he wrote, kids who didn't have perfect grades, weren't stars in sports, and had no extraordinary outside interests. He'd fought the fear, struggled to manage the pressure. But it crushed him. He closed one letter with two words all in capital letters: "MAKE CHANGES."

Patrick was a sophomore at Corona Del Mar High School in Newport Beach when he died. Surrounded by million-dollar homes, his school is known for high-achieving students. Ranked No. 25 in the state among college preps, and No. 5 in Orange County, it sends nearly all its graduates to degree programs, many to the nation's most elite colleges. It also had a well-known dark side.

For years, students and parents had complained about a toxic culture that encouraged cheating. Nearly a dozen students were caught purchasing answers to Advanced Placement tests online, according to reports published several years ago. That preceded another notorious scandal.

No one remembers exactly when Timothy Lai arrived in Corona del Mar, but he quickly became a popular tutor known among parents for boosting their children's scores.

Like Singer, Lai sold certainty. He did it by hacking into teachers' computers and changing grades. After fleeing to South Korea, he was eventually arrested and sentenced to a year in jail. The news shocked some parents. Others, though, were outraged when school officials expelled eleven students for cheating. Why, they wanted to know, were only a few being punished when, they alleged, as many as 150 students may have been involved? A mother attacked the district for throwing "a handful of students to the wolves" for participating in a "culture of cheating [that] goes far beyond the students that you have marginalized."

Patrick kept his distance from the academic strivers. He joined the baseball and football teams and was well liked; the daughter of one of Orange County's Real Housewives invited him to his first formal dance. He made sandwiches for the homeless, talked to new kids at school, helped the disabled, tried to make everyone happy. He never left the house without saying "I love you," Kim Turner remembered.

Close to his parents, he golfed with his dad, a vice president at the Irvine Company, and cooked with his mom, an executive at the OC Alliance for Just Change. He hiked, fished, and skied at the Turners' vacation home in Idaho, the youngest of four athletic siblings in a close-knit family. He was a good student but didn't like fighting for grades. Rather than fill his résumé with internships, he built a business walking neighbors' dogs.

By sophomore year, the academic pressure was intense, unbearable, and inescapable. Patrick felt nobody at school valued students without perfect GPAs, the ones who prized character building over grade grubbing. He struggled to battle his fear of failing, to manage the competitive pressure to maintain a B average. It wasn't his parents pushing him, he said in a suicide note. It was the stress he felt at school. "It is purely the school."

Newport Beach is a bubble, he wrote, filled with kids and parents constantly comparing, bragging about how great they are, about straight As, about getting into the best colleges. "People don't understand how to be selfless. . . . So much pressure . . . to do well that I just couldn't do it anymore."

Kim and John Turner are determined to make sense of Patrick's death. "We had no idea he was in so much pain," Kim said. "We had no idea he was suffering." Their foundation, Patrick's Purpose, promotes kindness and mental health, and awards scholarships to teens headed to vocational school or community college. They want the world to understand what Patrick taught them. Chasing success, said John, "is like chasing ghosts."

They organized meetings in neighborhood clubhouses and community centers to give friends and classmates a place to talk about their fears and struggles.

"So many of them have told us they felt the same way Patrick did. They left hundreds of notes," Kim said. "There's so much hurt out there. It's a wake-up call for parents putting way too much pressure on their kids."

In the weeks following Patrick's death, Sean Boulton, the principal at rival Newport Harbor High, challenged the city to change its image and redefine success. In a letter, Boulton described a competitive culture, sickeningly familiar at affluent high schools nationwide, that leaves students feeling shame, isolation, and, ultimately, worthlessness.

"Our teachers and district have created and maintained a system that our community/country has demanded from us over the past 20 years since college admissions mania went into hyperdrive. . . . Schools endlessly discuss test scores, National Merit Scholarships, reading scores, AP scholars, comparisons to other school districts and this is when we start losing our collective souls—and our children."

In the end, he said, "It is the sum of our experiences that should always outweigh the sum of our bank accounts."

Patrick's funeral was held at the local Catholic church, officiated by the family's Presbyterian pastor and assisted by an Episcopalian priest and a rabbi. Thousands attended, including every member of the high school baseball and football teams. When John Turner expressed astonishment at the turnout, a friend explained: "Patty's death shocked everyone in our community. If it could happen to us, it could happen to anyone."

Rather than assign blame, Pastor Mark Davis sought to explain. He concluded his meditation with a warning: "At every level—from the most impersonal bureaucrat to the most impertinent parent—we are all part of the chaos. We're both victims and contributors to the chaos."

That chaos came into focus a year after Patrick died, when Rick Singer pled guilty to organizing the nation's largest college admissions criminal conspiracy. Prosecutors said that over seven years, dozens of wealthy parents paid a total of $25 million to Singer to get their kids into elite colleges. Celebrities, financiers, and executives were charged with hiring Singer to use bribes, rig tests, fake scores, and lie on applications to pick the locks at the country's most elite universities. After her arrest, model and actress Lori Loughlin told reporters she did what "any mother would do" to get a child into college. She didn't mention that very few mothers have a net worth of millions.

Like many parents Singer bewitched, Adam Wheeler felt an intense desire to rise above his intellectual caste. Wheeler also discovered it was a lot easier to cheat his way to college than go through regular channels. His scheme, undetected for years, portended the rise of Rick Singer.

Though one of the best, Wheeler was not the first would-be Horatio Alger to crash the Ivy League gates. As far back as 1987, Princeton accepted track star James Hogue, a grifter posing as a self-taught orphan with an uncanny resemblance to Kevin Bacon. A decade later, Columbia accepted Esther Reed, one of nine children born to a single mother who died shortly after Reed dropped out of high school. Reed stole a missing woman's identity, scored 1400 out of 1600 on the SAT, forged her application, and earned a 3.2 GPA at Columbia before serving three years in prison for fraud. And in 2006, Yale accepted forger Akash Maharaj. He did well enough as an undergraduate to win the English Department's Henry H. Strong Prize for an essay about his literary alter ego Jay Gatsby. He was sentenced to five years' probation.

In ways few did at the time, Wheeler instinctively understood how digital technology could help him get an elite college degree. Wheeler transformed himself from a hardworking middle-class teen into a notorious con artist, cheating his way into Bowdoin, Harvard, and Stanford, winning academic prizes worth nearly $100,000.

The story of Wheeler, reconstructed from the public record, seems a less menacing version of Patricia Highsmith's *The Talented Mr. Ripley*. Though the high school Wheeler attended rarely sent kids to the Ivy League, he understood Harvard defines success.

Neither Wheeler nor his parents have talked publicly in the decade since his arrest. "We went down periscope at Adam's request," his father, Richard Wheeler, said recently. "Adam wanted to put it behind him. Our family has focused on healing and moving forward. The privacy we have sought provides the opportunity to do so."

The outlines of his life, though, come into focus in *Conning Harvard*, a deeply reported book written by Wheeler's Harvard classmate Julie Zauzmer. Wheeler attended Caesar Rodney High School in the white, working-class town of Camden, south of Dover, Delaware. His mother worked in a decorator's shop and his dad taught drafting at his high school, named after Delaware's delegate to the Continental Congress. "We were all kind of nerdy," a classmate told Zauzmer, "but Adam was the nerdiest."

A neighbor remembered Adam gladly walking her dogs and always refusing payment. He played in the band, loved literature and Frisbee, and graduated in the top 10 percent of his class. Lacking pedigree, pricey test prep, admissions consultants, and essay coaches, he was still determined to attend an elite college. His SAT scores didn't qualify him for the Ivies, so he focused on Bowdoin in Brunswick, Maine, the first school in the nation to make test scores optional and ranked No. 6 among the nation's best liberal arts colleges.

When it came time to complete his application, Wheeler puzzled over the essay prompts. Some, like "What matters to you and why?," are fairly straightforward. Others, not so much. "Generations of students have found connection and meaning in Bowdoin's 'The

Offer of the College.' Which line from the Offer resonates most with you?"

Wheeler found an essay in a book, copied it, and sent it off, Zauzmer reported. Bowdoin accepted him. Within his first year, he was suspended for plagiarizing. Rather than return to Bowdoin, Wheeler applied to Harvard. Using sophisticated digital skills, he changed test scores, forged letters of recommendation, and faked transcripts showing he had attended Phillips Academy and MIT. He claimed fluency in languages he didn't speak, authorship of books he never wrote, and invitations to lectures about Zoroastrian cosmology that he never delivered.

At Harvard, Wheeler fabricated and plagiarized undetected for two years, according to published reports. Wheeler earned the prestigious Hoopes Prize, the highest research honor Harvard bestows on undergraduates. He racked up enough successes to make him eligible for Rhodes and Fulbright scholarships. In the final round for the Rhodes, a committee member recognized Wheeler's essay as the writing of Pulitzer Prize–winning scholar Stephen Greenblatt. The jig was up. Or so it seemed.

After withdrawing from Harvard, Wheeler applied to Yale and Stanford. Yale called Wheeler's high school and discovered his fabrications. Wheeler confessed and apologized. A few weeks later, Stanford accepted him. To support himself before moving to Palo Alto, Wheeler used his Harvard identification for an internship at a nearby hospital. A staff member recognized him, and the police arrested him. He appeared in court, reporters and television cameras trailing, wearing a denim jacket and T-shirt, his downward gaze hiding soulful blues eyes and boy-band good looks, a hint of stubble on his chin.

Financially destitute, he pled guilty to larceny and identity theft. He promised to repay Harvard $45,806 and to never identify himself as a Harvard student. He served five weeks of a suspended one-year sentence. In short order, he was back in court. In another application for an unpaid internship, he said he had been a student at Harvard.

This time the judge had little mercy. She sentenced Wheeler to a year in prison and ten years' probation ending in 2021, scolding him for striving and for "thumbing his nose at the system."

3

The Rise of Rankings

News You Shouldn't Use

The same year Adam Wheeler was jailed for cheating his way into Harvard, Amy Chua's Tiger Cub was celebrated for getting into college the old-fashioned way. Beauty, brilliance, talent, and connections paved the path to Harvard for Chua's daughter, the news site Above the Law reported. In "Tiger Mom Triumphant: Her Cub Got into Harvard!" David Lat explained how.

"As we all know by now, Sophia made her Carnegie Hall debut at the tender age of 14," but also had "one other significant factor in her favor . . . : legacy status, as the daughter of two Harvard-educated parents. . . . Speaking from my own personal experience . . . 'sending a child to a top college is the ultimate vindication.' And colleges don't get more 'top' than Harvard (which is #1 in the current *U.S. News* rankings)."

Not long after Lat's gushing Tiger Cub report, I was sitting among hundreds of families in a suburban high school auditorium at a workshop to teach us the secrets of college admissions. A balding, bespectacled admissions consultant, collar open, sleeves rolled up, shirt untucked, stood in front of a screen twice his size and emblazoned with his company's logo. Scrolling through my phone, I heard something that jolted me to attention.

"Forget Harvard," the consultant said, pointing out, as Lat had in his paean to the Tiger Cub, that Harvard has a single-digit acceptance rate, the lowest in the nation. To bring his point home, he gave a pop quiz.

"Write down your top three college choices," he said. "I'll read a list of colleges. When you hear the name of one of your colleges, check it off."

His list was a litany of *U.S. News & World Report*'s top-ranked colleges.

"Raise your hand," he said, "if your list has a college I didn't name."

Only a couple of hands went up. He stared in mock disbelief.

"There are two thousand four-year colleges, and you're all focused on the same twenty-five? Why?"

The responses were as recognizable as the colleges he named. Parents want exclusivity, prestige, trusted brands, bragging rights. They want guaranteed returns on investments. They want the connections that entitled the Tiger Cub to slide easily into Harvard. But they don't want to resort to the sordid exploits that landed actress Lori Loughlin in jail. They just want to do right by their kids. But how?

By the time they're shuffling into high school auditoriums for annual college nights, most families have a pretty good idea of the trouble ahead. They have an inkling that the path to college is shrouded in fog that gets thicker and darker the closer kids come to high school graduation. They've heard the admissions landscape shifts faster than quicksand and they want to avoid being swallowed whole. For advice, they turn to *U.S. News*'s "Best Colleges" rankings.

For decades, *U.S. News*'s at-a-glance superiority rankings mostly impressed upper-class parents. But over time, "Best Colleges" fed the rest of America's obsession with the "likes" and ratings that created Rotten

Tomatoes, Facebook, Yelp, Amazon, and Instagram. In the three decades since its launch, "Best Colleges" has become the Lonely Planet of admissions, leading overwhelmed and confused families to apply to about a hundred schools with the highest academic hurdles. As competition to clear those hurdles escalated, a cascade effect pushed to ever-higher heights the average test scores and grades needed to qualify. To make their children competitive, parents began hiring armies of tutors and consultants, spending billions of dollars on admissions prep, an industry that barely existed before "Best Colleges" rankings appeared.

"Best Colleges" permanently altered the landscape of higher education, helping to launch the high-stakes academic arms race that has come to characterize modern college admissions. As information, rankings aren't inherently bad. They merely "fill a need that would have been met by someone, if not *U.S. News*," said Kevin Carey, director of education policy at the nonpartisan New America research foundation in Washington, D.C. Carey argues for replacing flawed rankings like *U.S. News* with better ones "based on the right measures that would create healthier competition."

Until that happens, though, *U.S. News* leads a crowded field of similar products, the object of ongoing scorn. *U.S. News* rankings amount "to little more than a pseudo-scientific and yet popularly legitimate tool for perpetuating inequality between educational haves and have-nots—the rich families from the poor ones, and the well-endowed schools from the poorly endowed ones," economist, essayist, and social critic Peter Sacks wrote more than a decade ago. Scores of critics have agreed with him. A recent Stanford study concluded that the best way for students to find a right-fit college is to "ignore the rankings."

Despite ample warning, families, colleges, even financial institutions use rankings to assign value and prestige to higher education. Why?

Look no further than Robert Morse, the wizard behind the curtain who controls large swaths of higher education's complicated empire.

The chief data strategist for *U.S. News & World Report*, Morse is inscrutable, an unremarkable "Beltway wonk: rumpled, self-effacing, mildly preppy," Malcolm Gladwell wrote in a profile of him for the *New Yorker*.

Started as a "news-you-can-use" story in a 1983 issue of the magazine, college rankings became a wildly lucrative business that redefined higher education and allowed *U.S. News* the financial edge it needed to bury its corporate rivals *Time* and *Newsweek*. Despite its virulent critics, "Best Colleges" has prospered, stoking competition among colleges to recruit top high school students, and among students to snag places at its top-ranked schools.

Morse and a small team of rankings zealots packaged and sold "Best Colleges" as objective and scientific even as *U.S. News* consistently refused requests from scholars to peer review the data. Using publicly available information and leaks from insiders, researchers discovered the rankers used biased methods to rig the results to reflect their priorities.

Though its formula has changed over the years, "Best Colleges" continues to measure one constant: institutional wealth. Top-ranked colleges are the richest, armed with the largest endowments and financial assets. Competition to get into those colleges has caused acceptance rates to plummet and average test scores and grades needed for admissions to soar. More students competing for the same number of places supercharged the admissions industrial complex and spawned the hysteria and anxiety families associate with applying to college.

Robert Morse is a contradiction, both gruff and genial, seemingly unaware of his role in forcing the least advantaged colleges to compete in the Hunger Games of higher education. He expresses such surprise at how seriously colleges take rankings that he conjures the image of Captain Renault, the police prefect in *Casablanca* who protests as the waiter hands him his winnings, "I'm shocked, shocked that there is gambling going on in here."

After a Politico investigation argued that *U.S. News* rankings promote economic inequality, Morse responded with the same sort of message he has repeated for nearly three decades. While acknowledging that some of the criticism was fair, he saw no link between "Best Colleges," the academic arms race, and growing inequality on campus. Invoking Captain Renault's "round up the usual suspects" defense in a column for *U.S. News,* Morse essentially blamed higher education for causing its own crisis and called Politico's investigation a "bizarrely constructed article, built on false premises and filled with conjecture rather than facts."

Morse joined *U.S. News* in 1976, as an ambitious twenty-eight-year-old with an undergraduate degree from the University of Cincinnati and a master's degree from Michigan State University (*U.S. News* ranked them No. 143 and No. 80, respectively, in 2021). *U.S. News* editor Marvin Stone hired Morse to work in the magazine's economic unit, monitoring the consumer price index and forecasting business trends. Two particular trends interested Stone: college enrollment and rising tuition.

College enrollment was increasing fast—47 percent between 1970 and 1983—as baby boomers took full advantage of plentiful government subsidies for degrees. The precipitous rise in college costs was even more intriguing. Average tuition increased 70 percent between 1976 and 1983, from $2,275 to $3,877, according to the National Center for Education Statistics. (That rise continued from 1980 to the present, an 800 percent average increase at public colleges—from $2,500 to the current $23,000—and an 800 percent increase at private colleges, from $5,000 to the current $45,000.)

College degrees were becoming one of the most expensive consumer products average Americans buy over a lifetime. And yet, shoppers could find more information about the relative worth of $20 toasters than they could about the value of six-figure college degrees. Stone figured parents forced to pay for pricey degrees would probably want to buy a guide to help them identify premium, high-status brands that promised reliable returns on investments. Rankings gave consumers much-needed advice, and also extended the magazine's successful "News You Can Use" features.

The magazine's marketing department produced the first rankings, mailing college presidents surveys requesting they rate the top 10 schools in the nation. The first rankings appeared in 1983 and again in 1985, splashed across eight magazine pages. The results were unsurprising. Stanford was first, Harvard second, Yale third, Princeton fourth, a sorting that has remained largely unchanged for four decades. (In 2020, Princeton was first, followed by Harvard and Yale; Stanford was sixth.) Except in ties, rare in the early days, it was a zero-sum competition. If one college won, another lost. Harvard, Yale, Princeton, Stanford, Columbia, the University of Chicago, and MIT have ranked first among peers since 1983.

"Best Colleges" was perfectly timed to exploit a tectonic cultural shift. In the 1980s, Ronald Reagan glorified markets, encouraging materialism and consumerism and creating anxiety that the rankings fueled. Reagan attacked higher education as a privilege, not a right. "Greed is good" became the decade's coda. "Best Colleges" didn't cause consumer-driven status seeking, but the company's executives were prescient enough to monetize it quickly. In 1984, Ivy League–educated real-estate mogul Mortimer Zuckerman bought *U.S. News* from its employees and began retooling the magazine's brand from a newsweekly to a rankings machine. Within a year, Stone was gone. By 1987, Robert Morse was the director of the "Best Colleges" project.

The decision to pair Morse with veteran newsman Mel Elfin was inspired. With no journalism training, Morse was a business wonk so soft-spoken, one reporter said, that "if he were an actor cast as an introverted accountant, [he] would be criticized for overplaying his role." Elfin, by contrast, was a brash Brooklyn-born street fighter with a Harvard degree—a high-octane, influential Washington insider schooled in the sharp-elbowed world of competitive weekly newsmagazines.

Elfin rose up the ranks to replace Ben Bradlee as *Newsweek*'s Washington bureau chief, becoming a confidant of *Washington Post* publisher Katharine Graham. Defiant and famously acidic, a colleague recalled, Elfin was "strung tight as a high wire." During tense conversations he snipped at his hair with children's scissors, defending his staff against complaining politicians and subscribers alike. As one particularly intense and loud argument between Elfin and his reporters wafted down the hall, an eavesdropping junior editor asked another, "What will we tell their widows?"

Elfin decamped to rival *U.S. News* in the mid-1980s after losing an internecine battle at *Newsweek*. Elfin, the big-picture editor, packager, and engaging writer, and Morse, the numbers cruncher, formed the rankings tag team. For the next decade, they parlayed status mania into a multimillion-dollar franchise, filling an unexploited market niche to feed a competitive culture.

In the absence of any widely accepted definition of "academic excellence," Elfin and Morse created one. Though rating the quality of a college degree is nothing like ranking the relative worth of a Honda Accord over a Toyota Camry, Morse and Elfin's *U.S. News* team did it anyway. Surveying college executives and collecting whatever statistical data they could convince schools to hand over, they conceived subjective measurements. The formula for the "Best Colleges" was fairly simple, remaining more or less the same for a decade. They combined and weighted five basic metrics:

Selectivity, a competition to recruit students with the highest test scores and grades.

Yield, a competition to entice the best students to accept offers of admission.

Reputation, a competition to seek the highest status among other colleges.

Graduation rates, a competition to keep students enrolled, or reject students with hardships that might cause them to drop out.

Institutional resources, a competition to amass the most wealth.

More telling was what "Best Colleges" left out. The metrics never measured actual learning or sound educational practice, or the discipline students mastered over four years of study. Calculating how much or how well students learn would require comparing thousands of programs, surveying millions of alumni to define success and satisfaction, and assessing how well students master the critical thinking needed to discern differences between fact and opinion. "Best Colleges" never tried to measure learning. Instead, the authors relied on subjective conclusions they could obtain data to confirm. "Student Selectivity," "Institutional Resources," and "Academic Reputation" accounted for 50 percent of each institution's ranking for years.

When "Best Colleges" changed its formula to include endowment wealth, public universities fell out of the top 20, replaced by wealthier private schools. Northwestern, Johns Hopkins, the University of Pennsylvania, and Vanderbilt rose in national stature, allowing them to go from accepting 40 to 50 percent or more of their applicants to rejecting anywhere from 85 to more than 90 percent. The University of California dropped in rank from No. 5 to No. 22; the University of Michigan from No. 7 to No. 25; the University of Illinois from No. 8 to No. 48.

It was as if Michelin had decided to rank restaurants based on price and profit instead of the quality of the food and dining experience. "They changed the methodology . . . and guess what?" one critic noted. "The blue-blood colleges with 300 years of history moved up, and those darn publics were put into their place." Eventually "Best Colleges" had to produce another list, "Top Public Universities," separate from the "Top National Universities" dominated each year by Stanford, MIT, and the Ivies.

"Best Colleges" became a thick guidebook the size of a hardcover dictionary, published in the fall, timed to the start of the school year. *U.S. News* dated the rankings book a year ahead to give it a long shelf life. The company recruited sponsors and advertisers, re-branding degrees as high-status products with price tags, aiming their buyers' guide directly at consumers to help them shop for colleges. The first book sold more than a million copies, a payoff far beyond the editors' expectations. The magazine's "exclusive rankings" issue sold 40 percent more than the standard edition.

Fat with ads and corporate sponsors, "Best Colleges" arrived with a thud on the desks of alarmed college presidents. The ivory tower was under siege.

Ignoring, acknowledging, or co-opting a growing chorus of critics, Morse and his team collected as much free data as possible, stock-piling unique content before other news organizations even realized what *U.S. News* was doing. They collaborated with key players in the emerging admissions industrial complex, like-minded companies hoping to profit from selling higher-education data. They recruited the College Board, the nonprofit SAT testing company; then Peterson's, one of the nation's largest test prep businesses, to produce a Common Data Set.

Promising college data collectors they'd use the information for noble purposes—to help families make informed choices—"Best Colleges" processed the data into ever-more lucrative admissions products. In 1993, *U.S. News* appeared online, eventually allowing millions of families to search "Best Colleges" from a personal computer, and an unprecedented number of students began applying to elite colleges.

Competition went into hyperdrive. Choosing a college became "a high-stakes economic and social transaction," the *New York Times* said. Rejections soared as elites accepted fewer and fewer applicants. *U.S. News* marketed "Best Colleges" as America's "No. 1 selling college guide." As "Best Colleges" gained market strength, educators grew increasingly worried.

"Academics resented them; they thought they were an offense to the industry, they thought they were misleading to students and fostering this competition," said Richard Freeland, former Massachusetts education commissioner and retired president of Northeastern University. Rankings were widely regarded among academics as crass, simplistic, and misleading, Freeland said. "The metrics mirrored conventional wisdom that confirmed the wealth, status, and prestige of elite colleges."

As far back as 1986, two dozen university presidents trekked to the Georgetown offices of *U.S. News* to gripe, a ritual that continued for years, said Alvin Sanoff, "Best Colleges" managing editor in the early days. "As many as three presidents a day" came by, he said.

Sanoff, a veteran *U.S. News* editor with degrees from Harvard and Columbia, joined the rankings team in 1992. He sat at a cramped desk piled with notebooks and folders, facing a bulletin board tacked with a mess of schedules, letters, and small pieces of handwritten notes partially hidden by a Rolodex and a push-button landline telephone.

Unlike Morse, Sanoff was a shoe-leather reporter with decades of experience checking facts, deleting opinions, and enforcing objectivity. Sanoff tried to bring order to the chaos. He tried "to get people the best information about . . . the best values in college education," his son Geoff told the *Baltimore Sun* in his father's obituary. "Sanoff took criticism 'very seriously.'"

Sanoff heard a lot of criticism in the early days. Academics called, complained, wrote letters demanding the company cease and desist what they viewed as its annual rankings sham. The survey was flawed, they said, a popularity contest that did "a disservice to thousands of high school students seeking direction in choosing a college," the *New York Times* reported. Stanford's president, Donald Kennedy, called "Best Colleges" a "sort of beauty contest."

"Everybody who thought about it after thirty seconds knew most of the people who were filling out those surveys had no idea what they were talking about," Freeland said. "I filled them out all the time. It was probably just the honest thing to do. Just fill it out because we thought we should. But all you're really doing is replicating conventional wisdom. I think that's what they wanted. They wanted to know what the conventional wisdom was."

Acceptance rates at top-ranked colleges were plummeting, making them even more exclusive and attractive. High school counselors complained that rankings fomented status hysteria, that teenagers and their parents mindlessly applied to high-ranked schools with little regard for skyrocketing costs. Very few people really knew how the numbers worked, said Nicholas Thompson, an early "Best Colleges" critic. *U.S. News* imposed a double standard. While pressuring colleges to release proprietary data and revealing enough about the "Best Colleges" formula to imply legitimacy, company officials kept the complex formula opaque, locked in a black box to make fact-checking and thorough review impossible.

While a Stanford student, Thompson led a student boycott against the rankings. As an editor at the *Washington Monthly*, he sharply criticized Morse and Elfin. The editors controlled "Best Colleges" like a fiefdom, with Elfin having "an almost paternal devotion to the rankings," Thompson said. Elfin "seemed to have known that the only believable methodology would be the one that confirmed the prejudices of the meritocracy: The schools that the most prestigious journalists and their friends had gone to would have to come out on top." The rankings described the perfect college as "rich, hard to get into, harder to flunk out of, and has an impressive name."

"Best Colleges" caused a decades-long uproar. "Beyond being just offended by the whole idea that a commercial magazine would presume to rank institutions, there were substantive reasons that they were destructive," Freeland said. "Some things about them are pretty questionable. One of the most questionable is what they leave out. They didn't give any credit for diversity or for educating low-income kids. Critics thought rightly that this was driving institutions to pursue the same model of quality when that same model of quality wasn't necessarily useful in a system that prides itself on a diversity of its institutions."

Middlebury College president Olin Robison called "Best Colleges" a "fraudulent exercise [that] sells a lot of magazines," in a 1989 *New York Times* article. Robert Atwell, president of the American Council on Education, told a *Times* reporter he regarded "Best Colleges" as an "annual travesty." "Best Colleges" used statistics to bolster weak arguments, critics said, creating a false air of scientific certainty based on opinion surveys masquerading as fact developed by amateurs behind a curtain of secrecy. In a widely publicized poll, administrators graded "Best Colleges" 1.97 on a 4.0 scale. At a national meeting of higher education officials, one admissions officer compared *U.S. News* to Satan.

The rankings team listened politely, then used the complaints to demand even more data from colleges, ostensibly to make their product seem more scientific and less commercial. Schools that refused faced punishment.

Reed, a top-ranked liberal arts college, began boycotting the *U.S. News* survey in 1995, concerned about its methodology. The next year, Reed fell from the top to the bottom tier, next to Richard Stockton College of New Jersey, No. 153, "an outcome more punitive than logical," Sanoff said. It became clear that resistance was pointless.

Instead of fighting, colleges manipulated the data to boost their own rankings. When the *Wall Street Journal*'s Steve Stecklow pried open the black box, his investigation unleashed more woe than Pandora herself could have.

Stecklow exposed widespread data-collecting inconsistencies in "Best Colleges" and implicated schools in the resulting deception. By manipulating the data they provided, colleges could better their *U.S. News* rank. One included math scores of foreign students but excluded their substandard English scores. Others omitted scores from poorly qualified foreign and remedial students. New York University, Boston University, even Harvard were rank-boosting through data manipulation, as were lesser-known colleges like Colby, Bard, and Christian Brothers University, the report revealed.

Critic Peter Sacks called on the Ivy League to muster the courage to band together, oppose the rankings, and finally defeat them. "I'm talking about the really big dogs, Harvard, Yale, Princeton, the University of Michigan, and the University of California," he said, "to step up and do what's right."

Only one did: Stanford president Gerhard Casper.

Casper wrote a scathing letter to James Fallows, the newly appointed *U.S. News* editor, attacking the specious formulas and misleading conclusions. He eviscerated the rankings with the precision of a neurosurgeon, dissecting the faulty logic; absurd, subjective categories; and changing formulas that led readers to believe "some schools have suddenly soared, others precipitously plummeted."

He was skeptical, he said, that the quality of a university could be measured statistically. "Even if it can, the producers of the *U.S. News* rankings remain far from discovering the method." Casper urged the company to move toward greater honesty with its readers and away from false precision. "Instead of tinkering to 'perfect' the weightings and formulas," he asked, could it not "question the basic

premise? Could you not admit that quality may not be truly quan-
tifiable?"

He challenged Fallows "to lead the way away from football-
ranking mentality and toward helping to inform, rather than mislead, your readers."

Executives promised to modify the survey, but Casper got tired
of waiting. He ignored the magazine's demand to supply subjective
information and instead posted online other data that he believed
more accurately defined a college's quality. The next year *U.S. News*
dropped Stanford from No. 1 to No. 6, behind Harvard, Princeton,
and Yale.

Critics continued to hammer *U.S. News*. To quell the rebellion,
Fallows commissioned the National Opinion Research Council to
analyze "Best Colleges" metrics. The results were damning, confirming what rankings foes had long suspected. The report faulted the
rankings for what they left out, specifically measures of education,
learning, student experience, and curriculum. Attacking the magazine's statistical analysis, the study concluded that the rankings "lack
any defensible empirical or theoretical basis." The subjective weights
and measures used to design "Best Colleges" formulas produced
findings "difficult to defend on any grounds other than the *U.S.
News* staff's best judgment on how to combine the measures."

Elfin was unapologetic. "We've produced a list that puts Harvard,
Yale, and Princeton, in whatever order, at the top. This is a nutty list?
Something we pulled out of the sky?" he told the *New York Times*
a few months earlier. "When you buy a VCR for 200 bucks, you
can buy Consumer Reports to find out what's out there. When you
spend 100 grand on four years of college, you should have some independent method of comparing different colleges. That's what our
readers want, and they've voted at the newsstand in favor of what
we're doing."

Not long after the public squabble, Fallows left *U.S. News* and Elfin retired. Higher education had only slightly changed its opinion about "Best Colleges" over the years, Elfin told the *Times*. "It's moved from a period of open hostility to grudging dislike." Cleaning out his office, Elfin packed up photos of himself with every US president he'd covered, starting with Johnson. When a reporter asked him to identify his greatest accomplishment, Elfin had no doubt. The rankings, he said. "This is what's going to last." Elfin's *New York Times* obituary confirmed his hunch: "Newsman Who Built Up College Ranking Guide Dies at 89."

Sanoff left *U.S. News* shortly after Elfin to work in the flourishing enrollment-management industry. For the next decade, he and Morse preached the gospel of rankings in private meetings and at public conventions, in articles published in national magazines and newspapers, building allies out of critics. They convened advisory councils with deans and high school guidance counselors, met with scores of visiting academics. They listened to complaints, then pivoted, explaining to anxious officials how to rise in the rankings.

Morse kept on keeping on, consolidating the power of "Best Colleges." Students were applying to top-ranked schools in record numbers, sinking elite college acceptance rates to single digits, intensifying stress and competition among the aspirational classes. The release of "Best Colleges" each fall produced front-page news, prime-time segments, millions of digital page views, and "howls of anger . . . in the offices of colleges and university administrators throughout the land," Sanoff wrote.

Some colleges used rankings to compete. Others, like Northeastern, used them to survive. "We always admitted there were lots of problems with the rankings, but it's useful information for the marketplace," Freeland said. "We needed a way to compete. As a strictly pragmatic thing, we grabbed onto it. It was the only avenue out there. It was a tool we could use, so we used it."

Toward the end of his life, systemic corruption troubled Sanoff. "Elite schools are like warring software companies, trying to best the other to land the students they want," he wrote. "The fact that some institutions are willing to engage in the equivalent of trying to find a loophole in the tax code says a great deal about the perceived stakes."

Responding to what they considered legitimate concerns, the editors continually fiddled with weights and categories before publishing another edition, Sanoff wrote in a scholarly article, "The *U.S. News* College Rankings: A View from the Inside," published a month before he died. That fiddling caused big problems. Altering the formula even a little from year to year invalidates annual comparisons. Though editors knew tinkering voided year-to-year results, they did little to publicize the flaw, Sanoff said, except to include a footnote explaining how that year's rankings "are not directly comparable to those published in previous years." Without valid comparisons, there are no winners and losers. Without winners and losers, there is no competition. Without competition, there is no news to break, no headline to shout, no revelations to sell, no academic arms race to chronicle.

"Those within the magazine have always known that year-to-year comparisons of a school's ranking are not valid in years when changes are made in the methodology," Sanoff confirmed, a point the magazine "has not always stressed . . . in talking with other news organizations."

Not long after Sanoff's funeral, a national coalition of liberal arts colleges attempted again to defeat "Best Colleges." The organization's leaders urged members to refuse to return the subjective "Best Colleges" Academic Reputation survey, calling it a popularity contest that colleges manipulated to their favor. The strategy worked. The response rate for the reputational survey plunged to its lowest level, 46 percent from 68 percent a decade earlier. It was, the *Chronicle of Higher Education* reported, "a possible sign that organized criticism of the rankings has sunk in."

Morse and *U.S. News* defended "Best Colleges" with the ferocity of a third-tier newsmagazine battling for survival. Brian Kelly, the magazine's editor, ignored a paltry 50 percent return rate, and told a *Times* reporter, "the vast majority of presidents and academics are still supporting the survey." Reiterating the Morse message track, he said that the magazine applauded any effort to come up with new data, even as he rejected their concerns. "Best Colleges" is a consumer guide for families, not a peer-reviewed academic article, he told Inside Higher Ed. "We do not publish the rankings for college presidents."

Like *U.S. News*, Morse emerged from the battle stronger, if not a bit gloating and perhaps a tad disingenuous. "The colleges themselves have been a key factor in giving us the credibility," he told *Time* magazine a few years later. "When the public sees that the schools are wanting to do better in our rankings, they say, Well, if the schools want to improve in these rankings, they must be worth looking at."

Give him credit for guts and top marks for discipline: Morse has remained on message for decades, rarely deviating from the official party line. Rankings are painstakingly tabulated using the best information available, the most sophisticated system out there, he repeats over and over. The rankers weigh each factor that goes into tabulating the final product using "our accumulated judgment." *U.S. News* has no role in setting standards for any college; rather, rankings arm families with good data. It's not social science. "We're not doing peer review." The company champions greater transparency, standardizes data, and tweaks the formula when necessary to measure "which schools are the top in academic excellence."

U.S. News has expanded the rankings brand to high schools, graduate schools, and hospitals; to cars, travel destinations, hotels, cruises, countries, states, cities; hundreds of thousands of pages of data—a digital dive so deep that clicking through the website is exhausting and overwhelming.

Looking back on the decision to rebuild his publishing empire on rankings, Zuckerman acknowledged the risk to a *Post* reporter. "I thought it had a real chance," he said. "But nobody had ever done this before." "Best Colleges" allowed *U.S. News* to surge ahead in the race to harness and monetize digital content, its audience numbers reaching "3 million and climbing—fast." "U.S. News & World Report Returns to the Ranks of Profitability" the *Post* announced in 2013, citing $10 million in earnings on more than $40 million in revenues.

"What we're doing is different from journalism," Morse told me. "We're creating news and information rather than covering or analyzing events."

Pruning traditional news from its mission, the company morphed into an advertising and marketing powerhouse, *AdAge* said, producing content from "a marketer's perspective," doing "monster business in lead generation, or, as its president and CEO Bill Holiber calls it, performance marketing."

In an admiring profile, the *Post* described Morse as an "unassuming celebrity" honored with memorabilia and "promotional gewgaws," like commemorative cups with his likeness that the company distributes at national conferences alongside a six-foot photographic cardboard cutout. Flipping through hundreds of "Best Colleges" pages stuffed with ads, reporter Richard Leiby described higher education as having become "a massive corporate enterprise that churns out typhoons of marketing hype. Colleges even get a one-day advance notification about their rankings so they can prepare press releases."

Morse proudly declared "Best Colleges" the winner in 2014: "We're like the 800-pound gorilla of American higher education," he told the *Post*. "Important enough to be the subject of doctoral dissertations, academic papers and conferences, endless debate, and constant media coverage."

"Best Colleges" has spawned dozens of copycats: *USA Today*'s "USA's Choosiest Colleges," *Business Week*'s "Best Graduate Schools of Business," third-party content aggregators like Niche and Chegg, and every conceivable list from "Top Party Schools" to "Best College Dorms" and "Best College Water Parks." It created new ranking categories to answer every possible critic, from "Best Undergraduate Teaching," "Best Public Universities," and "Most Innovative Schools among National Universities" to "Top Performer on Social Mobility."

"Best Colleges" fed the global rankings industrial complex, with guides published in two dozen countries including Canada, China, Britain, Germany, Poland, Russia, Spain, and Taiwan. It produces millions of page views on publication day, tens of millions around the globe, traffic running at thousands of megabytes per second. The sheer numbers can paralyze families fearful of making wrong choices. Rankings are chaotic, bewildering, confusing, oppressive; Andrew Ferguson described just how overwhelming in *Crazy U: One Dad's Crash Course in Getting His Kid into College.*

At the end of an interview, Morse handed Ferguson several pounds of "best colleges" guides, one 1,800 pages, a stack a foot thick. Morse told Ferguson that his son might want to start sifting through the magazine's college website too. It had more than a hundred thousand pages of information.

"A hundred thousand pages!" Ferguson replied. "Great!"

If Morse had doubts or felt pangs of conscience about the anxiety rankings created, he hasn't shown them much publicly. Criticism doesn't bother *U.S. News* executives as much as it has made them feel "slightly jaded from being under attack all the time," Morse told *Boston College* magazine. "In the editors' view, they're providing a service the public seems to need and want. After all, the rankings are among the magazine's top-selling issues."

Morse keeps "Best Colleges" cranking to the tune of a ringing cash register. By building rankings into a multimillion-dollar global force, he toppled the ivory tower and brought armies of academics to their knees. Gone were the days when college presidents challenged the rankings' authority. Fearing what might happen if their schools fell in rank, they played the game. Nothing, it seemed, could knock "Best Colleges" off its lofty perch, not even the demands of six angry US senators.

In a letter to *U.S. News*, the senators requested changes, publicly accusing "Best Colleges" of creating "perverse incentive for schools to adopt or maintain policies that perpetuate social and economic inequalities." When the *Post* called Morse for comment, he declined.

Instead, Brian Kelly sent a 650-word letter largely dismissing the senators' complaints. "We have used the best available data. . . . [We] change our methodology when new or better data becomes available. . . . We will continue to study this data, take feedback, and make refinements as necessary. . . . We welcome the chance to meet with you."

The political circus was a familiar sideshow. Attacking "Best Colleges" distracts politicians from taking the most important step to neutralize rankings: restoring funding to public colleges and providing sufficient financial aid to struggling students.

Rankings are a frustrating moving target, an exercise in public trust. Do we trust colleges to report accurate statistics to *U.S. News*? Do we trust *U.S. News* to publish accurate data in "Best Colleges"? Do we trust a content-creating corporation that refuses to let experts and journalists review its facts and findings?

The *U.S. News* strategy of demanding transparency and accountability from everyone but itself has allowed the company to avoid responsibility for the damage "Best Colleges" has caused.

Each time dissenters raise legitimate points, *U.S. News* executives respond with the same "what about" litany that diverts attention away from crucial answers, replying: What about the change in methodology we made to emphasize student outcomes? What about our ongoing debate about how to best measure a college? What about our evolving methodology? What about the transparency we've driven in higher education? What about our attempts to address socioeconomic status by incorporating the percentage of students on Pell Grants? What about how well we serve the millions of students and families who come to our website to research colleges?

What about all that? I called Morse for answers. I found a thoughtful, serious, reasonable man shaking his fist at history, aware of but seemingly unconcerned about his role in creating and stoking a college admissions hysteria that had barely existed before he came along. As we discussed the "Best Colleges" origins, Morse stopped to say he'd be happy to talk more after I'd cleared the interview through *U.S. News* communications director, Enxhi Myslymi.

Myslymi, a Fairfield College graduate—"definitely not one of the elites!" she chirped—was bubbly but unyielding. Her team controls media access, she said, and Morse was a busy man. She'd respond to my request in a week or two. It seemed somehow fitting that a twenty-six-year-old graduate of a second-tier college had the power to keep Morse bunkered in a Georgetown office.

I asked why it would take so long to decide. She equivocated, then explained. "If I can be frank, as you know, there's been lot of criticism and takedowns of the rankings. We'll take your request back to the team to decide if he can talk to you, but I can't promise anything."

A week later she replied. "While we appreciate you contacting us to speak with Bob Morse, we will not be able to accommodate this request."

4

The Academic Arms Race

Make *Moneyball* Admissions Work for You

Soaring tuition, multimillion-dollar college presidents, celebrity faculty, luxury student housing, campus water parks, and hyper-competition for the highest test scores and grades all coincided with the rise of "Best Colleges." *U.S. News* sponsored an academic arms race that destabilized higher education and turbocharged a nascent industry called enrollment management.

Even for faculty like myself, enrollment management is baffling and mysterious. Working behind closed doors, analysts manipulate econometric models to predict how many students will enroll and how much to discount tuition to persuade students to attend. To maximize revenues, enrollment managers created rules that irrevocably altered college admissions, encouraging students to borrow more money than they can afford to repay, leading to $1.5 trillion in student debt. The road to affordable colleges has become impossible to navigate, and many families trying to stay ahead of the changes are destined to fail.

Jack Maguire couldn't have known how misused enrollment

management would become when he started plotting strategies to save his beloved alma mater Boston College in the 1970s. Maguire is known as the father of enrollment management, higher education's Billy Beane, a *Moneyball* guy decades before baseball adopted sabermetrics.

Just as Beane did for a struggling baseball franchise, Maguire recognized the power of harnessing data. Trained in theoretical physics, Maguire brought a scientist's sensibility to the task of reviving a dying college, inventing an analytical system that led a revolution. Maguire used formulas, algorithms, and intuition to devise admissions strategies that doubled applications and grew revenues. He was so successful, Boston College emerged from near insolvency in a few years and eventually became what it is now—an elite global brand and one of the nation's wealthiest universities.

Maguire relied on a counterintuitive approach once little known in higher education called financial aid leveraging. He tore down the traditional silos separating offices that recruited, funded, retained, and replaced students. He ignored academia's distaste for commerce, embraced marketing, and used students, alumni, and faculty to encourage students to apply.

Most daringly, he raised tuition and awarded merit scholarships to entice the most desired students to enroll. The college used the increased revenues to reduce its debt and subsidize campus improvements. Maguire called his strategy enrollment management.

"Today, if you're not doing some version of what Jack invented, you're out of the game. You're just behind the competition," said Richard Freeland, former Massachusetts commissioner of education. "He made what once was entirely an art into a science and a very powerful one."

Maguire was an early detractor of "Best Colleges," which used a formula he thought hurt schools with missions to educate the least advantaged. He voiced his concerns to Morse early on, he said, sending letters suggesting changes to make the rankings more equitable. He urged the magazine to reduce the value given to SAT scores and to weight more heavily student retention and graduation rates.

U.S. News made some changes Maguire and others suggested but kept a formula that has consistently defined excellence using wealthy, elite colleges as the standard. Before the academy fully realized the threat "Best Colleges" posed, it was too late. College presidents were faced with a scorecard and required to play the game or risk a punishing fall in the rankings.

In the absence of shared values, enrollment managers used "Best Colleges" to define academic quality, worsening the hypercompetition families now take for granted. *U.S. News* lay siege to the ivory tower, encouraging colleges to adopt policies that benefit the most privileged at the expense of everyone else.

Relentless cuts to tuition subsidies that started with Ronald Reagan worsened under George Bush and Bill Clinton. Average tuition costs skyrocketed as need-based financial aid decreased. Enrollment managers used merit scholarships to recruit students with the highest test scores and grades, discounts that favored affluent graduates of wealthy high schools.

Seduced by the status that top-ranked colleges convey, aspirational students relentlessly pursued the highest grades and test scores. Their parents were spending, collectively, millions of dollars for tutors and consultants to provide every possible advantage. The obsessive sorting "Best Colleges" encouraged launched an academic arms race between the haves and have-nots and a yawning divide between elite colleges and the rest.

"The whole business of getting enrollment management right is very, very Darwinian. Getting it right is messy," Maguire said. "You'll succeed not principally because you're smarter than everyone else or that you're tougher than everybody else. You'll succeed because you're best capable of adapting to change." As the power of "Best Colleges" grew, so did enrollment management, a multimillion-dollar industry that hatched "a bazillion" consultants, Maguire joked, dozens of companies, some subsidiaries of multibillion-dollar corporations.

I met Maguire on a cold day in Concord, Massachusetts, at the headquarters of Maguire Associates. Maguire loves to tell stories, and his modest office is filled with memorabilia from the myriad colleges and universities he's advised over five decades. In his eighties, Maguire is as passionate as he was when he arrived at Boston College as a young faculty member. He returned to his alma mater in 1968 to teach physics with a newly minted doctorate from Rice University. The college was on the verge of bankruptcy, enrollment declining, $30 million in debt, endowment at zero.

Typical of private Catholic schools, Boston College was founded in the nineteenth century to educate the country's growing immigrant communities. In the 1960s, the school reimagined itself as the "Catholic Harvard of the East," Maguire said. "We didn't want the bread-and-butter immigrants anymore." The applicant pool shrank, and the college lost the tuition revenue it needed to keep the doors open.

When the director of admissions quit, the president hired Maguire to replace him. Working with Vice President Frank Campanella, a Harvard-educated business executive, Maguire started analyzing Boston College's tuition pricing. For comparison, he collected data from nearby Boston University, whose president was transforming the school from a faltering college into one of the nation's leading private universities.

Boston University charged higher tuition but was expanding enrollment as steadily as Boston College was losing it. In the comparative data, Maguire saw odd contradictions. Even with Boston University's higher sticker price, the average tuition students paid at both colleges was the same. He traced the explanation to the tuition discounts each college gave students.

To recruit and retain high-achieving students, Boston University was discounting tuition, on average, 40 percent, Maguire found. At Boston College, the discount was about 17 percent. "Boston College had a much lower sticker price and a much lower discount rate." But net tuition revenue per student was about the same. "The better position was BU's."

Maguire raised sticker prices at Boston College and gave discounts to students the college valued most. Full-paying wealthy students subsidized the rest. "That full sticker price reaps a lot more revenue that can be reinvested more easily for all kinds of good things like better buildings, better paid faculty, bringing in more diversity," Maguire said.

Robin Hood pricing became more common as colleges struggled to meet the growing financial needs of middle- and low-income students. "I don't like that 'Robin Hood' term, but I guess I'm invoking it," Maguire said. "I guess it's better to rob the rich to pay the poor than the Donald Trump approach, robbing the poor to pay the rich."

By the 1990s, adverse and unpredictable changes had permanently altered the college admissions landscape. The government's unrelenting cuts to tuition subsidies for middle-income and disadvantaged students forced colleges to find other funding sources or significantly increase the number of wealthy students they enrolled. The rigid "Best Colleges" formula made it financially difficult for colleges to determine their own goals and visions.

Enrollment managers figured they either played the rankings game or risked losing the revenue they needed to stay competitive in the marketplace. As *U.S. News* gained more power to dictate the definition of academic quality, the arms race intensified. "Had institutions not abdicated their natural claim to define quality in higher education, *they* would have been the ones to determine what to measure and what to consider optimal outcomes," Maguire said. The rise of "Best Colleges" rankings "fueled a preoccupation with school status in the competitive battle for students."

Maguire urged his clients to define enrollment strategies based on institutional values and principles, not according to the demands of a commercial magazine. "Every college has the power to define what specifically distinguishes it from other colleges—its institutional DNA," Maguire said. "It's not about survival of the biggest, or best, but fittest—fittest within a particular niche."

But the pressure to maintain or boost rank became inescapable. *U.S. News* algorithms reward colleges with higher rankings for spending money on everything from student services to faculty salaries. To keep spending heavily, colleges needed to raise tuition and admit more rich kids. To continue allocating resources to meet the "Best Colleges" prescription, college enrollment managers created their own algorithms to serve the rankings and maximize revenues.

To enroll the high-achieving students needed to boost selectivity, colleges awarded merit scholarships to wealthy students with little or no financial need. To lower acceptance rates, they used aggressive marketing strategies to attract and reject as many applicants as possible. On and on it went, spiraling out of control—courting donors, hiring celebrity faculty, increasing applications and rejections, awarding discounts to enroll high-achieving students to boost status and rank. The battle for the best students led to hypercompetition on high school campuses. To get into highly ranked colleges, students needed ever-higher grades and test scores.

"The rankings don't tell you about quality, they tell you about market strength," Freeland said. "Academics thought *U.S. News* gave the suggestion that one institution was objectively better than another institution, and it was fostering competition."

Some colleges rebelled. They cajoled. They assembled advisory groups and committees. They signed petitions. They held meetings. They boycotted. They wrote op-eds. They launched competing rankings to measure values they held dear, like "Colleges That Change Lives." They called "Best Colleges" rankings "corrupt," "pernicious," "misleading," "perpetrators of inequality," "a scam," "deeply flawed," "a tyrannical tool," "a list of criteria that mirrors the superficial characteristics of elite colleges and universities," "more damaging to higher education than any other enterprise out there."

Others decided it was easier to reverse engineer the "Best Colleges" formula and transform themselves into luxury brands. Two colleges in particular emerged big winners: Washington University in St. Louis (No. 16 in 2021) and the University of Southern California (No. 24 in 2021). Analyzing the strategies the colleges used to climb to the top of the *U.S. News* firmament, University of California researchers found a common denominator between the two: billions of dollars in capital.

The studies affirmed what critics had long been saying: money buys rank.

Top 20 colleges are exclusive, uberwealthy private schools with billion-dollar-plus endowments, something that hasn't changed in decades. No college ranked in the top 20 has moved into the top 10, a Harvard study found. Boosting rank requires huge infusions of cash, hundreds of millions of dollars directed to areas that promote upward movement in *U.S. News* variables.

Washington University and USC shared another crucial factor: strong leaders committed to winning a marathon, not a sprint. One of those presidents, Steven Sample, arrived in 1991 at USC. Back then, USC was derided as the University of Spoiled Children, a safety school that accepted more than 70 percent of its applicants. Determined to boost USC's rank, Sample went on a $100 million spending spree, significantly improving financial resources and faculty salaries, both crucial to "Best Colleges" ratings.

To increase student selectivity, USC poured millions into merit scholarships, discounting tuition for high-achieving applicants regardless of family wealth. USC eventually moved from No. 51 to its current place at No. 24, tripling tuition to $59,260 and rejecting 89 percent of its applicants.

To help offset the cost of that climb, the university occasionally engaged in unethical fundraising, including trading access for donations, the *Los Angeles Times* found. Sample retired in 2010 and died in 2016. His successor, Max Nikias, resigned in 2018 with a $7 million payout. Afterward, the university was publicly criticized for prioritizing fundraising over rectitude. "Instead of cultivating an environment of reflection and reasoned debate, the university sprinted toward growth," William Tierney, a USC professor of education, wrote in the *Los Angeles Times*. USC's connection to the Rick Singer scandal, Tierney told a *Financial Times* reporter, "is tied to all the others largely because of the previous administration's desire to improve dramatically in a very short time."

While impressive, USC's accomplishment was nowhere near as climactic as that of Northeastern University. Northeastern soared from No. 162 to its current No. 40—a 122-point improvement versus USC's 29 points. *Boston Business Journal* called Northeastern's achievement "one of the most dramatic since U.S. News began ranking schools."

Freeland took over Northeastern in 1996 with a mandate to stop the hemorrhaging enrollment and boost rank. He immediately hired Maguire to help. Maguire remembers Northeastern at the time as treeless, squat, and institutional. "Kind of like this," he said, kicking a cardboard box.

Despite its unremarkable campus, Northeastern played a remarkable role in Boston. At a time when Massachusetts had no public liberal arts colleges, Northeastern was the largest private university in the nation, educating the city's immigrants and working class and providing solid low-cost degrees with traction in the marketplace.

Massive government subsidies to higher education in the 1960s made it possible for the University of Massachusetts to open a branch in Boston a few miles from Northeastern's campus in the city's sketchy South End. Students flocked to the ocean-view public school in a neighborhood far more affluent than the area surrounding Northeastern. Faced with growing turmoil in the city and low-cost state competition, Northeastern couldn't attract the enrollment it needed to survive.

By the 1990s, Northeastern was a struggling third-tier commuter school with little residential housing within a few miles of a dozen better-funded colleges and universities drawing thousands of wealthier applicants. Freeland arrived at Northeastern at a pivotal moment.

U.S. News was redefining educational quality as status and prestige, giving no credit to colleges for educating needy students from underresourced urban high schools. Rather than publicly oppose "Best Colleges," Freeland saw a way to use the rankings to Northeastern's advantage.

"If you're Northeastern and you're the bottom of the barrel, and everyone thinks you're this third-rate institution that serves local kids and can't go anywhere else, how do you convince them otherwise that you're actually a lot better than that? We always admitted there were lots of problems with the rankings." Even so, he happily embraced them. "It was very controversial at the time. I knew no one who wasn't disdainful of the rankings. Everybody hated them. It was almost embarrassing. I took a lot of gas from people for taking it so seriously."

Now retired, Freeland keeps an airy office on campus filled with art and books, facing a wide, tree-lined street and Fenway Park. His brown corduroy jacket, blue button-down shirt, chiseled features, and salt-and-pepper hair project an image of intellectual authority. A scholar trained in American Studies, Freeland sees Northeastern's rise in the context of the power rankings have over higher education.

Unable to compete, private colleges like Northeastern had to change or die. "We had to rethink our competitive model," Freeland said. "Who to serve, what to be." Freeland promised the Northeastern board that he'd break into the top 100 from No. 162 during his ten-year tenure as president. Freeland's mandate to crack the code was more difficult than he'd imagined.

He spent the next decade "disaggregating the formula," he said, forming an institutional research staff, appointing higher education's first marketing executive, and assigning a vice president to reverse engineer the "Best Colleges" blueprint.

Enrolling more affluent, high-achieving suburban students improved the university's graduation and retention rates, a significant portion of the university's "Best Colleges" score. By improving student selectivity and graduation rates, Freeland achieved two "Best Colleges" boosts at once. "You got independent value on the rankings for improving the quality of your students. You got a second bump because those students also tended to bump up the graduation rate. We got pretty sophisticated about this." The end result? "Best Colleges" rewarded Northeastern with better rankings for reducing the number of disadvantaged students whose poor high school preparation and ongoing financial hardships forced them to drop out.

"By the time we got into this, we could pretty much say if we move the needle this much on this metric, this is how it will affect our overall ranking. Ultimately, we developed policy interventions based on that research. We were pretty successful." Freeland's institutional research teams used algorithms to tell enrollment managers which sorts of students to accept and how much to discount tuition to convince them to enroll.

The campus filled with bulldozers, cranes, and construction workers as Northeastern spent hundreds of millions of dollars to raise thirteen new student residences. Tree-lined walkways and architecture that broadcast prosperity grew and flourished among utilitarian concrete cubes. Freeland spent $400 million on new construction, $3 million a year on marketing, and many hours with his staff parsing the "Best Colleges" formula.

His team had regular access to Robert Morse, he said, and he met with him a couple of times. Morse surprised him. "I expected a kind of hustler. He was thoughtful and reasonable. And also tough-minded. He'd say things like 'Yeah, you're right. I agree with you intellectually, but it wouldn't work in the magazine.'"

Toward the end of Freeland's presidency, his deadline looming, he traveled to Georgetown to lobby Morse to change a particularly vexing metric he felt unfairly hurt Northeastern's ranking. "Best Colleges" had penalized the university for a successful cooperative education program that placed students in full-time employment during alternate semesters. Since a significant percentage of them worked off campus, Freeland wanted to subtract co-op students from the university's total enrollment, boosting the dollars-per-student spending ratio, an important measure on the "Best Colleges" scale.

Morse refused, Freeland said. He remembers Morse telling him, "You're right, that's absolutely persuasive. But I can't do it, because if I do that for you, someone will knock on our door with another story to tell." The clock ticking, Freeland returned home to discuss the situation with colleagues. "We finally decided he knows we're right intellectually, so why don't we just do it? Let's not ask permission, let's just do it and see if he whacks us. So we did it. And they let it go."

Northeastern broke into the top 100 two weeks after Freeland retired in 2006. Applications doubled. Average test scores rose more than 200 points. The university jumped sixty-four places. Northeastern today is a wealthy "Best Colleges" powerhouse, a university that once accepted 75 percent of its applicants but now rejects more than 80 percent. Its $55,566 annual tuition in 2021 was more than three times what it was when Freeland started. The board awarded Freeland a $2 million bonus and replaced him with a dean from the University of Southern California. "There's no question that the system invites gaming," Freeland told a *Boston* magazine reporter. "We made a systematic effort to influence [the outcome]. . . . That was life or death."

College became "a consumer affair," higher education marketing executive Robert Sevier wrote in a business journal article. Students were seen as "consumers" purchasing products they enjoy. "We sell experiences." Embracing luxury retail marketing strategies, they launched building booms that produced lavish housing never before seen on college campuses. Inspired by Disneyland and Starbucks, college executives replaced spartan, smelly gyms and dormitories with resort amenities and plush apartments. They built fitness centers with lazy-river swimming pools, water slides, hot tubs, saunas, rock-climbing walls, and Zumba classes. They offered students housing extravagances few Americans can afford—concierge services, rooftop pools, outdoor theaters, fifty-inch flat-screen TVs, showerhead speakers, granite countertops, stainless steel appliances, floor-to-ceiling windows, terraces, sweeping views, and $2,000-a-month rents.

Recruiting costs increased 68 percent, from an average of $750 per student at private colleges in 1980 to $2,357 in 2017. Multimillion-dollar recruiting and telemarketing campaigns became standard. Colleges partnered with the Common Application, allowing students to submit as many as 20 applications electronically with the click of a button. They bought millions of names from testing companies that sell student data for 47 cents a name in $7,710 packages and $17,750-a-year fees. Differences between the higher education and luxury markets flattened as the power of "Best Colleges" grew. Small colleges—especially those with missions to educate the disadvantaged—were going out of business at an alarming rate.

Strategies to boost rank became standard among aspiring presidents and boards of trustees. They doubled tuition. They launched revenue-generating but academically unproven online programs. They reduced need-based financial aid to give tuition discounts to high-achieving affluent students to enhance institutional prestige.

They recruited wealthy, full-paying foreign students and persuaded the poor and middle-class to assume onerous debt.

Even students with no interest in selective colleges were bombarded with telemarketing calls and blizzards of junk mail, emails, and texts enticing them to apply. More applications allowed colleges to send more rejections, which made them appear more selective. Some schools sent students completed applications, waiving fees, "simply for the rankings," said Jack Blackburn, dean of admissions at the University of Virginia. "It's not just weak colleges and universities doing that. There are also some pretty well-established places."

"Best Colleges" managing editor Alvin Sanoff left *U.S. News* to work for Maguire and began writing about the rankings' failings. He faulted *U.S. News* for flawed metrics but also blamed colleges for dishonestly manipulating data to boost rank. College presidents put rankings at the center of marketing campaigns to mislead families, he said, using deceptive advertising. He singled out a bottom-tier school that sold itself as "ranked among America's best colleges" in a magazine advertisement. "The fact that even a bottom-tier school uses rankings to market itself illustrates how higher education has increased the visibility and impact of the rankings."

Sanoff died in 2007, the same year the president of Sarah Lawrence College refused to play the rankings game. An eminent, writing-intensive humanities college modeled on Oxford and Cambridge, Sarah Lawrence joined a movement to drop the SAT and ACT as an admissions requirement. High-stakes admissions tests did little to predict student performance, President Michele Tolela Myers said, but did "bias admission in favor of those who could afford expensive coaching sessions."

Absent SAT scores from Sarah Lawrence, *U.S. News* said it would calculate the school's ranking by assuming an average SAT score roughly 200 points below its peer group's average. Sarah Lawrence's ranking went into free fall. It was banished to the "unranked."

Myers felt extorted. "In the absence of real data, they will make up a number," she wrote in the *Post*. She called "Best Colleges" "ranking roulette," gambling in a house that stacks the decks. "The message is clear. Unless we are willing to be badly misrepresented, we had better send the information the magazine wants."

Fallout from the 2008 Great Recession worsened hypercompetition among colleges and among students searching for affordable degrees. The government cut funding to higher education 20 percent between 2008 and 2013, a Pew study found. Public universities scrambled to compete with private colleges for the wealthy students they needed to meet revenue targets.

Looking for low-cost strategies to boost rank, colleges instituted "spring admission"—accepting full-paying students or athletes with weaker credentials after the deadline to report data to *U.S. News* had passed. They offered "binding early decision" to lock in half or more of their first-year classes in early December by requiring accepted students to agree to whatever financial aid they offered, a strategy that favored the wealthiest.

Even after "Best Colleges" dropped a metric called "yield"—the percent of accepted students who enroll—enrollment managers still used it to broadcast their popularity. Administrative bloat grew. So did armies of low-cost untenured adjunct faculty. The number of college administrators increased 60 percent, ten times the growth of tenured faculty members, between 1993 and 2009, Bloomberg reported. Tuition and fees increased nearly five times the rate of inflation between 1980 and 2018. Student debt reached historic highs—a total of $1.5 trillion.

College presidents bemoaned rankings publicly but extolled them privately to appease trustees and donors looking for bottom-line validation. They "read it, feed it, and fidget all summer until the new edition arrives, and then wave it around like a bride's garter belt if their school gets a favorable review," Andrew Ferguson observed in *Crazy U.*

Few presidents saw an upside to attacking *U.S. News.* "If you're at the top of the heap, why do you want to do something that might threaten that?" one explained in the *Chronicle of Higher Education.*

Boards of trustees promised huge bonuses to presidents for boosting rank. Higher rankings increase alumni giving and endowment gifts, and influence foundation grants. Bond-rating companies like Moody's and S&P use rankings to evaluate financial stability. A botched attempt to improve graduation and retention rates—an important *U.S. News* metric—at Mount St. Mary's University in Maryland forced a new president to resign.

President Simon Newman suggested professors "drown the bunnies" by flunking struggling students quickly. "This is hard for you because you think of the students as cuddly bunnies, but you can't," he said. "Just put a Glock to their heads."

The "Best Colleges" scorecard became a cheat sheet. Schools with honor codes and penalties for plagiarism inflated SAT scores and graduation rates. They manipulated data to appear more selective. They rewarded applicants for retaking the SAT to get higher scores. They inflated the percentages of full-time professors. Cataloging all the misrepresentation, falsification, and cheating would bore even the most ardent rankings critics. So many colleges misreported data that *U.S. News* punished only the most flagrant, with penalties that rarely deflated status or impacted rank, a survey of news reports revealed.

College admissions had become a gambling hall with quants betting on which and how many students would come. "The pressure is real," said Bruce Poch, former director of admissions at Pomona College. "God forbid you go down in those numbers."

Even Sarah Lawrence happily reclaimed its seat at the rankings table after Michelle Tolela Myers left. "Frankly it is good to be back in the rankings," Sarah Lawrence vice president Thomas Blum told the *Post* after the college submitted test scores it had once withheld. *U.S. News* lists are "primary source material" for many students and parents, he said. "They do recognize we are a national liberal arts college. It does not hurt to have that kind of recognition."

Though the "Best Colleges" formula has changed over the years, it continues to measure institutional wealth. A 2019 social mobility index, worth 5 percent of a college's score, is at best a fuzzy metric. Another new measure to address inequality, "graduation rate performance," is so convoluted it requires a statistics degree to unpack:

> A comparison between the actual six-year graduation rate for students entering in fall 2012 and the predicted graduation rate for the proportion who graduated six years later in 2018. . . . The predicted graduation rate is based upon characteristics of the entering class, as well as characteristics of the institution. If the actual graduation rate is higher than the predicted rate, the college is enhancing achievement or is overperforming. If its actual graduation rate is lower than the predicted rate, then it's underperforming. *U.S. News* divided the actual rate by the predicted rate. The higher the ratio, the better the score. This indicator of added value shows the effect of the college's programs and policies on the six-year graduation rate of students after controlling for spending per student, the proportion of undergraduates receiving Pell Grants, standardized test scores and high school class standing of the entering classes, and for the first time, the proportion of undergraduates who are first-generation. Also, the proportion of science, technology, engineering and math, or STEM, degrees out of the total degrees granted was a variable used to calculate the predicted graduation rate for each school in the National Universities ranking

category only. To determine whether an awarded degree was considered STEM, *U.S. News* used the U.S. Department of Homeland Security's STEM Designated Degree Program list. The list includes a diverse array of degrees in general STEM areas such as biology and engineering, as well as specific STEM degree tracks in nontraditional STEM fields, such as business statistics and digital communication and media.

The statistics that do matter—the percentage of students with loans and the average debt they hold—are locked behind a "Best Colleges" paywall. Trying to access "10 colleges where students graduate with the least debt," I was directed to pay $40 for a full listing.

Google "college rankings" and over a billion choices appear, an overwhelming overload of information. Rankings are "a joke," commentator Frank Bruni wrote in the *New York Times*. The *Atlantic's* George Packer described parents battling to get their children into elite schools as a frantic scramble for status, with the most prized acquisition "an acceptance letter from a university with a top 10 *U.S. News & World Report* ranking."

Only a tiny fraction of the millions of high school applicants will attend elite colleges. The rest will go to one of the vast majority that accept most of the students who apply. The average acceptance rate at private colleges is 66 percent, and more than 70 percent at public schools. Since nearly all applicants will find a college willing to take them, why the stress? Why the anxiety? Why the sleep deprivation? Why have hundreds of thousands of words been written about an academic arms race ruining the emotional psyches of an entire generation, robbing them of childhood? Why are obsessed parents spending millions of dollars, legally and illegally, to pump, primp, and preen their children for college?

The hysteria is a needless reaction to a numbers game driven almost entirely by commercial interests. The academic arms race isn't about the struggle to crash the gates of elite colleges. It's a battle for access to affordable degrees.

"Best Colleges" has effectively deceived families into believing the only schools worth attending are the ones ranked highest. Competition for places at selective colleges has become so fierce and costly that nearly half the nation's eligible low-income students are too discouraged to even apply, a Jack Kent Cooke Foundation study found. Decades of tuition hikes, government cutbacks, and a national obsession with elite colleges has distracted Americans from demanding that lawmakers restore tuition subsidies and public funding to universities where the majority of students attend classes and earn degrees.

The children of the wealthy will always find a seat at a good college if they can pay full tuition. The real victims are families competing for affordable degrees against players using loaded dice on a tilted craps table. "The way the college admissions process worked today, no one had a chance," CEO Devin Sloane wrote in a letter to the judge explaining why he paid $250,000 to bribe his son into USC. "The system was broken and unfair."

It is unfair, but not for someone like Sloane. It's unfair to teenagers from resource-starved public high schools whose financial aid goes to expensively prepped rich kids' merit scholarships. It's unfair to students whose tuition payments offset the administrative bloat needed to beat "Best Colleges." It's unfair to colleges fighting to educate the least advantaged students without the resources to game the rankings.

"The system operates like a casino, and the top-tier schools with billion-dollar endowments will always win," Maguire said. "Only they can afford to gamble on the year-to-year ranking shifts. All the other players would do well to cash in their chips and leave the casino."

5

You Will Fail Without Us

The Tyranny of the Test

A ce the test. It's the one true thing I knew about college admissions. A high SAT score is the key that unlocks the numeric lock on the Ivy League gates. But what's the secret number? To find out, I attended a Yale information session when my third child was in ninth grade.

Arriving after dark, I made my way across cracked asphalt parking lots toward Santa Ana High, one of the largest and poorest secondary schools in Orange County, California, home base for Rick Singer's criminal enterprise. Walking past withered landscaping, I joined a gathering crowd of casually dressed parents, some chattering in Spanish. We moved like a herd into the auditorium, a building sagging from age, filling circa-1970s wooden chairs that creaked and groaned as we sat.

Yale's assistant director of admissions approached the podium. It was a low-tech presentation, a few people sitting in folding chairs on a brightly lit stage. He recited an unfamiliar litany of facts, opinions, and unsettling advice. Two remarks so stunned me I thought he was kidding, or trying to discourage students from applying: The most successful Yale applicants had been preparing for admissions since preschool, he said. And, he added, Yale regularly rejects numerous students with perfect SAT scores.

How are there so many kids with perfect test scores? Why would any college—even Yale—reject a teenager with an accomplishment as impressive as a perfect SAT score? Something about the SAT was seriously out of whack. I resolved to find out what it was.

As my daughter journeyed through an eerily opaque admissions industrial complex, I felt adrift in misinformation from so-called experts. They obfuscated with pleasantries and platitudes about how applicants should present themselves: Be genuine. (But create a personal brand.) Follow your passions. (But market yourself.) Live a balanced life. (But earn a 4.5 GPA.) Give back. (But score a 1540 out of 1600 on the SAT or 34 out of 36 on the ACT.)

Applicants needed much higher scores to get through the same gates that their parents, with comparatively lackluster SATs, had sailed through easily. Average test scores to qualify for elite colleges and merit scholarships had climbed higher and higher. As scores spiral upward, families correctly recognize that to attend those colleges or win those scholarships, they'd have to pay for test prep. The global expansion of the College Board and the ACT allowed the test prep industry to expand at a furious rate. Costs range from $40 an hour to $20,000 packages sold to monied families in the nation's wealthiest enclaves.

Taking and retaking tests for better scores became as common as paying for prep. Students who prep not only do better, they push up average scores needed to get into selective colleges. Worse, colleges use test scores to decide who gets scholarships and institutional grants.

I attended information sessions, I read books, I talked to dozens of parents trying to understand the arcane world of high-stakes admissions testing. I organized workshops for the PTA so we could figure out the differences between the SAT and the ACT, a distinction that wasn't clear to any of us.

The mysteries of standardized testing hide a shameful truth: Scores correlate with income. Students from families earning more than $200,000 a year scored 400 points higher on the SAT than students from families earning less than $20,000, according to a study by the College Board, the purveyor of the SAT test. The wealth gap is directly related to the rise of the test prep industry. Students who pay for prep do better than those who can't.

Even something as basic as a $150 graphing calculator provides students advantages unavailable to those who can pay only for the $8 model. A significant number of students arrive to the test without a calculator because they can't afford or don't realize they can use one. A senior at a public high school in Idaho wrote about a girl in her exam who lacked "this privilege hack." When the girl asked the proctor if she could borrow a calculator, "she was told none were available and that she didn't need one."

The highest-quality private tutoring—at hundreds of dollars an hour—can raise scores enough to put students on the radar of elite colleges and make them competitive for merit scholarships. As few as twenty hours of test prep can add as many as 115 points on the SAT, and just six to eight hours produces an average 90-point increase, according to College Board data.

The College Board and the ACT, billion-dollar nonprofit companies that sell nearly all admissions test products, provide immense profit opportunities for their partners in the test prep industry. Tens of thousands of corporations, businesses, and entrepreneurs aggressively compete for the money parents spend on prep. I've sat through dozens of pitches from SAT and ACT prep companies and heard time after time misinformation presented as fact and designed to incite anxiety. Overwhelming parents with graphs and charts, consultants pitch $400-an-hour tutors to prepare students for elite colleges, even though fewer than 4 percent of all college applicants attend the nation's most selective schools.

With so few students eligible for top colleges, how did a few dozen entrepreneurs catering to snobby parents grow into a shadow global education market, with $1,500-an-hour tutors, $50,000 weekend boot camps, and publicly traded companies battling for global market share?

I got my answer at a Kaplan session held at a public high school hosted by the sales rep of that billion-dollar-plus company.

Test prep is the great equalizer in the brutal world of college admissions, he said, punching emotional hot buttons: "More students than ever applying." "Incredibly competitive." "I'm not trying to scare anybody here. . . ."

But?

"These tests determine what school you'll go to. It's the top factor in deciding college admissions and scholarships. You can't do it on your own."

Afterward, parents swarmed him, rock-star style, shoving forward to ask questions; get advice; pick up his business card, flyer, and brochures. Middle school parents told him their children had taken the test three times, hoping to score high enough for scholarships.

"What's the cost?"

"How do I sign up?"

No worries, he said. "We have a discount for all the parents attending tonight!"

My friend Dana Collinson found an equally enticing deal with the Princeton Review. Her daughter was in her senior year, had a good SAT score, but needed a boost to qualify for merit scholarships at her first-choice college. Dana liked the Princeton Review's "money-back guarantee." It was more than she wanted to spend, but the company upgraded her for free to its "Ultimate Course" that came with a 150-point improvement guarantee. Dana signed the contract and paid the Princeton Review more than $1,000, figuring it was a no-lose gamble. Her daughter would either improve enough to get a merit scholarship, or Princeton would refund her money.

Her daughter "worked really hard in class and at home doing all the homework. Her in-class test scores went up," Dana said. "But when it came to the actual test day, there was virtually no improvement. Very disappointing—after fourteen sessions and a lot of hard work!" Dana asked for her money back. The company refused and referred her to language in the contract. Customers can enroll in unlimited classes to improve scores, she was told. But Kaplan doesn't issue cash refunds. "It was *very* misleading," she said. By then it was too late. The application deadline had passed. Her daughter was accepted to American University, her dream college, but was denied a merit scholarship.

Dana unwittingly discovered the unwritten rule of high-risk admissions testing. It's nearly impossible to identify the best coaches and tutors from the thousands peddling wares. Years of personal experience and scores of interviews with families like the Collinsons have taught me that there is often little correlation between price and quality, especially at test prep corporations. A $25-an-hour college student might help more than expensive Kaplan and Princeton Review classes.

More test takers and more test prep have inflamed competition. At Georgetown, for example, half the students accepted in 2007 scored between 26 and 32 on the ACT. In 2015, half scored between 31 and 35. At Harvard, 25 percent of those admitted in 2014 had perfect SAT scores. Test prep made perfect scores more common than ever. Prepped applicants were causing serious score inflation. That's what Jon Boeckenstedt, vice provost at Oregon State

University, found when he analyzed the numbers. On the ACT, for example, fewer than one student out of 100 scored 34 or better in 2002. Five times as many earned those scores in 2018.

Competition to get into selective colleges and win merit scholarships reached a fever pitch. So did competition to sell tests and prep to as many students as possible. With billions of dollars at stake, the ACT and the College Board ruthlessly maneuvered for global market share, creating a testing gold rush with major unintended side effects. An unstoppable chain reaction engendered widespread cheating in the US and abroad. Sophisticated international gangs were systematically exploiting lax test security and profiting from some of the worst cheating scandals in testing history.

By the time Boo was finishing her junior year, her public high school had encouraged her to sit for so many exams she'd been standardized-tested to the point of anxiety-ridden absurdity. She'd taken the PSAT, five SAT tests at five different sittings; three SAT Subject Tests and one ACT for a total of seven admissions testing sessions. She'd also taken five Advanced Placement tests, the culminating exercise of prescribed coursework that purports to be the equivalent of college classes—and prerequisites for many selective schools.

My husband and I stood by, confounded and confused, by what college admissions had become since we'd graduated in the 1970s. I have no recollection of my own SAT score, but I took the test once and was admitted to the two colleges I wanted to attend, UC San Diego and Occidental College. I chose Occidental, had a transformational experience, and felt indebted to Jim Montoya, the admissions director who'd accepted me into a class that went on to include successful doctors, lawyers, academics, journalists, entrepreneurs, and multimillionaires.

Just before Boo's senior year, a college classmate and former Stanford admissions officer invited Montoya and me to his wedding.

In the many decades since I'd last seen him, Jim had become an executive at the College Board. Sitting next to Jim at the reception, I complained about the perversity the College Board had brought to admissions, the bitter struggle students face trying to better scores by hiring high-priced tutors and retaking the test over and over.

With good humor, Jim advised me to stop worrying, that Boo's SAT scores would get her into a great college. The next week, he left for China, to promote and expand the College Board's business in Asia.

Few people outside the industry realized at the time how important Asia would become to higher education. But the College Board was prescient. As admissions globalized, the College Board and the ACT collected record revenues.

It was no accident that the College Board's biggest moneymaker became Advanced Placement courses and testing. By convincing high school administrators throughout the US, Asia, the UK, Canada, and Latin America to increase the number of college-bound students in Advanced Placement classes, the College Board earned more than $200 million in 2013 from fees students paid to take AP tests, and millions more from teacher training, merchandise, and proprietary prep books and practice tests. By 2018, the College Board had contracts with twenty states to support AP courses. The number of students taking AP tests nearly doubled, and the company earned $480 million in revenue, according to the *Chronicle of Higher Education*.

It was against this backdrop that I went to lunch with a high school friend, a multimillionaire Harvard Business School graduate. He told me it makes good economic sense to invest in tutors and consultants even if it means spending $100 an hour.

I gulped. Wouldn't it better to save the money for tuition?

No, he said, and explained the "Golden Ticket" rule—a greatly misrepresented and largely misunderstood admissions principle. A

Golden Ticket admits kids into a college—typically one of the hardest to get into—that charges only what families can afford to pay. Getting into one of them won't guarantee riches and an anxiety-free life, but it will allow middle-class and low-income parents to send their children to private college without going bankrupt or taking on hundreds of thousands of dollars in debt.

The few schools that promise to charge only what families can afford have the highest admissions hurdles, accepting about .01 percent of the nation's total applicants. They evaluate students holistically, without regard to a family's finances, basing admissions decisions on grades, test scores, and a host of indescribable attributes that make the process so murky.

In our case, I did the math and was shocked. A Harvard or Yale degree would cost $10,000 a year less than a degree from the University of California. Other highly selective public Ivies and small liberal arts colleges—Williams, Amherst, Swarthmore, Pomona— also knock 30 to 90 percent off the tuition sticker price for accepted students with family incomes less than $200,000.

My friend explained another little-understood fact. Less selective colleges and universities use high test scores and grades to award hefty merit scholarships to recruit the top-scoring students to improve their rankings. The more AP classes students take, the higher their grade point averages. High grades and top test scores translate into free money—substantial grants and scholarships that result in huge tuition discounts.

Only a few students get the biggest discounts, the best scholarships and the most money, generally those with enough money to pay for tutors, test prep, and admissions consultants. Everybody else battles for financial aid scraps. The for-profit test prep industry—$1 billion strong and growing, according to IBISWorld research—"is a natural free-market response to the way the SAT and ACT are used in our society," said Robert Schaeffer, a longtime

SAT and ACT critic, and founder of FairTest, a nonprofit advocating for fairness and accuracy in testing. "We don't blame them for what they do."

He blames the test sellers. Schaeffer has dogged the testing industry since the 1980s, when he and Monty Neill launched their nonprofit to battle the inequalities admissions testing promotes. FairTest was the first to shine a bright light on the unfairness of standardized testing, noting correctly that results most accurately reflect family income rather than native intelligence. If so many upper-middle-class and wealthy students are fighting for limited discounts, raising the bar on what it means to be academically qualified, how do working-class and poor students fare? "Really badly," Schaeffer said.

Fear motivates parents at all income levels, and that fear drives the test prep industry. They all sell the same message: You will fail without us.

Albert Zeng was sitting on a bench waiting for his mother to pick him up after his session at Ardent Academy, a test prep center in Irvine, California. He was jittery. The pressure was on. The coming weekend, he was taking the SAT for the fifth time. The $10,000 his mother, June, estimated she'd spent on tutoring had resulted in higher scores but not to the level likely to get Albert into UC Berkeley or Stanford, the schools he dreamed of attending.

He was fifteen, a sophomore, a full year younger than most students who take the SAT for the first time. Competition at his school, Irvine High, was fierce. Students cram schedules with AP courses, as he planned to, and earn As in them. Albert worried that he might not get those As—seen as a basic requirement, not a stellar achievement—when the number of advanced courses started piling up in his junior year. Then he remembered, smiling slightly for the first time, that his sister had a B in a class, and she got into Dartmouth. "Oh, no, no, no, no, no," his mother said, laughing but entirely serious about squelching this idea. "That was in her senior year, when the colleges don't see grades. No Bs until then."

Whether Albert liked it or not, testing companies had changed the way high schools prepare students for college. Too often they enroll as many students as possible in AP classes, often with little regard for an individual's ability to succeed. By the time our youngest child was in high school, the admissions-testing landscape had drastically worsened, and the average test scores to get into affordable colleges had risen steeply. Her principal routinely ignored recommendations to limit AP class sizes to no more than 25 students even after I sent him the College Board guidelines that warned: "With more than 25 students, the course will lack the critical classroom atmosphere that allows each student to interact with the teacher." Her AP Spanish, English, World History, and Economics classes had nearly 40 students, her AP Biology had 35, and her AP Calculus had 30.

Parents are powerless to force high schools to reduce class size. I had several meetings and countless exchanges with the principal regarding AP class sizes. He refused to budge. If Stevie needed more instruction, he said, hire a tutor. In a final email, he wrote: "I think the bottom line here, is we are going to have a difference of opinion. You have stated quite clearly that you believe a [AP] class with 36 students is untenable for the teacher. I very much disagree with that claim. Thank you for your time."

As average scores ratcheted up, so did cutoff thresholds for merit scholarships. Large chains like Kaplan, Princeton, Test Prep Gurus, Varsity Tutors, and Elite Educational Institute ("helping students reach their academic goals since 1987") were hawking online classes and peddling profitable prep sessions in windowless classrooms.

Looking for help, I googled "best test prep Orange County" and followed a trail to an office park in Irvine, one of the nation's first planned cities. Like Koreatown in Los Angeles, Irvine is a mecca for tutoring companies and independent admissions consultants. I pulled off the I-5 freeway and into Jeffrey Office Park, a four-block warren of one- and two-story cookie-cutter buildings and businesses to prepare students for college admissions.

Nearly every office offered tutoring, testing, and college admissions prep in English and Chinese. Each lobby I visited had newspapers, magazines, and phone books in Korean, Chinese, or Japanese, sometimes all three. In a half day there I didn't see or talk to anyone who wasn't Asian. "It's a breeding ground for excellence," said a for-profit college coach who screens applicants for Harvard, her alma mater. "The discipline, the resources here—they're a magnet."

Irvine has neat, organized, tree-lined streets, with houses and shopping centers so disarmingly similar it's easy to drive for miles and see no new vistas. The city is renowned for rigorous public schools and for the University of California, Irvine, ranked one of the nation's ten best public universities. Only 5 percent of Americans are Asian, but Asians make up 40 percent of UCI's students and 20 percent of those enrolled at Ivy League colleges.

Students begin arriving at Jeffrey Office Park after school and on weekends in everything from BMWs to minivans. Sullen, downcast, their backpacks slung over slumping shoulders, they head into offices, up stairways, and into black-box classrooms crammed with plastic chairs and cramped laminate desks. "I have to stay focused," said one teen. "I'm under a lot of pressure." She and her friends described the tricks the companies teach them, some fair, some cheating. Slow readers do better on the SAT than on the ACT, but because the College Board forbids calculators, math is harder. (The College Board has since relaxed its no-calculator rule.)

"It's much better to take the ACT," she said. "You can program equations into your calculator."

"Isn't that cheating?" I asked.

"I don't think so," said another.

"Nobody says you can't do it. They even show you how."

"Who shows you?"

"Everybody. The teachers."

When I met with an executive at one of the companies, I asked him specifically how his tutors provide students with an advantage. "We teach them how to program their calculators," he said, showing me on his computer a how-to list of the forbidden formulas needed to ace the ACT. Students are allowed to preprogram formulas for the test, he assured me.

OK, I said, but I had my doubts.

Later that night, I dug into the ACT website. The ACT requires students to wipe clean calculators, to "remove all documents and programs with algebra system functionality." But because the rules are rarely overtly expressed and sometimes unenforced—even the ACT buries the prohibition deep in its website—students cheat. Just how much they cheat became apparent when the ACT was at the center of the largest cheating scandals in 2016.

Unscrupulous entrepreneurs and for-profit testing centers had been obtaining and selling advance copies of tests online, bribing proctors and hiring ringers to help students cheat on exams. They were even charging customers to attend hotel seminars where they provided answers to test questions. The news agency Reuters uncovered egregious conflicts of interest between the ACT and an Asian testing company, quoting students, administrators, and tutors at test prep centers claiming widespread fraud.

Chinese and South Korean companies regularly advertised ACT exam questions and answers. One company, Huafu Education, offered to sell test content for $762, telling a reporter, "What we're offering is exactly what you'll see on test day." At different ACT centers—some charging students up to $10,000 a year to prep— officials and proctors ignored or assisted student cheating, Reuters reported. Fed up, at least one teacher resigned. If colleges knew about the cheating, a teacher said, "they wouldn't want to accept the students anymore. It's outrageous."

Reuters discovered an even more pernicious problem. Cheating at test prep centers is "not the work of outsiders" but is occurring within "a system controlled and policed by the ACT organization itself." A half dozen centers sold test prep and exam questions while at the same time administering the exam—a conflict of interest that violates ACT policies. Rather than take responsibility, testing officials told Reuters they blamed "organized fraud rings . . . who, for a lot of money, are seeking to undermine the system."

As long as the testing companies remain the gatekeepers to elite colleges and merit scholarships, parents will cheat to help their children get better scores. The worst pay criminals like Rick Singer to bribe psychologists for fake disability waivers to get extra time on tests. Others seek advice from companies selling tips on how to legally exploit lax testing loopholes. Message boards advertise ways to use a federal student disability designation—called a 504 plan—to buy more testing time.

The advantages always go to the families who need it least. Wealthy students get additional testing time far more often than everyone else, a *New York Times* 2019 analysis showed. In the country's wealthiest areas, "the share of high school students with the designation is double the national average. In some communities, more than one in 10 students have one—up to seven times the rate nationwide."

A local test prep company, AR Academics, was refreshingly honest about how it helps high-paying clients game the test. AR uses legal loopholes to harvest previous exams, a company official explained at a public information session. Since testing companies reuse material so often, students are familiar enough with exam questions that they get higher scores.

AR serves wealthy clients along Orange County's Gold Coast, where median home prices reach $4.35 million. A friend told me her daughter was prepping at AR and she was thrilled with the results. Her recommendation was enough for us to consider hiring the company, despite living thirty miles north and facing the prospect of hellish rush hour traffic to get to its Newport Beach headquarters. Then I heard the prices. AR was requiring a $1,650 nonrefundable prepayment, including a $150 materials fee for a packet of previously administered exams.

On average, clients were paying $2,500 for one test prep cycle. Multiply that times the recommended three-test cycle and the bill reaches $7,500.

No wonder kids from wealthy families score better than everyone else, reinforcing what a University of Minnesota study calls "existing patterns of social inequality." The *Journal of College Admission* concurred. Standardized testing perpetuates an "unequal playing field of higher education participation." Private test prep tutors and companies are the "driving force of entrepreneurial admission." At elite universities with the best need-based financial aid and merit scholarships, test score averages are stratospheric. They range in the mid-30s (out of 36) for the ACT and more than 1500 (out of 1600) for the SAT. A 10- or 20-point coaching effect is significant if it helps students cross the cutoff threshold, one academic study concluded.

Finding an effective tutor can be as futile as trying to locate a lost ring on a crowded beach. The quality of high-end tutoring and test prep is rarely discernible, the pricing seldom straightforward. Details are sketchy, contracts convoluted, refund policies fuzzy, unnamed tutors assigned at the last minute.

Though bios are sometimes available, tutors hardly ever allow parents to vet them. Test prep is an array of confusing choices: $3,250 for this package, $4,500 for that package; $35 to take a diagnostic test; $80 an hour or $85 an hour or $70 an hour for prepaid packages of nonrefundable lessons depending on the type of tutoring, the tutor, the academic class, the standardized test.

Chungdahm ReadWrite had among the oddest pricing policies I found when I was investigating test prep a few years ago. Parents pay a $1,000 deposit, then sign a "tuition agreement" that specifies the cost based on student point increases, for example, "Parent agrees to pay $1,000 for the first 2-point increase in ACT score and $500 per 1 point thereafter."

The multimillion-dollar company C2 Education pitched programs that promise to meet individual student needs. "I almost fell backwards when I saw the pricing," one parent said. "It was $11,000 for a one-year program to get my daughter ready for SAT, AP exams, and college essays. Of course, we couldn't afford it. But really, folks? Really? Don't they realize most of us are trying to save money for college? Ugh."

Not only do the College Board and ACT earn millions for fees they charge students to take their tests, they profit from ancillary products and services, add-ons that can increase the per-test cost up to $200. Even knowing that reusing old tests advantages the wealthy—and inflates scores—they continue the practice, despite dozens of documented cheating instances.

Recognizing the enormous profit potential in recycled tests, prep companies from Newport Beach to Seoul rush to harvest and sell them to well-off clients.

One student hired a Shanghai SAT cram school and received an answer key, called a *jijing*, that allowed him to go into the test knowing about half the critical-reading questions. He scored a perfect 800 and was admitted to UCLA, Reuters reported. To demonstrate how easy it is to cheat, whistleblowers in China and South Korea emailed College Board officials full copies of tests or significant portions of them. "Basically, the only way to survive in the industry is to have a copy of the test" in advance of a sitting, a test prep coach in South Korea told Reuters. "It's like doping in the Tour de France. If you don't do it, someone else will."

Technology makes cheating easier and socially acceptable. More than 35 percent of teens said they used smartphones to cheat on homework or tests, a 2018 Pew Research study showed, and 65 percent said they saw others use phones to cheat. Even before Rick Singer, news reports were rife with accounts of students and adults breaching computer systems to change grades, steal final exams, use private social media to share screenshots of test questions—all in the quest to get into college.

In Korea, dozens of tutoring centers distributed the SAT to clients prior to test dates. In New York, high school students were paying college students to take tests for them. On Reddit, twenty-one pages of test questions were posted. The Chinese website Taobao, run by Alibaba, advertised at least eleven vendors selling copies of the SAT, offering dozens of versions, with ads showing photos of test booklets. Trying to keep tests secure is a game of whack-a-mole, so futile that when a European school in Taiwan sent tests and answer sheets in lockboxes to the US for grading, the boxes arrived with the answer sheets missing.

Like gods on Olympus, corporate and college executives battle for market share and intellectual superiority, operating in a universe far removed from everyone else. Millions of words have been spilled, and research dollars spent, arguing whether grades or standardized test scores better predict success. Here's my answer: a debt-free college degree best predicts a successful, healthy life.

So why can't everyone have one? Because the people with the power to shift the paradigm choose not to. As the scholar Nicholas Lemann correctly points out in his standardized testing exposé *The Big Test*, "You can't undermine social rank by setting up an elaborate process of ranking."

This is where the story gets complicated—and political.

It begins with Gaston Caperton, the former governor of West Virginia. He took over the College Board two decades ago, doubling its revenues to nearly $1 billion. He expanded the testing company's goods and services, marketing aggressively in China and India. He convinced thousands of high school principals to adopt AP classes, increasing the number of students taking Advanced Placement almost sevenfold to 2.2 million in 2013, up from 330,000 in 1990.

Like the ACT, the College Board has capitalized on selling student information, minutiae so detailed that admissions officers can ask to buy all the names of girls in the Pacific Northwest with scores of 720 on the chemistry SAT Subject Test. I discovered this additional revenue stream while attending a workshop a few years ago in a luxury Newport Beach office building on elite college admissions, sponsored by two pricey admissions coaching companies.

One of the speakers, Arun Ponnusamy, worked for Caltech admissions until he joined the for-profit coaching company Collegewise, where he is now the chief academic officer. Caltech regularly paid the College Board about 40 cents for each test taker's name, email, and street address; the ACT charged 41 cents, he said. (It's recently risen to about 47 cents a name.) Colleges use the data to woo particular types of students they want, maybe more girls with top scores in chemistry, or boys with high marks in the humanities, or more applicants wealthy enough to pay full tuition.

As the ACT grabbed larger and larger segments of the admissions testing market from the SAT, College Board revenues began to decline in 2009. Meanwhile, an unknown former Wall Street consultant named David Coleman was quietly lobbying states to adopt the Common Core, national standards used to teach English and math from kindergarten through twelfth grade. By 2011, forty-six states had adopted the controversial Common Core, what the *Washington*

Post called "one of the swiftest and most remarkable shifts in education policy in U.S. history."

When the ACT overtook the SAT as the most widely used admissions test in 2012, College Board executives replaced Caperton with Coleman. Almost immediately, Coleman ordered a SAT revision to conform to the Common Core. He recruited Manuel Alfaro to design new standards.

Alfaro arrived with an impressive résumé and two decades of public- and private-sector experience in test development. Two years later, after having been dismissed from the College Board, Alfaro was "a disillusioned idealist," he wrote on his blog, "shocked by the reality I encountered." Executives ignored warnings about problems with poorly vetted questions on the revised SAT; he was instructed to create a "backstory" that "independent groups" had analyzed and endorsed an SAT and Common Core alignment, he reported in blog posts.

Using the backstory to persuade states to require the SAT instead of the ACT, the College Board pressured Alfaro to rubber-stamp the redesigned test to "hide the fact that they were taken directly from Common Core standards," he alleged. When he refused, the College Board fired him, Alfaro wrote, and rushed to produce a redesigned test to beat the ACT for Colorado's testing contract. The College Board won the Colorado contract, but Alfaro refused to concede, continuing to post what he saw inside the College Board. As more states adopted the Common Core curriculum, Coleman's team aligned the SAT to meet its standards, Reuter's confirmed. The end result? The College Board not only sold the SAT to lawmakers as a way to certify students had met state standards, it also raked in hundreds of millions of taxpayer dollars, investing millions of dollars in tax-free offshore accounts.

Shrouded in secrecy, the new, revised, Common Core–based SAT debuted in March 2016. Within hours of the first sitting, questions were posted on the website College Confidential and another called SAT Helper. A Chinese company hired forty students to take the test, harvest as many questions as possible, then report their findings at a hotel seminar in Shanghai.

In May 2016, Alfaro launched an online petition urging the federal government to investigate. "The SAT is a sham! Please help me shine a spotlight on the dark corners of the College Board: the future of millions of students is being jeopardized by the organizations and institutions that claim to make student success their top priority."

That's when Alfaro the whistleblower became the target of federal prosecutors. FBI agents raided his Maryland home in August 2016, seizing computers and documents, and putting the case under judicial seal. No information is available about what charges, if any, were filed against Alfaro. The raid soon silenced him and prompted the College Board to announce it was "pleased that this crime is being pursued aggressively," spokesman Zach Goldberg told Reuters in September 2016.

The case has remained sealed ever since. Alfaro's social media was deleted and he went so far underground it took a private investigator to find him in suburban Chicago. I left voicemails and a note on his door but got no response. When I called the US attorney's office, an official said no search warrant had been issued. The FBI searched his house without a warrant? What might they be hiding? And why? Hard to say. College Board officials refused to answer questions after weeks of multiple requests.

In public appearances, Coleman gave no explanation for the worst cheating scandals in College Board history, nor did he address Alfaro's accusations. He vowed to fix flaws in the redesigned SAT, promising to "simplify words" in the math section. "Using superfluous words is superfluous," he told colleges and guidance counselors at a Columbus, Ohio, conference. Later he said of the Reuters exposé, a Pulitzer Prize finalist, "I think the College Board should do everything it can because I'm worried about the perceptions in the article."

Perception matters. In a confidential document Reuters obtained, College Board officials warned, "Another large-scale incident could get attention of U.S. press and universities." The College Board dismissed suggestions to reduce the number of test dates overseas to help control cheating. Reducing test dates, the memo said, "would enable the arch-rival ACT exam to gain market share."

Overlooking cheating was apparently another corporate strategy to maximize revenues at the expense of the millions of students who are forced to play by sketchy rules. Why else would the ACT and the College Board knowingly minimize widespread and growing concerns? Instead, executives look for new markets to exploit. The federal mandate to test all 15 million public high school students opened up a $700 million revenue stream. Tapping the vein of taxpayer money, testing companies sold testing products directly to state governments, spending millions of dollars lobbying lawmakers to require public school students take their tests. They then turned around and used taxpayer money to promote their financial and political agendas.

At least nineteen states contract with the College Board to support Advanced Placement classes, and thirteen to offer SAT tests. Five states pay for both. The state of Michigan alone paid the College Board $50 million over three years to test students in grades eight through ten using the PSAT and another $53.1 million for SAT testing. The College Board has tested more than 3.7 million students as part of SAT School Day, when teens spend hours sitting for the corporation's exams at taxpayer expense. How much the College Board earns from taxpayers is unclear since the company won't say. But it includes "a crap-ton of extra services," said the National Center for Fair & Open Testing's Akil Bello.

It's a high-stakes game with an enormous jackpot. Companies battle to acquire as much as they can of the nearly $2 billion government spends to test students. More than 2.2 million students took the SAT in 2019, and the company sold more than five million Advanced Placement exams. Each SAT costs $64.50; Advanced Placement exams range from $94 to $142; Subject Tests cost $74. The College Board sells a dozen study guides on its website ranging from $19 to $30. The company's curious investment partnerships have grown almost 450 percent, from $110 million to $600 million, with no information or explanation, in 2018, according to the College Board's latest available tax returns.

"The testing companies are making a land grab," says Scott Marion, the executive director of the Center for Assessment, a nonprofit that helps states design and evaluate tests. "It's a little like the Gold Rush. . . . If the SAT is in 50 states, guess what, kids are going to take it."

A few states have spurned the testing companies and refused to use their products. Vetoing a bill that would have allowed districts to use the SAT or ACT to test math and reading, California governor Gavin Newsom said the tests favor wealthy students and "exacerbate the inequities for underrepresented students, given that performance on these tests is highly correlated with race and parental income," and are "not the best predictor for college success."

Yet the College Board continues to try to expand its reach with initiatives like the $6 Solution, a failed attempt to combat inequality. Financed by the College Board and billionaire Michael Bloomberg, the project focused on convincing poor, largely white, top-of-their-class, high-SAT-scoring rural high school students to apply to selective colleges.

Studying this cohort, Harvard scholars discovered that they had rarely considered selective schools, preferring instead public universities or community colleges. If disadvantaged students received a

$6 packet explaining how to apply to elite colleges, researchers predicted that as many as 46 percent more would enroll. The results proved otherwise. The College Board mailed the packet to 30,000 students. About 150 students enrolled—one-half of 1 percent. The $6 Solution quietly shuttered in 2018, a broken promise to the students the College Board had promised to help, author Paul Tough reported in *The Years That Matter Most*.

Instead of assisting the disadvantaged, the College Board prioritizes and promotes programs that serve itself and its partners. Results of its well-publicized alliance with Khan Academy to provide free online SAT tutoring have been mixed at best. Khan's Official SAT Practice program boosts some kids, just not the struggling students trying to catch up, Tough concluded after analyzing proprietary College Board data. The Khan SAT program allowed students already testing well "to increase their advantage over the rest of the pack," Tough found, but it did nothing to level the college-access playing field. "It had made it more uneven than ever."

Khan's partnership with the College Board, however, has helped the nonprofit academy to thrive. Khan reported more than $100 million in assets in 2017—double its net assets in 2014. Founder Sal Khan earned $871,054 in compensation in 2018. For the College Board, the alliance with Khan is about "fighting irrelevance" and reclaiming market share lost to the ACT, wrote Allen Cheng, CEO of PrepScholar, on his blog. Noting to his readers that the academy is a competitor, Cheng said he admires Khan, but called the contract with the College Board "a Faustian bargain." The union allows Khan to access the student data that the College Board collects and to use the company's powerful branding and licensing. In return the College Board can boast about giving away free test prep for the SAT. If Khan really wanted to level the playing field, Cheng said, the company would also partner with the ACT. Creating an ACT–College Board alliance "would double its impact and help a ton of students." But that will never happen. A deal with the ACT "would be a massive blow" to the College Board's goal to dominate the testing market.

Khan's test prep fails to teach students test-taking strategies, Cheng said, skills that provide crucial score boosts. To earn the highest possible points, students must acquire test-taking tools completely unrelated to mastering academic subjects: skipping the hardest and focusing on easier questions, developing a reliable SAT essay before the test, and approaching reading passages to balance time and accuracy. One critic compared Khan's online SAT tutoring to "trying to learn to play golf by watching Tiger Woods and then going to a driving range."

As millions of poor kids struggle to compete on high-stakes tests, the companies profiting from their pain appear to exist to enrich their first-class-traveling executives. The College Board stashes millions in offshore tax havens and hedge funds, sheltering gains in secret accounts, tax filings from 2014–2018 show, instead of using those revenues to improve the lives of the kids it claims to serve. It sells flawed tests to state governments and the public, then takes the personal data it collects from teenagers and sells it to colleges.

David Coleman, the company's leader since 2012, earned nearly $1.8 million in 2018. President Jeremy Singer took home more than $1 million. The seven highest-paid executives received a total of $23.8 million over four years ending in 2018. During that time, Coleman's compensation was $6.8 million; information officer Theresa Shaw's was nearly $3 million; vice president for global communications Stefanie Sanford's was $2.8 million; and senior advisor Cyndie Schmeiser's and vice president for AP tests Trevor Packer's were $2.4 million each.

Two other executives no longer with the company, Neil Lane and Steve Titan, earned a total of $2.76 million from 2014 to 2016. Though the board of trustees' members are supposed to be unpaid, one former representative earned $51,668 and free use of a New York City apartment. Steve Bumbaugh, the high-income vice president devoted to helping low-income students, earned $523,434 in 2018, typical for College Board top executives but five times the average $120,000 salary a nonprofit CEO earns.

Between 2015 and 2018 the College Board paid the Educational Testing Service more than $1.4 billion. The ETS, a $1.5 billion nonprofit test-development company, paid president Walter B. Mac-Donald $1.22 million, according to its most recently available tax returns. Its highest-paid executives earned between $327,000 and $822,892, for a total of more than $18 million in 2017. ETS board members earned as much as $103,000 annually for doing about two hours of work a week.

For the first time since our family was sucked into the standardized testing vortex, I understood the intractable inequality of opportunity that high-stakes testing brings to college admissions. The ACT, College Board, and ETS preach honesty, fairness, and equity while serving commerce, revenues, and growing market share to keep their revenue streams intact. Even the laudable goal of making testing optional fails to address the bigger questions of affordability and growing student debt.

As the COVID-19 pandemic worsened, more than two-thirds of all US colleges declared themselves test optional. Test-optional admissions is a start, but no panacea. The policy has yet to produce equal access to affordable degrees, though it is a strategic win for colleges. Test-optional colleges receive on average nearly 30 percent more applications, an increase that has allowed them to reject more students, improve selectivity, and better rank.

By their nature, high-stakes admissions tests are neither good nor bad. Test scores are a symptom of educational inequality, not the cause of it, supporters argue. If used to inform decisions rather than reject kids, high scores can boost the few students unlikely to be accepted for other reasons. But that slight benefit in no way outweighs the harm testing and rankings companies have inflicted on higher education. Testing companies obsessed with maximizing revenues, rankings companies obsessed with profit margins, and colleges obsessed with status have intentionally misused high-stakes admissions tests for decades. Students have become collateral damage, rejected from colleges they want to attend and, even worse, denied the scholarships and grants they need to avoid debt.

If colleges want to use tests to sort students and award tuition discounts—despite all the evidence that shows grades better predict college success—then they should remove incentives to misuse scores. In a proposal to end the testing battles once and for all, Jon Boeckenstedt, vice provost at Oregon State University, explained how easy it is to do:

- The US Department of Education stops collecting the high school test scores of incoming first-year college students.
- The College Board and *U.S. News & World Report* eliminate test score data from the survey questions they use to produce the Common Data Set.
- The National Association for College Admission Counseling, the College Board, and the ACT issue statements urging colleges to stop publishing and promoting test scores.

To that I add an amendment: stop using test scores to award merit scholarships and institutional grants. "Then colleges can use test scores all they want," Boeckenstedt said. "And presumably they'll be free to admit students with lower scores without fear of hurting themselves in the rankings."

The University of California going forward will evaluate students using more than a dozen other factors, including grades in honors and college-equivalent courses such as Advanced Placement; the quality of academic achievements relative to the high school opportunities available to students; special talents, achievements, and awards; academic accomplishments that take into account special circumstances such as disabilities, the need to work to support family; difficult personal circumstances; location of high school and residence; and being ranked in the top 9 percent of their high school class.

There's a reason the *Wall Street Journal* called the SAT the "Student Affluence Test." The SAT once stood for a measure of aptitude. Then it stood for a measure of assessment. Now the acronym stands for literally nothing. Coleman remains full of sound and fury, reinforcing the message that we have no choice but to play by the rules the testing industry hands us.

In an impassioned public plea, Coleman beseeched America in late 2019 to end the admissions madness the College Board helped create. He urged students to prep with Khan Academy, then take, and retake, the SAT. If that doesn't work, he wrote in the *Atlantic*, "we should offer many other ways for [students] to show their strengths to admissions officers."

Translated, that means test early, test often, and hire a tutor. In the end, that's what we did. We hired Guy McEleney, a family friend. Guy had no tutoring experience but had prepped himself for the ACT and scored 35 out of 36. He offered to tutor Stevie for free, but we paid him $25 an hour and served him a home-cooked dinner every week.

I requested a copy of the first ACT Stevie took, and they reviewed the questions she'd missed. When she took the test a second time, her score rose from 32 to 34, one point above the average for elite colleges. She was admitted to nearly every school she wanted to attend, settling on Harvard, with enough financial aid to make her degree affordable.

Did our family buy advantage? Yes, we did, with no regret. Did we pay thousands of dollars to the testing industrial complex? No, we did not. We paid $400 to a college student and saved $150,000 in college costs. It's the best investment we ever made.

6

The Myth of the Perfect Fit

The Siren Song of Exclusivity

The waning winter brings familiar rituals to Amherst, Massachusetts. In this small corner of New England, the admissions committee at Amherst College gathers in the decision room for its annual culling. Sitting around a brown rectangular table cluttered with highlighters, water bottles, coffee cups, and notepads, admissions officers assemble to choose who will be invited to study and live in their privileged community the following fall.

Nearly ten thousand students answer Amherst's essay prompts every year, hoping the college will decide they belong on campus as much as they want to be there. It can take applicants hours to parse prompts that end in inscrutable statements like these:

"But the most important value is insight—insight into the workings of the world. It may be because there is another guarantor of correctness in the sciences, namely, the empirical evidence from observation and experiments."

"No citizen, especially today, can exist in isolation—that is, I untranslated."

"Creating an environment that allows students to build lasting friendships, including those that cut across seemingly entrenched societal and political boundaries . . . requires candor about the inevitable tensions, as well as about the wonderful opportunities, that diversity and inclusiveness create."

Contemplating their answers, they no doubt dream of one day strolling Amherst's rolling green lawns and wandering its lush woods. Nearly 90 percent of them will have those illusions crushed every year. Only about four hundred new students join the anointed few housed and schooled in redbrick buildings on Amherst's two-hundred-year-old campus.

Deciding which of the ten thousand to accept—who will fit best at Amherst—is a grueling, months-long process that begins with readers for thirty geographic regions winnowing the pile to one thousand. Those lucky few go to the decision room, an airy space of light walls decorated with a few paintings and a chair rail, just big enough for a conference table. To give families access to that room, Amherst released a video featuring the committee's final deliberations. The members look like a slice of America: mostly white, a few of color, a mix of the middle-aged and twenty- and thirty-somethings, well dressed in a Gap and Ann Taylor style.

Katie Fretwell, a 1981 Amherst graduate, presided as dean in deliberations that reminded me of my own college's decision room. I'd spent long sessions with colleagues, sorting hundreds of applications, looking for students we believed would fit best on campus. Fretwell's Dickensian name aptly described the ordeal admissions officers and students face each year.

The most meritorious win seats at Amherst—but merit isn't enough. Essays need to touch hearts, or demonstrate obstacles overcome, or exhibit quirky passions or extraordinary athleticism. As they debated, and sunlight streamed through Colonial windows, I remembered hours of deliberations that took place during the six years I spent on Chapman's faculty admissions committee. Coolly professional, with little outward emotion save for occasional laughter, we moved steadily through lists of applicants in weekly meetings. Except for names and qualifications of students discussed, not much was different at Amherst.

Each officer pitched one of their regional finalists for a few minutes before the group rendered a quick decision with a ritualized raising of the hands.

Member: "With Kaitlin, her being an inside-the-box kind of gal."

Fretwell: "How many would like to admit?"

No hands up.

"Wait-list?"

Eight hands raised. Next.

Member: "He's a top tester."

Member: "He's got all As."

Member: "Four varsity sports."

Member: "First-chair trumpet in the orchestra."

Member: "Ready for this? 6.4 GPA on a 4 scale."

Fretwell: "Did he get all those 5s without AP courses?"

Member: "Yep."

Fretwell: "But we can't take 'em all."

Next.

Fretwell: "I'm questioning the edge here, however, in all her excellence. How many would like to admit?"

Three hands raised.

"OK, she goes to the wait-list."

Next.

Member: "The night before her AP Chemistry exam, she learned her father had an affair with a twenty-three-year-old prostitute."

Fretwell: "How many would like to admit?"

Seven hands raised. Next.

Member: "One parent is a business exec VP with a master's. Both went to Harvard. He's got three siblings who went to Harvard in classes '09, '11, '15."

Admit. Next.

Member: "His family financial situation took a huge hit and they lost their family store and all other assets."

Member: "Dad's alcoholism consuming the family. This is a quote from one of his essays: 'The alcohol consuming poor Muslim family down the street with whom no sane member of society would want to interact.'"

Fretwell: "How many would like to admit?"

Eight hands raised. Next.

Tom Parker, the college's now retired financial aid director, summarized the committee's feelings. "We're fully aware of the fact that the process is—I don't want to say flawed—but is making minute distinctions among extraordinarily talented kids. There are times, honestly, where I'm not sure why I put my hand up or failed to put my hand up. I'm kind of going with my gut here. I am cognizant of some lives being changed, literally. On the other hand, yeah. I do feel bad. The months of February and March are simply no fun."

I sympathized with Tom. Sitting at the table with my university's admissions committee, we reviewed scores of files in marathon sessions sustained by cold coffee, cookies, and chocolates. Given the stakes, the discussions were strangely amicable but also interminable. We took sides to accept or reject one student over another. We debated accepting less qualified wealthy kids to subsidize needy applicants, about the ethics of admitting moderate-, middle-, and low-income kids without giving them the financial aid they'd need to avoid massive debt.

The longer I sat on the committee, the clearer the architecture of admissions became. By the time files got to us, the real work was over. Enrollment managers and consulting firms had used algorithms and formulas to calculate how many admitted students to accept, and how to select the right ones to maintain or boost rankings, revenues, and prestige.

Logic, not emotion, determined the fate of most applicants. As we struggled to admit students we thought were the right fit, it became painfully clear that colleges and applicants define "right fit" very differently.

Colleges frequently tell students what they want to hear, then use a different formula to choose which students to accept. The excitement, affection, and passion that families feel for a particular campus often have little to do with how colleges identify and enroll the students they need to fill their first-year classes. The disconnect between what colleges and students want leads to a lot of disappointment. Too often the goals of students and colleges are diametrically opposed. Understanding how to think like a college helps families avoid falling into the traps schools deliberately set.

Families become so invested in finding the emotional right fit they frequently choose colleges that leave them with crippling debt. The average student graduates with $33,000 in loans, a financial burden that can't be wiped away in bankruptcy. Bankers don't care about right fit that goes wrong. Like death and taxes, payments come due.

Free-market lawmakers want to deregulate higher education even more, allowing markets and the private sector to control prices and access to degrees just as they do for jeans, coffee, and luxury cars. But choosing the right college is far more complicated than deciding between brands of jeans. A college education reveals its worth over four years, not in the thirty minutes it takes to figure out which pants make your butt look better. A system that embraces students as consumers and makes education a product bought and sold like jeans invites the uncertainty that characterizes college admissions today.

Though colleges have always used emotion to recruit students, the stakes are higher now. Applying for college has become so cumbersome, complicated, and expensive that the process is often, as one parent observed, "like throwing darts without knowing where the board is."

"Right fit" is so subjective that colleges can define it any way they want. And they do, to serve their interests. Algorithms and admissions officers sort applicants with 90 percent logic and 10 percent emotion—the inverse of the formula most families use to choose colleges. To boost rank and increase revenues, schools sell lifestyles.

Selective colleges promise admission to clubs so exclusive that membership is restricted to a tiny few. Graceful brick buildings, soaring white steeples, and imposing iron gates telegraph wealth and advantage, a sense of belonging and possibility that students will find their fit in the school's culture of prestige and privilege. Universities with billion-dollar football programs sell tailgate booze fests, elite Greek societies, lazy-river swimming pools, deluxe living quarters, and gourmet dining.

At recruiting gatherings in huge hotel ballrooms, fresh-faced admissions officers mouth platitudes while stunning images on gigantic television screens behind them feature well-groomed students strolling immaculate campuses bathed in the glow of fall colors. To visit those campuses, students spend on average $3,000 traipsing from one college to the next, each a Goldilocks looking for one that's "just right."

Those costs can soar to hundreds of thousands of dollars for private jets, concierge tour guides, and prearranged meetings with admissions deans and college presidents. Colleges barrage teenagers—

a tribe already vulnerable to emotional appeals—with mail and tele-marketing, their subtly masked promises aimed at snagging applications. They buy personal information about applicants in bulk from companies selling data, including the College Board and the ACT. They send students mountains of mail and flood inboxes with come-ons and invitations to apply.

Postcards, emails, and texts tout honors programs and tantalize with possibility: maybe full tuition plus room and board, maybe a gift laptop, maybe an application fee waiver, maybe paid internships or a hefty scholarship. Aspirational brochures and websites feature ivy-covered stone buildings and students ripped from the pages of an Abercrombie catalog. Students feel flattered by the unrelenting attention, unaware the invitations are often intended to inflate application numbers and boost *U.S. News* rankings.

All that marketing and advertising usually has little to do with how colleges enroll students they think will best fit on their campuses. Grades and test scores open the gates. Compelling narratives that reflect the college's values put applications on the table. But subjective and secret factors determine who's invited to first-year orientation. Many schools want desperately to boost *U.S. News* rankings. Some want students who embrace their religious dogma—College of the Ozarks, Brigham Young, Pepperdine, Oral Roberts. Others look for applicants aligned with their political agendas—Hillsdale, Liberty, Patrick Henry—or their socially responsible values.

Many give preferences to athletes, and to the children of alumni, faculty, celebrities, big donors, high-ranking university executives, and their friends. The biggest secret of all, though, is how family income impacts the way colleges sort applicants. Algorithms help enrollment managers award "just-right" discounts to persuade the most valued "right-fit" students to enroll.

Almost always that algorithm makes the same demand: admit more rich kids.

"That's the message that almost every enrollment manager hears each spring, either obliquely or explicitly," Paul Tough observed after chronicling the admissions director at Trinity College as he tried to fill a first-year class. The class size was too large. The tuition revenue was too small. Every full-need student admitted had to be offset by enough full-paying students to hit revenue targets. "There were too many full-need students . . . and not enough full-pay ones."

Students are far less focused on finances than colleges. More than 92 percent choose schools based on factors other than affordability, according to a Gallup poll. They often confuse "right fit" with the happiness that comes from being accepted to a "dream college." When the Princeton Review asked students and parents to rank their "dream colleges" the winners were most often:

- Harvard (3.2 percent acceptance rate)
- Stanford (4.3 percent acceptance rate)
- Princeton (4.9 percent acceptance rate)
- MIT (7.2 percent acceptance rate)
- Cornell (12.7 percent acceptance rate)
- Columbia (6.6 acceptance rate)
- University of Pennsylvania (7.7 percent acceptance rate)
- Yale (4.7 percent acceptance rate)
- UCLA (12 percent acceptance rate)
- New York University (16 percent acceptance rate)
- University of Michigan (Ann Arbor) (19 percent acceptance rate)

Of those eleven, only Harvard, Princeton, Stanford, MIT, and Columbia—with acceptance rates 7 percent or lower—promise to charge accepted students what their families can afford to pay without loans. And good luck getting in. Applicants are seven times likelier to survive Ebola.

Parents go to unfathomable lengths to make sure their children are accepted at top-ranked colleges. Some parents were hiring doctors to do performance-enhancing Tommy John surgery on their sons so the young pitchers could throw harder and faster, Chris Siedem, the founder of Perfect College Match, told a *New York Post* reporter.

Other parents faked photos of their children as evidence of charity work or pretended their kids had hearing loss to get them extra time taking tests—all scams, independent consultant Ron Foley said, "to get the kid into college." Rick Singer hired Rebekah Hendershot to help write admissions essays for the children of his wealthy clients. After Singer assigned the essay topics, Hendershot said she felt pressure from the parents to do the actual writing, she told a reporter after Singer was arrested for fraud. It was a line Hendershot refused to cross. Sitting in one client's mansion, Hendershot remembers a boy struggling to produce a personal statement. He had been instructed to describe himself as the impoverished son of a single mother. "The kid was very nervous, very upset," Hendershot told *USA Today*. "Rick had been telling him for weeks to write this essay. . . . But the kid was having trouble writing it because he couldn't imagine what it was like to be poor."

Wealthy parents have been known to subsidize nonprofit schools and medical clinics in developing nations so their children can claim on college applications that they started them, psychologist Richard Weissbourd noted in a Harvard study of admissions policies. Nicole Eisenberg banded together with other affluent parents to help their kids start a local charity and boost her son's admissions chances, she told the *New York Times*.

As her son approached college, Eisenberg and other parents in their Bloomfield Hills, Michigan, neighborhood solicited friends to donate to the charity, eventually raising $250,000. "Did we ask for sponsors for them? Yes. Did we ask for money for them? Yes. But they had to do the work." The family even considered making a hefty donation to their top-choice college but decided against it. "There's no amount of money we could have paid to have got him in. Because, trust me, my father-in-law asked." Eisenberg's son was admitted to two of the nation's top musical theater programs, the *Times* reported, along with nine more of the twenty-six schools that received his applications.

Despite the odds, nearly 200,000 applicants in any given admissions cycle are trying to woo Harvard, Princeton, Stanford, MIT, and Columbia with essays to prove themselves worthy, begging admissions officers to fall in love with them like suitors competing for dates on reality TV. They demonstrate their virtues with campus visits where admissions officers "sprinkle fairy dust on them," a financial aid officer at the College of William & Mary told me. "Then parents come to us and we give them a dose of financial reality."

By that time, it's usually too late. Besotted teens have fallen in love. They've met admissions officers, talked for hours with interviewers about favorite movies and food, about novels and current events, pop culture and museums. They've become intoxicated with a few schools whose requited affections are their only ambition. Emotion, not logic, is why parents send their children to colleges they can't afford. Emotions, though, don't pay the bills.

Figuring out how to finance a degree without going broke is what makes "right fit" so complicated. Colleges rarely give students enough grants to make attending truly affordable. The gap between what colleges charge and what families can pay is what led Valerie to begin her career as a physician's assistant in the summer of 2020 with $250,000 in debt. She had borrowed $80,000 to pay for her degree at Duke University and $170,000 to USC for graduate training.

Valerie grew up middle-class in suburban Southern California. Her father, a machinist, and her mother, a public high school teacher, encouraged her to excel academically, and she was particularly gifted in math and science. She chose to attend Duke over the University of California, Berkeley, because its generous financial aid offer made it the least expensive of her options.

She borrowed the maximum amount allowed using subsidized loans and her parents made up the gap with parent PLUS loans. She never questioned the loans, she said. "I'm eighteen years old and not financially competent." Her parents, both immigrants and educated outside the US, "didn't have a clue."

After graduating in 2015 with a biology degree, she returned home to begin applying to graduate programs, hoping to save money by living with her parents. She discovered that not a single public college in Southern California—out of more than two dozen—offers a physician assistant degree, in a state with forty million people, where health care is a significant and growing part of the economy.

Private universities being her only option, she enrolled in USC's Keck School of Medicine. Because USC offers no scholarships, she borrowed another $170,000 to complete the three-year degree. If she pays $3,500 every month, she can repay her loans in ten years. If she pays $2,300 every month, she can repay her loans in twenty years. If she pays $1,900 a month, she can repay her loans in thirty years and pay an additional $400,000 in *interest alone*, nearly twice as much as the median home price in the United States.

In the midst of the COVID-19 pandemic, she was searching for jobs, hoping a major health-care corporation might hire her at a salary high enough to afford the loan payments. She was also applying to practices that serve low-income communities as a way to earn partial debt forgiveness. The reality of graduating into an economic depression has her worried. "How am I going to pay back $300,000? I don't have the luxury to say I'll take one job over another. I'm going to take whatever job I can get."

Like Valerie and her parents, families get lost in the jargon of financial aid, trusting colleges and lenders, often confusing grants and loans. It takes most graduates at least a decade to repay their loans, forcing them to delay buying homes, investing for retirement, and saving for their children's education.

Few Americans holding the nation's collective $1.5 trillion in student debt fully understood, as teenagers, the financial burdens loans carry. The middle class has been hardest hit. Families with incomes over $69,000 make up 60 percent of all borrowing by parents and students, according to a 2019 American Enterprise Institute analysis. Nearly 90 percent of first-year students attending private college can expect to receive, on average, 50 percent off the sticker price. But like JCPenney's promise of bargains at checkout, colleges wait until the very last minute to reveal their final cost.

So how can families make the odds work in their favor? Avoid falling victim to the most common mistake applicants make: choosing to attend the most selective college that admits them even if it's unaffordable. Colleges lure applicants into that trap with the bait-and-switch scheme called early decision. Early decision is designed to boost institutional revenues and favors students from families able to pay full or near-full tuition. (Be forewarned: early decision sounds suspiciously—perhaps deliberately—similar to early action. Early action is a no-risk way to get into college early and still have the freedom to compare financial aid offers.)

Early decision restricts students from applying to more than one college and then requires applicants to enroll if accepted. Though applying early decision significantly improves acceptance odds, students make a financial Faustian bargain: they sign a contract agreeing to accept whatever lowball tuition discount the college offers, often a package that requires borrowing substantial amounts of money.

Nearly 30 percent of high-achieving students from families with incomes greater than $250,000 a year use early decision, according to the Jack Kent Cooke Foundation. The advantages selective colleges give early decision applicants are astounding. The University of Pennsylvania and Duke are among dozens of schools that admit half their first-year classes in early rounds.

Researching colleges in 2020, I discovered that students applying early decision to Northwestern, Vanderbilt, Tufts, and New York University had a three times greater chance of being accepted. Lehigh accepted 60 percent early versus 19 percent regular decision. Kenyon accepted 70 percent versus 33 percent. American accepted 81 percent versus 30 percent. Pomona accepted 16 percent versus 6 percent. Washington and Lee accepted 50.5 percent versus 18 percent.

Experts put Swarthmore in the category of "super users" of early decision, colleges that accept three times as many students early. "For the love of all that is good in this world, if Swarthmore is your first choice, and you're competitive, apply ED," a consultant urged her clients.

To woo those rejected in the first rounds of early decision, some colleges offer "early decision 2," a second round. Not long after the first-round rejections arrived in mid-December 2017, our family was invited to attend a Colgate University reception at a luxury hotel in Los Angeles's South Bay.

Marble floors, crystal chandeliers, white linens, fine china, and fresh flowers greeted us as we entered. Several dozen applicants joined a couple hundred family members, alumni, and Colgate officials dressed in business attire. We sat down and I started chatting. All the kids at our table had been rejected from Harvard, Princeton, Stanford, and Yale in first rounds of early decision.

"We didn't get into our first choice," one mother said. "That's why we're here."

Colgate consistently ranks among the nation's most elite liberal arts colleges. *Forbes* called it "small but mighty," No. 6 on its list of "10 Expensive Colleges Worth Every Penny." Niche rated it New

York's second-best college behind Columbia and ahead of Cornell. It was No. 4 for having "the best-looking guys," a college "filled with white, preppy kids."

The Colgate students reflected the college's reputation. They greeted us with firm handshakes, talked about why they loved Colgate, answered questions with confidence and certitude that was oddly comforting. We listened to several presentations, including one from a Colgate executive who walked us through a virtual visit to the college, a bucolic campus in upstate New York. Fall leaves. White steeple. Stone buildings.

"Sounds like Yale, only better," I whispered to the mother sitting next to me.

She frowned. I apologized. "I'm sorry. Did you go to Yale?"

No, she said. Yale had rejected her daughter in December.

The dean of admission and financial aid told us about the college's return on investment, about the high-paying, intellectually exciting jobs Colgate graduates get, and the network of alumni and professionals who mentor them. He offered the families gathered that day a special incentive. Double the chances of being accepted. All you have to do is convert your regular admissions application into early decision by the March 1 deadline.

Colgate accepted nearly 41 percent of its early applicants, he pointed out, compared to 23 percent of regular applicants. He ended the ninety-minute presentation with as close to a guarantee as I'd heard, a spiel akin to a time-share pitch, minus the loan officer and a contract. "We invited you because we believe Colgate is the right fit for you," he said, implying, but not quite confirming, for the students in the room that they would be accepted if they applied early. This was the opposite of the usual application scam to entice as many kids as possible to apply only to reject them. This seemed to me, sitting among the hopeful, to be a ploy to persuade kids who'd already applied to enroll using early decision.

"I think you should do it," a dad at the table whispered to his son, a recent Stanford reject. Dad worked in finance and the family lived in Palos Verdes Estates, the second-wealthiest zip code in Los Angeles, and No. 38 in the US.

"Colgate sounds like a great college," his dad said. "And you'll get in."

"I'm not sure," his son said, his voice trailing.

"Apply early. Really. You'll get in."

Fear and uncertainty about coming rejections made Colgate look pretty good.

I wanted some of that admissions Xanax. But unlike the banker from Palos Verdes, our family couldn't afford it. In its regular-decision aid package, Colgate offered nearly 25 percent off tuition, but expected us to pay $55,000 a year, a sum so far beyond our means it was ludicrous to consider.

Early decision would have plunged our family into decades of debt, drastically altering our lifestyle, leaving us no choice but to plunder our retirement savings. For the wealthy—more than half of Colgate's students receive no aid and pay nearly $77,000 a year to attend—early decision provides certainty, relief, and significant advantages.

It also restricts competition, the federal government concluded after a two-year investigation, prompting the American Council on Education to question the government's motives. Only a few hundred colleges offer binding early decision, Terry Hartle, the council's senior vice president, pointed out to a *New York Times* reporter. "Given that this doesn't affect many schools, or many students, it's the ultimate first-world problem."

Is it? Early decision has created financial hardships for moderate- and middle-income students unfamiliar with the arcane way colleges structure aid packages. For them, untangling a loan-filled binding early decision financial aid package is hardly comparable to less than impeccable service at a five-star hotel or too little legroom in business class.

Leah, her younger brother Justin, and their parents can attest to the financial desperation they felt after being snared in an early decision trap. Justin's parents faced a Hobson's choice. After being rejected early from Brown, Justin was accepted to Wesleyan in a second round of early decision. Wesleyan gave Justin a significant discount. But what the college expected the family to pay was far beyond their means. (Because they fear adversely affecting Justin's financial aid, the family asked me not to use their real names.)

With an annual income of less than $65,000, Justin's parents received an aid package that required the family to borrow nearly $100,000 over four years. After discounts, subsidized loans, and an on-campus job that would pay Justin $2,700, his parents had to come up with $18,000 every year.

The offer was ironic, given Justin had applied to Wesleyan early largely because the college pledged to charge families only what they could afford to pay. Justin and Leah grew up middle-class in Grand Rapids, Michigan. Her parents opened tailoring and bridal stores in the 1990s, earning enough to send money to family in Vietnam. Amazon and the 2008 financial meltdown destroyed the family business during Leah's first year of high school.

When Harvard accepted Leah in 2011, it was a game changer. The college awarded her enough aid so that she could graduate debt-free in 2015. She landed a high-paying job and gave her parents money to open a small sandwich shop. They live month-to-month, have no retirement savings, and support Leah's grandmother.

Because her parents speak limited English, Leah helped Justin manage his college applications. In Justin's junior year, they identified right-fit campuses.

Justin's first choice was Brown. Brown had joined the elite Golden Ticket colleges, promising to charge families only what they could afford to pay without loans. The university was in its third year of a public campaign to recruit moderate-, middle-, and low-income students and to prioritize applicants from diverse backgrounds, a commitment Justin felt included him.

Justin applied early. Brown's early acceptance rate is more than three times its regular decision rate—21 percent versus 6. It has the lowest academic requirements among the Ivy League. Justin's grades put him just below Brown's 4.0 average for accepted students; his ACT score was as good as 25 percent of the students Brown took. Three wealthier, white seniors from Justin's high school were also applying early. Justin worried that he wouldn't measure up. Leah reassured him that his hard work, resilience, grit, and commitment made him an excellent candidate.

Brown disagreed. The committee rejected him, accepting the three white students instead, Leah said. "They all say they want diversity but look at who gets accepted. I felt bitter." The rejection left Leah doubting Justin could find a college that the family could afford. Even if the University of Michigan waived the $15,262 tuition, he'd have to pay $15,000 for room and board, books, and fees. Same with Michigan State.

She and Justin strategized. Since Brown's rejection freed him to apply to another college in second-round early decision, they pivoted. Searching for a college that promised to charge families what they can afford to pay, they settled on Wesleyan. Wesleyan, a small, selective college in Connecticut, has a reputation for vibrant, open-minded, creative students like Justin. Applying to Wesleyan early more than doubled Justin's odds of being accepted.

Justin's grades put him a little above Wesleyan's 3.73 average for accepted students. As with Brown, his ACT score was as good as 25 percent of the students the college enrolled. The financial aid application Justin submitted to the federal government estimated the family was so strapped it was unable to contribute a single cent to Justin's college expenses. Though Wesleyan charges $74,500 for tuition and room and board, plus books and fees, the college promises enough aid to make degrees affordable. If Wesleyan accepted Justin, the family could relax, knowing they wouldn't face years of debt.

Justin worked extra hard on his application, making sure it was as accurate a picture of him as he could draw. When Wesleyan accepted him, the family celebrated. When they saw his financial aid package, they panicked.

Wesleyan had discounted the total price, offering Justin $3,500 a year in federally subsidized loans and a $2,700 campus job. Where, they wondered, would they get the $18,000 a year they needed to fill the gap? And why was the gap so large between what the federal government said they could afford and what Wesleyan expected them to pay?

Leah had a week to find answers before Wesleyan began notifying colleges to withdraw Justin's other applications. Her parents had no equity in their house, and most of the profit earned from the sandwich shop went back into the business. Their only hope was private lenders. If they borrowed $80,000 at 6 percent interest and paid $600 a month for twenty years, the total amount with interest came to almost $150,000, an inconceivable figure to a family living paycheck to paycheck. They felt cornered.

If Justin pleaded financial hardship and broke the contract, what if other colleges rejected him? Or gave him worse packages? Maybe they could convince Wesleyan to keep Justin on the accepted list while they waited for offers from the twenty other colleges where he'd applied? Was it worth asking? Was it possible to leverage a deal on a binding early decision contract?

Leah weighed their options. The federal government estimated Justin and his parents had no money to contribute to his college costs. Wesleyan said they had $18,000 a year. Leah screwed up her courage and asked Wesleyan officials to explain the disparity. They told her how to appeal. She submitted proof that the sandwich shop had no assets and documents to show her family's medical costs, the family's support for her elderly grandparents, and her parents' lack of retirement savings.

When students like Justin threaten to withdraw due to financial hardship, elite colleges like Wesleyan with billion-dollar-plus endowments have the financial resources to negotiate. For two days Leah made her case. On the third day, Wesleyan reduced the amount they expected the family to pay to $3,800 a year, $316.66 a month, plus flights home and almost $2,000 for books and fees. If his aid remains the same, Justin will graduate in 2024 with $14,000 in loans, far better than the $100,000 the family faced with Wesleyan's first offer. Playing by the rules, Leah negotiated an 86 percent discount off Wesleyan's sticker price. After settling with Wesleyan, Leah brokered an even better deal with Boston University for her brother's best friend—a full ride.

When does right fit go wrong? When financial aid falls short of what families need to avoid loans. Schools that use merit scholarships to recruit affluent students often award higher discounts to families with incomes greater than $100,000 than they do to students from families with incomes less than $20,000, according to government statistics.

Why do they do that? Because offering $10,000 merit scholarships to three less-qualified affluent students brings in more money than using the same $30,000 to award a single grant to a moderate- or low-income applicant. The only way to give more financial aid to rich kids is to take it away from middle-, moderate-, and low-income kids.

At selective colleges, full payers go to the front of the line. More than half of the students at Ivy League colleges have no need for financial aid. Dozens of elite colleges—Brown, Dartmouth, Princeton, Yale, and the University of Pennsylvania among them—enroll more students from the top 1 percent than from the entire bottom 60 percent, according to Harvard researchers.

At Brown, for example, nearly 20 percent of the students come from families in the highest-earning 1 percent of American households: the median family income at Brown is $204,000, the highest in the Ivy League. Almost 60 percent of the class of 2021 received no aid at all, paying the full cost of attending, $80,448 annually.

The idea that selective colleges discriminate against affluent whites in favor of low-income students of color is just plain wrong. Selective colleges enroll minuscule numbers of students receiving Pell Grants, federal subsidies for moderate- and low-income students. Elite liberal arts colleges like Amherst, Wesleyan, Pomona, and Swarthmore do a better job than the Ivy League, but the total numbers are still comically low.

With an endowment half the size of Brown's and one quarter the enrollment, Swarthmore enrolls a larger share of moderate- and low-income students, more than 20 percent of its first-year class. That's about eighty students total.

Princeton was feted a few years ago for boosting to 22 percent the number of first-year students receiving Pell Grants. The *Washington Post* praised Princeton for shedding "once and for all, the reputation of a tradition-steeped university that caters mainly to the preppy and the privileged." Laudatory reports followed in the *New York Times* and *60 Minutes*. How many students benefited from Princeton's largesse? Fewer than three hundred out of 1.34 million applying to college that year.

As costs rise and incomes stall, the gap between what colleges charge and what families pay has widened to a chasm, more than 30 percent since 2008, from $11,347 to $16,255 at private colleges. At public universities, the shortfall has increased 40 percent, from $6,468 in 2008 to $11,118, according to the National Postsecondary Student Aid Study.

When USC announced free tuition to accepted students from families with incomes under $80,000, one financial aid expert called it "a brilliant PR stunt." The free tuition offer fails to include room and board, books, and travel, expenses that, as of 2020, can cost up to $21,000 a year. Since 16 percent of USC's first-year students are moderate- and low-income, the new policy affects roughly five hundred students, most of whom already receive nearly free tuition.

The vast majority of moderate- and low-income students are never encouraged to apply to selective colleges like USC. Their biggest obstacle is access. "They can't get the deal if they can't get in," scholar Sara Goldrick-Rab told a Yahoo reporter. "This doesn't change anything for them."

USC's free tuition helped very few. But it bought a boatload of public goodwill the school needed to rehabilitate its image after being the main target in the government's investigation of the largest criminal conspiracy in history to influence undergraduate admissions. USC was one of the most popular schools among the wealthy clients of swindler Rick Singer. The Singer scandal is a textbook example of the right-fit fallacy, the natural outcome of a system run by people born on third base going through life thinking they've hit a triple. Singer fabulized the right-fit students colleges wanted and then charged parents to create the right-fit children they didn't have.

A generation ago, enlightened government recognized and subsidized public higher education as a collective benefit. Today, free-market lawmakers and their supporters promote unbridled competition that allows the most advantaged to hoard opportunity and restrict social mobility. Gaining advantage in a system stacked to favor the already advantaged requires long-term political, social, and structural changes that the establishment will no doubt oppose. In the meantime, families can navigate their own roads to a life of possibility and opportunity. Even when forced to pay to play, families can play to win. Here's how.

Step 1: Narrow your focus. Understand the connection between getting into college and paying for it. Long before financial aid packages arrive, families have to sort through dozens of campuses to find "right-fit" colleges, a process that can feel more excruciating than facing four five-figure annual tuition bills.

College applications are expensive. It costs $90 to submit to Stanford, and between $80 and $85 at more than a dozen other elite colleges in 2020. Add to that $50 for each SAT and ACT score, and $93 for each Advanced Placement test. Subject tests cost $44 for the first one, $18 for subsequent sittings, $26 if the test has a listening section. After sending four free reports to colleges, the College Board charges students $12 for each additional report, and the ACT charges $13. After one free AP score report, the College Board charges $15 for each additional report.

Applying to twenty colleges will cost more than $2,000 just in fees. That's a little less than the $3,800 federal Pell Grant most moderate- and low-income students receive to pay their entire college bill each year. Consider, too, the opportunity costs students pay in the time needed to properly complete a competitive application. Apply more deliberately to fewer colleges using affordability as a litmus test.

Step 2: Figure out how the sausage is made. Understand how colleges build financial aid awards, called "packaging." Knowing a few facts about the way individual colleges award financial aid provides clues about how they sort applicants.

Colleges divide aid packages into three parts:

Loans and work-study: The most affordable loans come with government subsidies. Riskier loans come from private lenders. Work-study gives students federally subsidized campus jobs they can use to pay for tuition or living expenses.

Free money: Free money comes from tuition discounts,

merit aid, scholarships, institutional grants, and need-based financial aid.

Out-of-pocket payments: From parents, grandparents, students.

How does it add up? Consider New York University. NYU may be a top choice for students and parents, but it's a rich-kid college. Despite its $4.3 billion endowment, NYU enrolled 54 percent wealthy enough to pay the full cost of attending in 2020. With housing, board, and books, the bill comes to more than $300,000 for four years, or $76,612 annually. For the 46 percent receiving aid, the average amount they can expect to pay out of pocket is $44,873. To know for sure how much, students have to submit an $80 application, then wait for an acceptance and a financial aid package to arrive.

Step 3: Find your financial fit first. Identify colleges that meet the definition of financial right fit at the *start* of the search. The language of financing degrees has become so complicated that most parents wait until offers arrive to start financial planning. Bad idea. Instead, choose colleges that promise enough money to make earning a degree affordable. Use the net price calculator *before* starting applications.

Keep in mind, "affordable" is so subjective that every college defines it differently. Colleges, not parents, control the definition. You may think affordable means paying 10 percent of your income for college. Colleges may think affordable means you pay 40 percent.

To find affordable off-the-radar colleges, talk to friends and family about the choices they made. Ask them about their experiences, regrets, what they wish they'd known before arriving on campus, how much it cost for them to attend. Target colleges that guarantee merit aid, then ask what grades, test scores, and activities students need to win the highest discounts. Apply to colleges where your grades and test scores put you in the top 5 percent of the applicant pool, better-ing your chances to win the highest discounts offered.

Step 4: Learn to play the game. About sixty colleges promise to charge families only what they can afford to pay, an amount prob-ably far more than families want to spend. Of those colleges, more than half reject students based on their inability to pay, giving afflu-ent and full-paying students extreme advantages. Nearly 20 percent of private liberal arts colleges said they admit full-paying students with lower grades and test scores over more qualified, less-wealthy applicants, according to a survey of admissions directors.

To recruit more students, less-selective colleges have started cutting or freezing tuition in the past few years. A few public colleges fol-lowed suit, charging out-of-state students what it costs for residents to attend. The trend to cut tuition is good advertising for colleges, but nothing much has changed for families. Because so few stu-dents pay sticker price, the tuition cuts replaced the heavy discounts families came to expect. The new reduced sticker price more closely resembles the discounted price students had been paying.

John Gibralter, president of Wells College in New York, a five-hundred-student liberal arts campus, cut tuition 27 percent, to $29,400. The new pricing addressed the artful deception inherent in higher education's advertised tuition rates, he told a *New York Times* reporter. "At some point, it is like smoke and mirrors," he said. "We decided it made sense for us to be more honest and authentic and to talk about the educational product at Wells. And we wanted that to be available to many more people who may not otherwise look."

Step 5: If you're wealthy, apply via early decision. Early decision gives families and colleges what they want most: certainty. For the two hundred colleges offering early decision, it's the Holy Grail.

Early decision reduces the guesswork each spring as colleges struggle to enroll enough students to meet financial targets and bal-ance budgets. In early decision, 100 percent of the students they accept enroll, compared to the 33 percent they get in regular decision rounds.

The Common App requires students to sign early decision contracts, and though the agreements aren't legally binding, colleges threaten severe consequences if students break those commitments. High school counselors can still withhold transcripts and letters of recommendation until they confirm the outcome of early decision.

Brian C. Rosenberg, who retired in 2020 as the president of Macalester College, explained the double-edged sword of early decision in a *New York Times* interview: "The problem that it creates, and the problem that's most endemic in our higher education system, is the students that stand to be most harmed are the ones already disadvantaged."

7

The High Price of Advantage

The Wild West of Tutors, Coaches, and Consultants

I entered an echo chamber of bewildering admissions advice and misleading messages on a warm fall night in 2015. I was among hundreds of parents attending "College Night" at our kids' public high school, two decaying 1960s-era buildings in downtown Santa Ana. Counselors had organized dozens of workshops to introduce the ordeal that awaited us.

My youngest was fifteen, a sophomore, and her counselor had been urging students to start prepping for the SAT since ninth grade. Was that really necessary? To find out, I joined a few dozen other tired parents crammed into a small classroom with gray linoleum floors, sitting at narrow, faux-wood metal desks to hear a private college admissions consultant talk about high-stakes admissions testing. As we waited for the test prep guru to arrive, the light bouncing off institutional white walls was so bright I felt a coming migraine.

From the back of the room, a man in an open-collared shirt, brown loafers, and a charcoal sports coat took a few jaunty steps to the front. He started lecturing us about "reducing test anxiety."

The irony was unsettling. His presentation quickly became an angst-provoking session of PowerPoints and scattergrams, charts and statistics showing how unlikely it is for students with scores and grades below those of the nation's highest 4 percent to get into "top colleges." Of those colleges, 1 percent charge families only what they can afford to pay. The rest, he said, tie scholarships to test scores and grades.

"How much do you think you'll pay for college?"

No one answered, so he did. "The University of California charges $30,000 a year. If you want to send your kids to a private college, that's $70,000—*a year*. More than *a quarter million dollars.* Unless."

He paused for dramatic effect. "Unless your kids earn high enough grades and test scores to win merit scholarships."

A few parents actually gasped.

"That's where we can help." His company, he said, "provides students life lessons and their scores go through the roof!" He detailed irresistible offers—free testing, great results!—and distributed folders stuffed with marketing brochures.

"How much does it cost?" a parent asked.

"This is an informational session," he said. "We're not trying to sell you anything."

"Really?" I muttered.

As he droned on, I scanned sixteen pages of advertising. No prices. I clicked through the website. Lots of claims, no evidence: "Highest SAT scores," "admission to top colleges," "Ivy aspirations," "400-point SAT jumps," "offices in six affluent Southern California locations."

Still no prices. The next day, I emailed the contact on the website. Within thirty minutes I had my answer. Twelve lessons, $400 an hour, and a vague promise about the quality of the product: "Student average improvements of 400 points on the SAT and 6 composite points on the ACT."

$400 an hour? Who can afford that? Turns out a lot of people.

College night is the most common portal parents like me take into the admissions industrial complex. Once inside, they find thousands of companies and entrepreneurs competing, cajoling, and capitalizing on parents' deepest concern: their children.

Lost in an unregulated marketplace built on aspiration, families encounter charlatans with no credentials, consultants catering to the whims of multimillionaires, and occasionally excellent professionals with first-rate skills. Tutors and coaches do TED Talks, national news interviews, pen columns promoting themselves, make robocalls, and send email pitches to thousands of potential customers, with videos showcasing satisfied clients now enrolled in Ivy League colleges thanks to their application assistance.

Many entice, drop names, and spout pseudotherapy in motivational message tracks, exploiting parental fear and vanity for financial gain. They tell parents how to manage, shape, and brand their kids to beat the competition. They dictate classes, activities, sports, schedules. They train students for testing like heavyweight boxers battling for a title. They frame essays, closely edit them, demand rewrite after rewrite until it's unclear whose work is being submitted.

News reports recount horror stories of application frenzy and excess. Journalists repeat unquestioned claims of 100-point score improvements from SAT coaches charging $1,500 an hour; families paying $200,000 to brand children for the Ivy League; $16,000 for weekend application boot camps.

How did it come to this?

As far back as the late 1980s, panicked baby boomers, worried their children would be shut out of elite colleges, began hiring former high school and prep school guidance counselors to work privately with their families. As the market grew, so did the number of con artists. "Victims of bogus, incompetent or unethical counselors have little recourse when they get no results, especially after they have paid all or most of the fee in advance," the *New York Times* reported as far back as 1991.

In the next two decades, that small band of hucksters grew into an unregulated militia armed with amazingly sophisticated weapons. One of them, Rick Singer, became one of the country's most sought-after fixers. He spoke the language of corporate commercialism that executives understood. "Getting into college is a lot like selling iPads or cans of Coca-Cola," he said. "It's all about branding. . . . If you don't know what your personal brand is yet, it's time to name it and claim it. Because you need a strong brand."

Nearly every step in the application process became a profit center in the college industrial complex. Companies launched college tours by private jet (packages top $30,000 per trip and can hit six figures for multiple hubs); they built hotels in college towns catering to "helicopter parents and the rise of the parent-child college tour" with $475 million in raised capital, the *New York Times* reported.

Admissions consultants range in price from a few thousand dollars to $1 million or more. The best known, like Kat Cohen of Ivy-Wise, sell "insider knowledge" for hundreds of thousands of dollars to wealthy families looking for an edge. Even the *New York Times* hawks precollege services, summer classes for thousands of dollars, one-day symposiums on admissions ($125 in person, $48 live stream), and programs for kids whose college acceptances failed to meet expectations—$21,500 for Gap Semester and $16,500 for Gap Summer.

The industry has grown to $2 billion annually, with ten thousand people working full-time, plus as many as fifteen thousand part-timers, a number that has quadrupled since 2005, according to the Independent Educational Consultants Association. And that number doesn't include the five thousand who practice outside the bounds of professional associations.

Fear became a popular sales tool. Consultants cited harrowing statistics and described brutal competition to gin up angst about a system that even the wealthiest parents began to believe was rigged against them. Honest consultants and excellent tutors might give students advantages, but could they do the dirty work it took to optimize admissions chances? Parents at all income levels felt pressured to step up their game. But how? And at what cost?

Applications had doubled and tripled for the limited number of places at selective colleges. Acceptance rates plummeted to single digits at elite schools: colleges like Stanford that once took 30 percent or more of their applicants were accepting 4 to 5 percent. There was so much information that made little sense. Trying to sort the good from bad was an overwhelming exercise in frustration.

Admissions anxiety became palpable even among teens bound for state colleges. Funding cuts and tuition hikes made it harder than ever to get into affordable public universities. New York, California, Michigan, Pennsylvania, New Hampshire, Vermont, Illinois, and New Jersey raised prices beyond what moderate- and middle-income families could afford. As affluent students abandoned high-priced private colleges to attend state universities, they heightened competition for low-cost subsidized degrees.

Uncertainty nourished an industry feeding off what one expert described as a "bottomless resource: the love and anxiety of parents." Elite college admissions had become a competitive sport in America's wealthiest enclaves. "Most parents probably have done something they're not proud of in order to help their precious darling have an easier time in this unnecessarily cruel and competitive world," education writer Anya Kamenetz, a legacy graduate of Yale, told Bill McGarvey for his essay "We're Sacrificing Our Kids' Mental

Health to the College Admission Industrial Complex." "Most of the privileged and well-meaning folks I know think nothing of purchasing their child access to a private school education," she said; that means "special tutoring and test prep, fancy extracurriculars or an expensive house in a 'nice' school district."

From New York City; Raleigh, North Carolina; and Shaker Heights, Ohio, to West Los Angeles and Silicon Valley, college-prep fast-tracking was starting in preschool. Parents were sending toddlers to private tutoring like Kumon and Sylvan Learning centers to get ahead. "Part of them are saying, 'This isn't right, 3-year-olds should be playing in the sandbox and putting together mixing bowls,'" University of California psychology professor Alison Gopnik told a *New York Times* reporter, "but then they're thinking that maybe if the kid next door is doing it, it'll be time to go to Harvard and my child won't have the same advantage."

Parents had reasons for hoarding advantages. The stakes were higher than ever. Post-Reagan, a degree became the only sure path to financial security. The more competitive and expensive the college, the more parents borrowed and the more they watched the dreams they had for their children dry up. The odds that children would outearn their parents had been rising with distressing regularity with each passing generation.

Baby boomers born in 1950 had an 80 percent chance of earning more than their parents. Generation Xers born in 1970 had a 61 percent chance. Kids born the year Reagan was elected and later have a less than fifty-fifty chance. For those born after 1990, the future is even bleaker, scholars predict. They're coming of age at the worst possible moment. The economy collapsed during the 2008 Great Recession, the average student debt load has increased nearly ten times, and the COVID-19 pandemic forced many of them into indefinite unemployment.

At the end of the George W. Bush administration, the world's financial markets collapsed, and free-market lawmakers made it nearly impossible for Americans without degrees or union protections to get ahead. Millions of middle-class Americans lost good-paying jobs in the Great Recession—jobs in manufacturing, assembly, telemarketing, mail delivery, cooking, and administrative support. After Bush's $700 billion bailout to banks and corporations, employers began replacing more workers with labor-saving machines and requiring degrees from those applying for new openings, according to a National Bureau of Economic Research report. Middle-class jobs for Americans without degrees were fast disappearing.

Median earnings for high school graduates fell from $31,384 in 1965 to $28,000 in 2013. Young adults with just high school diplomas are now three times more likely to live in poverty than they were in 1979, according to the Gap Year Association, an industry that encourages students to travel for a year "before accruing college debt."

Remarkably, even as debt and defaults rose, free-market conservatives argued that college had become unnecessary, contradicting mountains of evidence and citing none of their own. Wages for workers without degrees have scarcely risen in fifty years after adjusting for inflation, and men's wages have fallen more. With degrees, men accrue approximately $900,000 more in median lifetime earnings than those with just a high school diploma. Women with degrees earn $630,000 more, but still less than men, according to David Autor, an MIT labor economist who has studied the relationship between education and earnings.

Americans need degrees—and good ones—if they want to stay afloat in the laissez-faire economy. Families unable to pay full price for college have little choice but to borrow more as tuition and housing costs climb. Flush with cash from borrowed money, colleges built luxury housing for students, hired celebrity faculty who rarely taught, awarded college presidents multimillion-dollar salary packages, and redirected millions of dollars into merit scholarships, discounts they used to recruit the best-prepped—usually the most affluent—students to boost rankings.

To get those discounts, parents hired precollege consultants to supervise prep from middle school to senior year, and tutors to boost test scores and grades in the most advanced classes. They hired application and writing coaches to assemble professional-caliber résumés and portfolios. They flew their children to pricey summer classes "to turbocharge grade-point averages," the *New York Times* reported, "or load up on the AP courses. . . . [and] skip ahead and qualify for higher-level subjects."

Everyone wanted to buy the secret formula to get into top-ranked colleges. They wasted a lot of money trying. "When you're trying to deconstruct the secret formula for admission to any college, you're playing a fool's game," said veteran admissions officer Jon Boeckenstedt, vice provost at Oregon State University.

"Those of us who know how admissions really works understand that at the vast majority of colleges and universities, there is no secret: If you're good enough, you're in. . . . At the rest—those 50 big-name institutions—even if you're good enough, you probably *won't* get in. . . . Parents and students don't like to hear this. People want certainty. They want the key to unlock the door. They want *an answer*. You won't find that in selective college admissions. There may be clues, but there is never certainty."

From the fountainhead of the free market sprang thousands of merchants marketing a wide range of speculative, useless, outrightly fraudulent gimmicks sold as precollege advantages. Using pitches borrowed from boiler rooms, time-share spiels, and pickup artists, entrepreneurs created high-pressure scams with images of beautiful, luxurious campuses to inspire families to dream of attending high-priced colleges they'd never before imagined.

High school principals, counselors, and teachers became the consultants' sales force, making competition for college admission appear worse than it was. Principals launched "Get Ready for College!" days in kindergarten. They forced students in middle school to compete for precollege honors classes. They shoved as many high school kids as possible into college-level Advanced Placement classes for bragging rights, to boost their rankings, and to appease neurotic parents pushing students to compete at the highest academic levels.

Principals, administrators, and state governments paid the College Board and the ACT millions of dollars to test students during the school day. They invited consultants to sell services directly to families in sessions they called "college workshops," thinly veiled private-industry pitches aimed at ratcheting up anxiety about getting into selective colleges as a way to their sell services.

Tutoring and testing companies bombarded students with messages on television, online, in social media, and with swag bags. They have Ivy League–inspired company names—"Impress the Ivies," "Ivy Coach," "The Ivy Dean," "Ivy Academic Prep," "Ivy League Tutors," "IvySelect"—but no actual Ivy League affiliations.

My wealthy friends were paying top dollar for advice I wanted to get for free. I volunteered to become the PTA education chair at my kids' public high school and organized college-prep workshops. I started by debriefing the parents. A few admitted they had been paying admissions coaches for their kids since middle school. Fearing competition would disadvantage their children, some refused to divulge their consultants' names or admit how much money they'd spent.

The vast majority of the PTA parents were like me, though, thoroughly confused. We didn't know the difference between the ACT and SAT, or why a kid would take one test over the other. We didn't know if our kids needed tutors or how to find one if they did.

I wasted hours, days, weeks, months attending sessions at local hotels and prep schools, trying to decode the doublespeak of admissions officers and consultants. I searched for magic formulas, for logic and answers, confronting what my Occidental College class-mate Andrew Ferguson calls "the law of constant contradiction. . . . For every piece of advice or information a parent or child receives while applying to college, there is an equal and opposite piece of advice or information that will contradict it."

In Ferguson's book *Crazy U*, he describes the same feral looks I saw, the anxiety, "the unloosed competitive instincts" that follow The Pitch. The hype is true, consultants tell parents. The admissions climate is as bad as you've heard. Worse. They tell you to do more because there's always more to do. They offer an endless supply of services to buy, and tasks to perform, to strive for the perfection they say kids need to compete. They hold a "persistent low boil," Ferguson said, scary enough to keep parents riveted, "but reassuring enough to keep [them] from abandoning all hope."

Counselors distribute checklists, calendars, tables, and charts showing the courses students need for college. They urge sopho-mores to take the PSAT, find a passion, enroll in as many honors and AP classes as their schools offer, play sports, get internships, do research. Volunteer to help the disadvantaged. Unless you *are* disad-vantaged; then get a job to use as fodder in admissions essays about overcoming adversity. Flatter teachers, then prepare branded portfo-lios to give them the material they need to write glowing letters of recommendation.

I heard the same tropes Ferguson did—about thirty-six thousand valedictorians denied admission to the Ivy League; 12 percent ad-mitted to College of the Ozarks, harder to get into than Amherst, Williams, UCLA, Georgetown, Tufts, and USC.

I ranted to my husband. "This is what parents have to spend? This is what kids have to do to fight their way into the College of the Ozarks?" I was outraged, not just by the prices, but also because I felt thoroughly manipulated.

The College of the Ozarks, a deeply conservative Christian school, has a tiny acceptance rate because it has *no tuition*. It's free, a fact the consultants neglected to mention. The dozens of books I read, the myriad workshops I'd attended, the people I'd talked to all led to the same conclusion: This wasn't a world I wanted to enter. And yet I felt like I had no choice. It was a matter of financial life and death.

In the past decade, financial aid formulas changed drastically. Colleges were using grants and discounts to recruit highly prepped students to help them meet unstated goals, usually to boost their status and *U.S. News* rankings. Nearly all colleges seduce the best students to enroll with tuition discounts called "merit scholarships," unrelated to a family's financial need.

A few dozen exclusive colleges charge families only what they can afford to pay, but getting into the elite of the elites is like trying to hit the center of a dartboard blindfolded.

Monied children at private prep schools receive intense individual admissions counseling unavailable at most public high schools. As the process for finding affordable degrees becomes more opaque, middle-, moderate-, and low-income students nationwide are getting less of the free counseling they need to succeed.

Nationally, the average public school guidance counselor advises about 500 students each, twice the 250-student caseload the American School Counselor Association recommends.

It's no wonder parents look for help in the $260 billion, unregulated admissions industrial complex. A friend, an editor at the *Los Angeles Times*, felt like she was drowning when her youngest daughter started applying to college. Her daughter attended one of the county's best public high schools and scored 2300 out of 2400 on her SAT (including the optional essay section). She had straight As, was on the dance team, and had traveled to Africa to research water systems. But when it came time to pull together her applications, "she was at a loss," my friend said.

The counselors gave her a lot less help than she needed to submit a dozen elite college applications. Even though my friend and her husband, an engineer, had already put two older children through college, much had changed in the intervening years. For the two older kids, she'd prodded, yelled, read their essays, enforced deadlines, and paid the application and testing fees. The University of California accepted them, and that was it. She never considered hiring a private consultant.

Fourteen years later, her family—like ours—had entered a baffling, disorienting wilderness. College applications had become so unwieldy, "it was downright bizarre," she said. Some elite colleges required a half dozen or more custom essays; arts portfolios illustrated with videos and slide shows; professional-caliber résumés, one for academics and another for activities; letters of recommendation that demonstrated an intimate knowledge of the applicants' intellectual and emotional accomplishments and potential.

The advice she kept getting was befuddling. "Stand out from the crowd, go beyond anything expected. But make sure you're authentic and sincere. Be yourself, of course. Just, you know, unique. Are we going crazy yet?" Figuring out how to finance a college degree was equally intimidating; each college's financial aid policy was more convoluted and obtuse than the next. She had no idea how to parse the law of constant contradiction. "By the time we even thought of hiring outside help, all the local consultants were full-up helping clients they'd started counseling freshman or sophomore year."

A colleague had enthusiastically recommended Tess, a consultant seventy miles away. Tess had connections. She knew the hooks.

"She promised she would manage this nasty system for us."

"How much?" I asked.

"$350 an hour. I wondered what on earth was going on with me," she said. "I tried to look at the payments as an investment in my daughter's future."

Tess had urged her daughter to apply early decision to the University of Michigan, a school she had no desire to attend, "as a form of admissions Xanax," she said. Since Michigan would certainly admit her early, Tess said, it would reduce her daughter's anxiety.

"That's what $350 an hour buys?" I asked.

Stevie was finishing sophomore year and we were being bombarded with warnings to hire an admissions consultant as quickly as possible. I started investigating what was out there. What I found shocked me.

Cardinal Education CEO Allen Koh described himself in an unsolicited 2020 marketing email as "one of the world's leading authorities on applying to highly selective American universities." His company charges $350,000 to $1 million to venture capitalists, hedge fund managers, and foreign clients with kids in US boarding schools, Koh has said publicly. "It's almost like concierge service," a business built on referrals, he told a *Wall Street Journal* reporter. "If we get someone's boy into Stanford or Harvard or MIT the parents are fielding hundreds of calls from friends congratulating them and asking them how they did it."

Another company, Varsity Tutors, expanded to the UK in 2017, and has plans to move into South America, Australia, and Asia. The company raised $107 million in capital in 2018, with $50 million from Mark Zuckerberg and his wife, Priscilla Chan's, charitable foundation. But buyers beware. Rigid pricing packages allow companies to control session length and tutor choices. The sales teams push parents to provide personal information over the phone for "tutor placement teams," and to commit to high-priced packages in sales pitches that reminded me why I shouldn't have bought that monthly gym membership I never use. Online forums feature students complaining about high hourly prices and poor quality. Tutors criticize the company for giving them no training and error-filled study materials, for paying them $18 an hour while charging clients $69.

To find lower-cost options, Stevie's high school counselor suggested I google "best college counseling [*insert your hometown here*]." I waded through forty pages of listings and found not one that provided cost information. I hired a graduate student to call for prices.

A week later, she handed me a thirty-page price list.

I flipped through it, looking for the cheapest.

Premiere Prep: from $1,300 for four ninth-grade sessions to $9,000 for a year's consultation.

Next.

Great Expectations College Prep: $250 consultation fee; $160-an-hour generic counseling; $2,200 Gold Package, ten hours plus video, cognitive skills consultation; Founders Circle Package, $400 consultation fee, sixty hours for $13,800.

Next.

Elite Total Learning Care: $5,500 package, $2,500 application workshops; AP Prep $600.

Next.

Powerful Prep: $250 an hour for staff tutor, $600 an hour with founder.

Next.

Curreri Educational Consulting: $300 an hour, up to $10,000 for packages.

Next.

HS2 Academy: featured in the *Los Angeles Times* as an admissions company that makes Asian kids seem less Asian. Refused pricing.

Next.

The College Trail: "Helping you get into your dream college." First session half-price.

Promising.

The College Trail, located twenty miles south, had no prices on their website, just a phone number and lots of scary details about investment ratios in tutoring per capita and "an increasingly competitive regional academic market." I called and reached the voicemail for Rod. Rod said I'd come to the right place, please leave a message. I was so worn out, I just couldn't.

I called the multimillion-dollar companies whose owners the media regularly promotes: Kat Cohen of IvyWise; Mimi Doe and Michele Hernández of Top Tier Admissions; Anthony-James Green of Test Prep Authority; Elizabeth Dankoski of the Dream School Project; Jessica Yeager of the Dream College Summit; Joel Block and Paul Kanarek at Collegewise; Bev Taylor and her son Brian Taylor of Ivy Coach.

Ivy Coach, Top Tier, and IvyWise sell themselves as some iteration of America's best college consultants. I heard the same pitch over and over: extremely limited exclusive programs; book now, we're nearly full; clients start as early as fifth grade.

What made one first among equals?

Independent consultants charge anywhere from $85 to $350 an hour—the median is $160—and packages range, on average, from $850 to $10,000 according to the most recently available information from the Independent Educational Consultants Association.

They provide little information about quality beyond platitudes. Some make wild assertions, like restaurants claiming to serve America's best burgers. InGenius Prep has "the world's leading admissions experts." Collegewise is "the nation's largest college counseling company." Top Tier has "America's premier college consultants." Ivy Coach is "the world's leading college consultant."

Ivy Coach claims to serve "the international aristocracy. Government leaders, captains of industry, celebrated glitterati and scores of the world's high-net-worth families—and their children." No wonder Ivy Coach charges some of the industry's highest fees. The company filed a lawsuit against a Vietnamese mother said to have been "amongst the international aristocracy." The mother agreed to pay Ivy Coach $1.5 million to hire founder Bev Taylor to help her daughter apply to seven boarding schools and twenty-two universities, including Harvard, Princeton, and Columbia, the suit alleged. When the mom failed to pay more than half her bill, according to the lawsuit (which Ivy Coach eventually dropped), the company sued for the balance.

Prior to the suit, the industry's trade organization had expelled Ivy Coach for price gouging. The company defended its fees in a blog post, accusing the trade association of violating antitrust laws. "The parents of our students appreciate that it is worth investing to help their children earn admission to an outstanding school when they'd otherwise earn admission only to a pretty good school."

Is advantaging the rich wrong? "Is that unfair? That the privileged can pay?" Ivy Coach managing director Brian Taylor rhetorically asked a *New York Times* reporter. "Yes, but that's how the world works."

When I called Top Tier, a consultant told me Stevie's profile was good, but not quite good *enough*. Her company could brand her to get her into an excellent college, maybe an Ivy League, maybe even *Harvard*. She offered to enroll her in an exclusive, three-day, $16,000 application boot camp at a secret location in Cambridge, Massachusetts. What shocked me more than the price was her assumption that we could pay $16,000 for three days of application assistance, about what it cost for her sister to *attend* Harvard for a year.

"What a shame," I bluffed. "She's busy that weekend."

No worries, she replied. "We have another program, the Personal Boot Camp, three days of personal assistance from a team counselor who comes to you for $16,000 plus travel and lodging expenses. . . . Let us know your top two preferred three-day time frames and we'll secure the dates."

It was fascinating and horrifying, slogging through what Andrew Ferguson calls the "large, lucrative, and parasitic industry [that] has puckered up and suctioned itself onto the tumescent host of college admissions." For the next few months, I roamed college fairs, jostling among families swarming tables for Stanford, Columbia, and Yale, where copies of *Getting In: Insider Tips on College Admissions for Immigrant Families* sold briskly.

I paid $48 to attend the *New York Times* virtual admissions symposium streamed live from the Times Center, billed "as a comprehensive overview with insights from current and former admissions professionals from colleges and universities around the country covering a wide range of topics, from crafting a compelling application and personal statement. . . ."

I attended admissions dog-and-pony shows featuring young, freshly scrubbed, nattily dressed millennials screening slickly produced college promotional videos in hotel halls big enough to hold inaugural balls. I asked advice from a member of the Regional Admission Counselors of California about finding good, affordable in-state colleges, only to discover she represents colleges outside California hoping to poach West Coast students.

The fairs and events featured huge casts. They looked like they cost tens of thousands of dollars to produce. Who fronts the money for this? I wondered. Multimillion-dollar trade organizations, I discovered.

The National Association for College Admission Counseling, with $22 million in assets, supports fifteen thousand dues-paying college counseling professionals. NACAC collected $16.6 million in revenues from fees for conferences, membership, and educational services, staging admissions-themed trade shows around the globe. Recent chief executive Joyce Smith earned $400,000 a year, and NACAC pays $7 million in staff salaries. Its smaller rival, the Independent Educational Consultants Association (IECA), caters to private admissions consultants. The IECA generates $2.8 million in revenues, $2.5 million from fees and products: membership, conferences, trainings, events, and tours. Under the leadership of chief executive Mark Sklarow—$234,000 annual compensation—the organization grew 450 percent, according to its 2017 tax returns.

On the IECA website, I learned how some private admissions coaches use overburdened high school guidance counselors to find clients, and how that cozy relationship benefits the industry's parasitic sales force. The trade group urges members to cultivate high schools for referrals. Offer them coffee, breakfast, lunch. Assist them in training sessions. Provide promotional materials; donate books, maps, and other resources. Coauthor news articles. Underwrite admissions events and speakers. Become the experts they call for help. Attend forums on admissions testing, financial aid, and Naviance.

Naviance, a subsidiary of the $2 billion British company Hobsons, charges high schools to license proprietary software to help families position their children for college. Naviance allows parents to compare grades and scores to those of other students accepted at colleges their children want to attend. I logged into Naviance and saw scattergrams more anxiety provoking than any I'd seen. Only a few students from Stevie's public urban high school had been accepted to colleges that promised to charge families what they could afford to pay.

Counselors and teachers distributed industry pitches to students and nominated them for hundreds of pay-to-play programs with impressive-sounding names and price tags buried deep in marketing and advertising brochures. They announced solicitations over high school public address systems, promising to "nominate whoever wants to go," a Birmingham, Michigan, high school counselor told a *New York Times* reporter. Companies persuaded teachers to recruit students for their programs by offering them $500 grants and free hotel stays.

Shady appeals became so common that in 2009 the *New York Times* sent a reporter to investigate. "Congratulations! You Are Nominated. It's an Honor. (It's a Sales Pitch.)" exposed some of the worst pay-to-play players and practices. They promised a "lifetime advantage" and "valuable addition" to student résumés in programs reserved for the "elite," "distinguished," and "select," the *Times* reported.

Other companies with impressive-sounding names like Global Young Leaders Conference and Academic Programs International convey privilege and prestige. "Invitations to join," with vague promises of exclusivity and "special access experiences," arrived in the mail with fancy gold lettering and embossed medal seals on thick card stock. The presentations hoodwinked families into believing that these high-priced programs would meaningfully help teens get into all kinds of colleges.

For students isolated in rural regions of the South and Midwest, the invitations seem "really official and really prestigious," one teen said. She lived in a small Iowa town on the Mississippi and chose to attend the National Young Leaders Conference because of her counselor's recommendation, she told the *Times*. "I felt really honored."

Many kids from small towns have never traveled far from home, the counselor said, explaining why she had recommended nearly a dozen students for the National Young Leaders Conference. "For these kids, it is a big deal." The invitation's packaging "kind of reinforces that."

Parents were sending teenagers to villages in Latin American and African countries, to build playgrounds or coach kids' soccer in between tourist sightseeing. For $5,000 plus $1,500 airfare, high school students were building playgrounds in Tanzania, teaching English in Thailand, or joining construction projects in Peru.

Academic Programs International distributed glossy, full-color catalogs showing white teenagers posed with groups of smiling Black or brown children. "Oh, yes, it really helps with admissions," one staff member told a parent attending an information session. "A lot of students frame their whole essay around the experience."

In myriad interviews, families were shocked to discover most for-profit programs provide no advantage, especially at selective colleges where admissions officers are becoming wise to opportunistic market-driven programs. The majority, while legitimate and legal, are usually pointlessly expensive and in no way substitutes for authentic volunteering.

In fact, a 2016 Harvard report concluded that applicants were better off doing good works closer to home. The report, supported by officials of sixty colleges and universities, called for deemphasizing expensive overseas volunteering, in favor of urging students to volunteer locally. That's something Sheryl Hill wished she'd known before she sent her son Tyler on a People to People trip to Japan. The family had no idea until it was too late that the "honor" Tyler received meant nothing, "that it doesn't make a difference. That nobody cares."

After Tyler died, Hill discovered to her horror that the People to People Student Ambassadors nomination was a sales pitch from mass marketer Ambassadors Group Inc. None of that was clear when Tyler received a letter signed by President Dwight Eisenhower's granddaughter Mary nominating him to join an elite group of high school students as peace ambassadors to Japan. The letter listed eight presidents and had the seal of the State Department, Hill said. Hill believed the company was a nonprofit established by President Eisenhower.

"We thought Ty was getting the letter because of who he was," Hill said of her son, a leader, role model, and straight-A student who'd won his high school's history award. "I thought he was going to be a student ambassador of the United States. I didn't know this was a for-profit company. I never would have thought kids would be solicited like a commodity."

Tyler was barely sixteen, a spray of freckles across tan cheeks, when he boarded the plane for Japan a decade ago. Before he left, People to People assured the Hills that the company had the gold standard for student safety and provided a twenty-four-hour response team to handle medical emergencies, Hill said. The company charged the Hills nearly $7,000 but promised the experience would help Tyler build his college applications and introduce him to "a world of exciting special access."

Wearing a burgundy polo shirt and khaki pants, Tyler shot a dazzling smile to his mom as they waved goodbye. He had traveled extensively, was six feet two inches tall, and was in great shape, a star rugby, football, and hockey player; a scuba diver and skier. Tyler would be fine overseas, Hill told herself. But she was wrong. The for-profit company was a "head 'em up, move 'em on, and rake it in" scam, as she came to see it. "They put six in a room and fed them McDonald's. That wasn't what I expected."

Hill was completely unprepared for what came next. After climbing Mount Fuji, Tyler started feeling sick and asked his counselors to see a doctor. The counselors refused, sending him to his hotel room to work through it, the Hills alleged in a lawsuit they later filed. That night, he started violently vomiting and spitting blood.

The next morning, aware of Tyler's worsening condition, counselors left him alone in his room, the Hills' lawsuit alleged. Tyler tried to call the hospital and his family, but his cell phone died, and he couldn't figure out how to dial the local emergency number.

Though People to People denied that Tyler was left alone and refused medical attention, the fact remains that counselors returned to his room to find Tyler unconscious. They took him to the Japanese Red Cross Medical Center a few minutes away. Hours later, a counselor called the Hills in Minnesota to tell them Tyler's heart had stopped for more than an hour, doctors had resuscitated him, and he was on dialysis. The Hills rushed to Japan. Tyler died two days later of cerebral edema caused by dehydration. "A very slow, torturous death. He died by slow suffocation," his mother said, choking back tears.

Hospital officials told Sheryl that his death could have been prevented if he had received immediate medical care, the Hills said in their complaint against People to People. The Hills were grateful that the company hired a grief counselor to comfort them emotionally, only to learn later, they alleged, that he had given Tyler's medical records to the Ambassadors Group without their permission. The Hills discovered unbearable truths after filing a wrongful death suit to recover the cost of the trip, funeral expenses, and other damages. The company was part of a massive unregulated precollege student travel industry with no meaningful oversight, no mandatory crime statistics reporting, and "no accountability," Hill said. Ambassadors Group, once a $128 million, publicly traded mass-mailing and marketing company that dissolved in 2015, paid millions of dollars in licensing fees for exclusive use of the People to People name, CBS News reported, including the right to use Eisenhower's signature. The company sent recruitment letters to a long-dead boy in Iowa, a girl in Tennessee who had died at ten days old, and to a one-eyed cat buried in the backyard of an Arkansas family, according to news site Consumer Affairs.

Even after Tyler died, the family friend who wrote the boy's reference letter received a horrifying pitch illuminating the relentlessness of People to People's marketing machine. After thanking him for recommending Tyler, the letter asked him to nominate other students to participate in the Student Ambassador Program. It also had Mary Eisenhower's signature.

"They stop at nothing," Sheryl Hill told a *Seattle Times* reporter. In the *Times* article, People to People apologized for sending the pitch and once again denied leaving Tyler alone. Hill said she had asked Ambassadors chief executive Jeffrey Thomas to remove from the company's website inaccurate boasts about People to People's safety record and insisted that he change his company's safety standards. He refused, she said, "and told me that's my opinion."

The Ambassadors Group CEO, a Dartmouth graduate, earned nearly $2 million in 2009, the same year the Hills won a confidential lawsuit against the company. Hill is still angry over Thomas's public statement after the settlement. "He said Ty's death would have no impact on shareholder value."

Sheryl and her husband, Allen Hill, used the settlement money to launch the nonprofit Depart Smart to prepare students to travel safely abroad. "This is a huge industry—two or three times the size of the NFL, with no oversight," Hill said. "Parents naively assume that our kids are protected by laws."

People to People International continues. The company, a nonprofit, uses the multinational worldwide travel corporation ECE International to provide its travel services, according to the website. Since the early 2000s, Mary Eisenhower has served in various roles at People to People International, earning more than $670,000 between 2013 and 2018, the year her son Merrill Eisenhower Atwater took over as CEO, according to tax returns. Nearly 85 percent of the nonprofit's revenues went to salaries in 2018 and another $125,000 to office expenses and advertising. Eisenhower declined to talk about Tyler Hill. "I am bound by the settlement not to discuss it. Regretfully, I will not be able to help you."

So many people selling so much fake advantage stack the odds against families looking for high-quality help at reasonable prices. Here's how to avoid scammers and maximize returns on your investment.

Tip No. 1: After making a decade's worth of mistakes, I discovered a few truisms. Corporate chains hire overworked, inexpensive counselors with questionable experience, then charge families premium prices. Price doesn't necessarily correlate with quality.

Tip No. 2: To avoid paying chains for middling advice, look outside the box. I asked high school counselors for names of recent graduates admitted to the dream colleges my kids wanted to attend. I called the parents of those students and asked them what strategies and consultants they used. I even hired a couple of those students as low-stress coaches.

Tip No. 3: The best tutors and consultants I found when my kids were in high school ranged in price from $25-an-hour college students to $85 an hour for a PTA mom who was a therapist and moonlighted as an admissions coach. My kids wrote their essays in high school English classes and at inexpensive after-school classes with their English teachers.

Tip No. 4: The Common App centralizes all applications in one place, so students no longer have to input the same data over and over for individual colleges. Member colleges provide links in the Common App to school-specific instructions for athletics recruits and students applying to art and design schools. Only the most selective colleges use the Common App essay as a deliberative sorting tool, and only within the context of the many supplemental essays those schools require. For the majority of applicants, admissions committees regard the Common App essay as less important than grades and test scores.

Completing the Common App with seriousness of purpose is the best way to advantage your admissions chances. Start working on the application in June after junior year by filling in personal information. Since the company officially releases what is usually the same form every August 1, check to see if what you've done needs to be updated in August.

For the essay, consider the broad prompts as ways to

communicate something about you that admissions officers can't find elsewhere in the application. Identify one prompt that will best allow you to shine a light on an aspect of your personality that is different from all other students like you. Spend time organizing your thoughts, brainstorming ideas, and coming up with examples and anecdotes about yourself in a way that properly addresses the prompt. Ask a teacher and counselor for feedback to help refine the essay.

Tip No. 5: Regardless of where you live, consultants will charge what the market will bear. Competitive affluent parents in suburban and urban areas nationwide will pay top dollar to advantage their kids. When shopping for a consultant, make sure you're paying for quality, not hype.

Tip No. 6: Hire only professionals committed to helping find colleges tailored to your child's specific qualifications. Make sure they help your family build a list of colleges in three categories: safety colleges that will certainly admit, match colleges where chances are good, and dream colleges that are a stretch.

Tip No. 7: Ask a lot of questions. Are consultants familiar with the college campuses on your list? Have they visited those colleges? Do they know the staff? If they do, make sure you ask them to provide specific names of the people they know. If they can't, then ask them why not. They may be lying about a network they don't have. Be wary of tutors or consultants who don't conduct friendly pre-interviews with applicants, preferably for free. If they don't ask basic questions about grades, test scores, academic strengths and challenges, passions, interests, and emotional and social depth, then look elsewhere.

Tip No. 8: Make sure consultants thoroughly understand how the colleges on your list award financial aid and can explain that to you. The consultant should help students find exceptional schools that want them enough to discount tuition to recruit them, where they're standouts and not just another applicant at an ultracompetitive, expensive college.

Tip No. 9: Look for nonprofits in your town or county that offer free or low-cost admissions counseling. Since high school counselors often have no idea how to find outside admissions assistance, do a little digging. Start by googling "nonprofits to help with college." One of the largest, the National College Attainment Network, helps millions of students apply to college through its nationwide member network. A complete directory of its services, costs, and members is available on its website (https://www.ncan.org).

Tip No. 10: Find a consultant committed to reducing anxiety, someone focused on finding the best, most affordable college for your family, not trying to sell you rankings or prestige. When hiring a high-priced consultant or corporate chain, do a thorough background check. Check credentials and references, get to know the counselors, find out how long they have been in the business. Most important: never pay the full amount up front.

8

Admissions Hooks and Scholarship Scams

Pay-to-Play Access and Skyrocketing Costs

Pay-to-play admissions has expanded into a multibillion-dollar market that favors "the rich and powerful," a belief held by two-thirds of Americans, according to a 2019 *USA Today* / Suffolk University poll. "Money talks, and they don't like it," Suffolk University Political Research Center director David Paleologos told a reporter. "Across all demographics, Americans find college admissions unfairly favor the wealthy and the well-connected."

Parents were paying thousands of dollars to private consultants to get their kids into college, then mortgaging their futures by borrowing tens of thousands of dollars more to pay for degrees. "As any student and parent outside the top 5 percent income class who pays for college can tell you, the need for money comes first," writes author Sara Goldrick-Rab in *Paying the Price: College Costs, Financial Aid, and the Betrayal of the American Dream*. To earn degrees in the US, she wrote, nearly all families "must quite literally pay to play."

Scammers selling predatory goods and services exploited families, taking advantage of their very real fear of falling down the socioeconomic ladder. The scams start years before families pay their first tuition bill. Thousands of consultants and companies extract billions of dollars from parents desperately seeking advantage. They sell bogus honors and control access to thousands of scholarships in a pay-to-play market so opaque and tangled it's impossible to differentiate the legitimate from the rest. Identifying the corporations and private equity funds behind the companies selling scholarships requires a forensic accountant. I know. I hired one to help me.

This wasn't always so. From the end of World War II to the election of Ronald Reagan, government subsidized higher education to power past the rest of the world economically. Millions moved out of poverty and into what became the world's largest middle class. Equal access to college was a cornerstone for America's vision of a Great Society embraced by Presidents Johnson, Nixon, Ford, and Carter.

Then came Ronald Reagan. A laissez-faire radical and fierce warrior for the free market, Reagan pledged to "make America great again," which meant, among other things, a return to the days when college was reserved almost exclusively for white Americans of means. Reagan and his followers fundamentally changed the way Americans thought about higher education.

Promising to "send the welfare bums back to work," charge students for degrees, and end "intellectual curiosity" subsidies, Reagan demonized students and appealed to Americans sick of paying taxes to help strangers. As governor, Reagan attacked the University of California—considered a model of egalitarianism—as a haven for left-wing communist sympathizers, protesters, and sexual deviants. As president, he convinced voters to elect like-thinking free-market lawmakers to restrict equal access to degrees. As far back as 1982, the US commissioner of education, Ernest L. Boyer, predicted that Reagan's disdain for public education would do long-lasting damage. "The serious impact of Ronald Reagan," he said, "has been his failure to affirm public education as an essential need for strengthening the nation."

Reagan convinced Americans that government is bad. "The nine most terrifying words in the English language are: I'm from the government, and I'm here to help," he said. His British counterpart, Margaret Thatcher, was franker: "Economics are the method. The object is to change the heart and soul."

For a growing number of Americans, the dream of upward mobility through college became a downward descent into financial insecurity. As government withdrew financial assistance to students, entrepreneurs and corporations filled the void with schemes and scams. To find legitimate sources of financial support, families were forced to wade through a new layer of complexity. Students searching for financial aid often fell victim to opportunists. Profiteers lured students with the promise of scholarships, then sold the data they collected from unsuspecting families and friends.

For the slightest possibility of a scholarship, students are required to hand over valuable private data for free to companies that resell it for millions of dollars. Dangling the possibility of free money, some companies have seduced millions of students to submit surveys filled with personal information. Those companies then turned around and sold student information to mass-marketing vendors. The mass marketers used the data to send spam emails back to students, filling their inboxes with an endless barrage of pay-to-play marketing pitches and scholarship "competitions."

Entering scholarship competitions might require signing up via Facebook or "liking" an organization's webpage. That can give marketing companies access to the profiles of every student who enters, as well as to the profiles of "competing" students and friends. Scholarship "winners" are often chosen via social-media popularity contests, providing sponsoring companies with thousands more potential customers. Other competitions require students to write essays promoting not the students but the companies themselves: in other words, free promotion for the company but few benefits for most students submitting advertising content. Corporate opportunists collect the data for resale to other companies ready to take advantage of the vulnerabilities of students and their families.

Often using random drawings to choose winners, companies give students prizes too small to make a dent in college costs. But the scams keep alive the myth that big-time scholarships can be won by responding to clickbait stories promoting winners of extremely rare large awards.

Thanks to the spectacular growth of the data-collection industry, information about the nature of these scholarships has never been more accessible or more depressing. Hundreds of companies—from producers of duct tape and e-cigarettes to those selling obscure financial instruments like surety bonds—now offer scholarships to promote products. They cajole as many students as possible to apply, and advertise on websites like Fastweb and Chegg, themselves moneymaking enterprises.

The federal government sent millions of families in 2020 links to 825 digital pages listing eight thousand scholarships. They encouraged anyone who filed an application for federal grants and loans to "look through the whole list," a mind-numbing waste of time spent wading through untold numbers of pitches from private companies like Recruit Connect Inc., LeverEdge Inc., Nitro Inc., AlgaeCal, and Amtrol Inc.

Since no federal laws currently regulate consumer data brokers, precollege pay-to-play marketing schemes operate freely and largely unregulated. Free-market lawmakers and lobbyists have blocked every attempt to force the industry to become more transparent.

For every parasitic pay-to-play company whacked down, another springs up to feed off the admissions corpus. The College Board and ACT now compete with newcomers like My College Options, Slickdeals, and ScholarshipPoints, which is owned by Edvisors, which is owned by the Las Vegas–based College Loan Corporation. Though legitimate scholarships exist—small awards reserved for teens of certain religions or interested in specific careers, or from civic organizations like chambers of commerce and parents' employers—those few get lost in a barrage of fake possibility.

Students would be better off finding part-time jobs or researching financial aid policies at their top-choice colleges than wasting weeks and months in a futile search for a few hundred dollars.

When my friend Karin was investigating scholarships for her daughter in 2015, she discovered that ScholarshipPoints, for example, required students to submit surveys to "earn points" to increase their chances of winning scholarship lotteries. Slickdeals was awarding prizes to students based on the number of other students they persuaded to sign up to become Slickdeal members. JW Surety Bonds had invited students to write well-sourced original essays about its obscure corner of the insurance business so it could collect thousands of dollars of Web content. She found out that, after awarding one student $1,000, the company posted the rest of the essays online without paying losers a dime for their efforts.

Duck Brand, a subsidiary of ShurTech Brands, sponsors a $10,000 scholarship for the best-designed prom outfit assembled entirely from duct tape—which students purchase out of pocket. The company's judges choose finalists, who go on to the "community voting" round. While contestants campaign for online votes, the company collects voter email addresses for validation. By doing so, the company gets an overload of website traffic, free publicity, and a long list of email addresses for future marketing.

The cruelest blow might be what happens after scholarship checks arrive. Colleges require those lucky winners to report outside awards so they can deduct the money from financial aid packages. In the end, many students get no benefit at all.

Private-industry scholarships may be dead ends for students, but they're cash cows for plucky entrepreneurs like Richard Rossi. Rossi directs the National Leadership Academies, one of a dozen precollege pay-to-play programs sold by the nation's largest precollege pay-to-play mass marketer, Envision. Envision flatters students with broad compliments about their intelligence and achievements while pitching pay-to-play programs that students infer will help them get into college.

The programs cost hundreds and sometimes thousands of dollars to attend and have impressive-sounding names: National Student Leadership Conference; Junior National Young Leaders Conference; Congressional Youth Leadership Council; Global Young Leaders Conference; National Youth Leadership Forum; Game and Technology Academy.

Scores of people have logged onto the Better Business Bureau website to complain about Envision and its corporate owner, WorldStrides Educational, which is owned by Lakeland Holdings LLC, which is owned by equity investors who paid $344 million for the company's stock in 2016.

The complaints describe a frustrating litany of scams, rip-offs, and misleading, hard-core no-refund policies. "The International Scholar Laureate program sounds like an amazing opportunity because it's marketed in such an appealing way but trust me IT IS NOT! IT IS A SCAM! They say it's an educational opportunity to participate in conferences with leading business companies and entrepreneurs and create a project to help solve a global economic issue, but it's an over-glorified scam."

The scholarship discounts the company offers rarely knock more than 10 or 15 percent off trips that cost $5,000 plus airfare and spending money, a parent complained to the Better Business Bureau. "If you do the payment plan, you pay more. Their travel insurance sucks. No matter what bad thing happens on the trip they will refuse to refund you the money."

When the *New York Times* looked into the National Leadership

Academies in 2009, reporters found at its center Richard Rossi, the academy's executive director. Rossi had founded Envision in 1985, and was hawking Envision's Congress of Future Science and Technology Leaders when a *Times* reporter caught up with him.

After buying data from a third-party scholarship vendor, the congress sent high school students letters signed by a Nobel Prize winner, the *New York Times* reported. In the letter, Nobel laureate John Mather praised students for being nominated to attend "a highly selective national program honoring academically superior high school students."

Thousands of eager students, pictured in a *Times* photo in khaki pants, collared shirts, modest dresses, and low-heel shoes, paid nearly $1,000—a total $3 million in revenues—to cram into a sports center in 2018 in Lowell, Massachusetts. They heard from motivational speakers like oceanographer Sylvia Earle and Google Science Fair winner Shree Bose.

The *Times* questioned Rossi about the seemingly disingenuous flattery and misleading mass marketing Envision used to lure students, describing the conference as "selective" because it accepted only students with at least a 3.5 GPA. "Does that make it less appropriate to tell them they are special?" Mr. Rossi asked. "In my mind, no." Rossi sold the business in 2011.

Can free-market America go any lower than using the promise of admissions advantages and scholarships to exploit teenagers? Yes, it can. Yale, the University of Maryland, Emory, Washington University in St. Louis, the University of California, and Stanford have in the past rented their campuses to Envision. Stevie received an invitation to enroll in an Envision-sponsored program at George Mason University in 2016. It promised: "Attending will differentiate [*insert your child's name here*] from her peers when applying to college, and it is certainly something she will want to highlight on her college applications."

When I was researching high school enrichment, I found myriad programs beyond what Envision was selling. I discovered that for $20,000 students can "become a Stanford student . . . at high school summer college." Brown was charging more than $7,000 for a month, and selling environmental leadership programs in Alaska; Florida; Italy; Spain; and Washington, D.C., with specialty courses for English-language learners and a STEM program for rising ninth- and tenth-grade students. A seven-week, $13,000 prebaccalaureate program was giving students the chance to earn Brown University course credit that "may provide students with advance standing." Or not.

Even as they profit from them, selective colleges are wise to revenue-generating marketing schemes. George Mason warns students enrolling in its Envision partner precollege programs that those classes are unlikely to "have a significant bearing on the college admissions process." A Tufts admissions officer was more candid about the proliferation of programs like Envision. She was seeing more applications "from students citing attendance at these workshops as an achievement," and flatly concluded, "this doesn't really give them any advantage," in a 2009 *New York Times* article.

Colleges are hardly without fault. They profit from programs that rarely give advantage and reward the children of the wealthy with the certainty everyone else craves. That certainty is almost always reserved for the upper reaches of the upper classes, according to *Wall Street Journal* reporter Daniel Golden. In *The Price of Admission*, Golden exposed "affirmative action for rich white people," preferences that far outweigh any benefits affirmative action gives students of color. Roughly 60 percent of elite college acceptances go to "non-academic preferences," leaving 40 percent of the places for everyone else to compete to win.

Academia has created a system that encourages families to leverage advantage however they can. Colleges lower standards to accept children of alumni and faculty, celebrities, donors, and friends of powerful executives, categorizing them as "special consideration" or "special interest" applicants. In crass exchanges of multimillion-dollar pay-to-play donations, they accept the unqualified children of billionaires, like Charles Kushner, Golden reported.

Jared Kushner's dad, Charles, had built the family business into a billion-dollar real estate investment and lending behemoth in the deregulated 1980s. Charles sent Jared to the exclusive Frisch prep school, expecting he'd go to Harvard. When Frisch counselors failed to adequately support Jared's Harvard application, Charles found another way. He met with Harvard's president, Neil Rudenstine, and pledged a $2.5 million donation. "There was no way anybody in the administrative office of [Frisch] thought he would on the merits get into Harvard," Golden reported. "Then, lo and behold, Jared was accepted."

While Jared was at Harvard, Charles Kushner was secretly evading tax laws, making illegal campaign contributions, and threatening to retaliate against a cooperating witness and her husband—his own sister and brother-in-law. His was "one of the most loathsome, disgusting crimes that I prosecuted when I was US attorney," former governor Chris Christie told a reporter. "And I was a US attorney in New Jersey, so we had some loathsome and disgusting crime going on there."

Charles Kushner—who has consistently denied that his dona-tion affected Jared's Harvard acceptance—pled guilty, served a lit-tle more than a year, and returned to running the family business, worth $1.8 billion in 2016, according to *Forbes*. After marrying Donald Trump's daughter Ivanka, Jared Kushner became one of the most powerful men in Donald Trump's administration. Charles Kushner received a full pardon from Trump in 2020.

Golden won a Pulitzer Prize for exposing college influence ped-dling and became a minor celebrity among the *Wall Street Journal*'s wealthier subscribers. When a high-tech tycoon asked him how much money he'd have to donate to get his academically average daughter into an Ivy League college, Golden was dismayed. "They regarded my series not as investigative journalism but as a how-to guide." Golden didn't need to teach rich people how to use their power and influence to get their kids into college. Most of them had figured it out already.

Billionaire David Shaw split a $37.3 million donation among five Ivy League schools and Stanford starting in 2011, when the oldest of his three children was two years away from college. Two graduated from New York's exclusive Horace Mann School and went to Yale. The third, Jacob, attended Stanford's summer jazz program for teens, Daniel Golden and Ava Kofman reported in a 2009 article. Jacob and his mom, the financial author Beth Kobliner, wrote a children's book when he was nine, with illustrations by Pulitzer Prize–winning cartoonist and screenwriter Jules Feiffer. "They live in a large, makes-you-want-to-kill apartment, it's so spacious and gorgeous," Feiffer told Golden. "They offered me real money, and I was in the market for real money."

Shaw's donation is a pittance compared to the $70 million that rock music impresario Jimmy Iovine and rapper Andre Young, known as Dr. Dre, donated to USC in 2013. After Dr. Dre's daughter was accepted to USC in 2019, he posted on Instagram: "My daughter got accepted into USC all on her own. No jail time!!!"

He aimed his dig at the wealthy-but-less-rich-than-he-is celebrities and executives who paid criminal consultant Rick Singer to bribe their unqualified children into selective colleges. "We're not talking about donating a building so that a school's more likely to take your son or daughter," said Massachusetts federal prosecutor Andrew Lelling about Rick Singer's scam. "We're talking about deception and fraud."

Three USC faculty members reflected popular indignation about Singer's clients in a post for the online journal The Conversation. "If the scandal reveals anything, it is that some affluent parents will stop at nothing to make sure their children win in the high-stakes game of college admissions."

Getting into exclusive colleges is more competitive than ever. A million-dollar gift just "doesn't have the impact it used to have 20 years ago," Princeton's former director of gift planning told a Pro-Publica reporter. Consider what Philip Esformes, a Miami nursing home magnate, did to get his son into the University of Pennsylvania. While investigating Esformes for running the largest health-care scam in history, federal agents discovered he had paid $400,000 of his ill-gotten gains to Singer, some of it to bribe USC to accept his daughter as a soccer recruit. At the same time, Esformes was cutting side deals with the University of Pennsylvania head basketball coach, Jerome Allen, bribing him with hundreds of thousands of dollars and bags of cash to better ensure the college accepted his son Morris.

Esformes apparently understood the advantages elite athletes have in the college admissions game. Colleges routinely lower academic standards to accept applicants who do expensive country club sports like fencing, crew, sailing, water polo, and equestrianism. Sports have become a form of affirmative action for wealthy white students, according to researchers with the independent Jack Kent Cooke Foundation. "The popular notion that recruited athletes tend to come from minority and indigent families turns out to be just false," researchers found. "At least among the highly selective institutions, the vast bulk of recruited athletes are in sports that are rarely available to low-income, particularly urban, applicants."

Morris Esformes graduated from the University of Pennsylvania in 2019, a few months before his dad was sentenced to twenty years in prison for paying bribes and receiving kickbacks in a massive $1 billion Medicare scam that targeted the disabled, elderly, and poor. Coach Allen, now an assistant coach for the Boston Celtics, avoided prison by pleading guilty and testifying against Esformes.

In one of his final decrees, President Trump commuted Philip Es-formes's sentence and released him from prison.

Though Esformes's behavior is extreme, his attitude is not. High-ranking college executives encourage wealthy donors and open doors for their children. At the University of Illinois, top officials overruled lower-ranked admissions officers and admitted the children of donors and lawmakers. At the University of Virginia, a fund-raiser goaded the admissions office to accept a rejected student. At the least, the student "must be on WL [the wait-list]," the official insisted, the *Washington Post* reported in 2017. A handwritten note explained why: "$500K."

As many as 25 percent of American parents said they would bribe college officials to get their kids into college, according to a 2019 YouGov poll; 34 percent said they would pay a college-prep consultant to take tests for their children. In "Confessions of a College Admissions Officer," Hillary Reinsberg described parents offering cash, dinner, even better jobs in exchange for getting their children into the top college where she worked.

Dozens of parents living in Chicago's affluent suburbs dared to redirect money intended for needy students to their own children. By giving up custody and appointing friends and family guardians, their financially independent pseudo-orphans became eligible for grants reserved for the poor, according to news reports. "The middle class . . . are working so hard and cannot send their kids to college" because of the rising cost, consultant Lora Georgieva told the *Chicago Tribune* in 2019. "I believe I am representing the voice of the middle-class people who are screaming for help to be able to send their kids to college."

Cheating has become mainstream. "Upper-middle-class status-hungry strivers and their families, prep schools, guidance counselors, and college admissions coaches are already doing [it] all over the place," an admissions officer at a Virginia state university told the *American Conservative* magazine.

"The average GPAs at some public high schools in upper-middle-class striver zip codes are 4.54—because they offer so many watered-down Advanced Placement courses. Grade inflation is so bad [that] it is common these days to see kids whose GPAs are so high as to be mathematically impossible . . . This way of falsifying transcripts has become nearly universal in the most status-conscious schools."

Jia Tolentino shamefully admits she helped white upper-class children con their way into the University of Texas so she could pay for graduate school. Parents in Houston gave her $150 an hour to coach "entitled teenagers through the application process," ghostwriting essays, "helping them cheat," she said in an essay for the magazine *Jezebel*. "I always ended up rewriting their essays in the end."

Tolentino sat across tables "from white girls in oversized T-shirts, white boys in basketball shorts, sweet kids with good hearts and sleep still in their eyes, who told me—either very nicely or very snidely, never anything in between—that it was harder for white people to get into college now than anyone else, because of affirmative action. They said this as their parents wrote me $450 checks to 'edit' their essays."

As difficult as it is to stop cheaters in the US, it's even harder overseas. Parents seeking American degrees for their children often barter for goods and services in a lawless market economy rife with corruption. Consultants called agents, some of whom have worked at American colleges, prey on wealthy foreign families willing to pay any price for elite college degrees. Their aspirations opened up another profitable opportunity for American pay-to-play brokers and swindlers. One of them, former Harvard lecturer Mark Zimny, used his company IvyAdmit to dupe rich Asians like Hong Kong jewelry magnate Gerald Chow.

In one of their first meetings, Zimny told Chow to read Daniel

Golden's *The Price of Admission* to understand how money talks. After Chow paid Zimny $2 million to help get his sons into elite American universities, Harvard—a top choice—rejected them. Zimny was eventually arrested, convicted of wire and bank fraud and other illegal conduct, and sentenced to five years in prison. He was released in September 2020.

Precollege pay-to-play is "totally out of control overseas," an international recruiter at a selective liberal arts college told me. Especially in Asia, "students have the ability to buy whatever they want." As college costs skyrocket, and average family incomes fall, small and midsize colleges need full-paying international students to subsidize middle- and moderate-income American families, he said. Corrupt foreign agents make it nearly impossible to distinguish students with potential from the liars and the cheaters.

When admissions officers see red flags—a large jump from one SAT test score to the next, or one polished essay and another filled with typos—they pay attention. "We do the best we can to weed out the frauds from the rest. We trust transcripts, test scores, and teacher recommendations. But overseas, those can be questionable. There's a tacit understanding that everyone is going to look the other way. I don't ask students, 'How much of this application did you forge?' We assume nothing. My job is not the fraud police. I don't go into each application wanting to catch somebody."

Though some colleges will expel students if they discover fraud, it's almost impossible to build a case. "It's all circumstantial evidence. I can't prove a student forged anything." Regulating the industry would be a great start, he said, "but I don't see that happening."

All parents want what's best for their children. But that desire can lead them into moral and ethical traps apparent only after they're ensnared. Wealth is no safeguard, as celebrity Felicity Huffman proved. At her sentencing for bribing a tutor to take tests for her daughter, she told the judge: "In my desperation to be a good mother I talked myself into believing that all I was doing was giving my daughter a fair shot." Huffman served eleven days in a federal prison. A year later, her daughters were on their way to Vassar and Carnegie Mellon, and Huffman was "looking forward not backward," *Vanity Fair* reported.

That was not the cheery outcome for victims of precollege profiteers exploiting working-class Black families in a rural corner of Cajun Louisiana. The T.M. Landry school, located in the "Crayfish Capital of the World," promised parents to place their children at elite colleges. In good faith, parents paid $7,200 tuition and sent their children off to school while they worked shifts in factories, customer service, retail, and housekeeping.

Physical and emotional abuse was part of a strategy teachers used to prepare students to compete in the admissions game, the *New York Times* reported in 2018. "That is how the real world works," the *Times* quoted the school's founder, Michael Landry, as saying. Landry and his school falsified transcripts, padded résumés and applications with nonexistent clubs and fictitious classes, embellished letters of recommendation, and rewrote essays, filling them with stories that "played on negative racial stereotypes" and "bore little resemblance to the students' real lives," the *Times* wrote. Though he admitted to hitting his students, Landry has denied other allegations.

Landry posted videos of the lucky few students opening acceptances from Harvard, Yale, Princeton, Brown, and Columbia that appeared on national television shows like *Today* and *Ellen*. Publicity from the videos helped the school collect more than $250,000 in donations in 2018. When the *Times* reporter asked Landry to explain his alleged dishonesty, he equivocated. "At the end of the day, if we got kids at Harvard every day, I'm going to fight for Harvard," Landry said. "Why is it O.K. that Asians get to Harvard? Why is it O.K. that white people get to Harvard?" Police investigated and cited Landry for simple battery. No other charges have been filed.

Pay-to-play college admissions is so ingrained in American culture that we're no longer able to see how systemic it is. "We've become drunk on exclusivity," Scott Galloway, a professor at New York University, told an education reporter. "We've created luxury brands so we can continue to offer more to the children of the rich while preying on the hopes and dreams of middle-class parents."

Until lawmakers make low-cost or free college available to all eligible students, parents must navigate the world of pay-to-play consultants alone. Here's how to bust the most common myths families hear on the road to college:

Myth No. 1: The more money private-sector consultants charge, the more secrets they have and the better qualified they are to get kids into the dream colleges they want to attend. Corollary: My [*insert name here: friend, neighbor, PTA pal, daughter's best friend's mom*] recommended this great private counselor who will get my kids into college.

Parents rarely know what questions to ask to properly sort scammers from legitimate consultants. It's the Wild West out there. There's no licensing, no certificates required, no special degree that consultants are required to earn. "Just put the star on your chest and go out there," said Lynda McGee, a Los Angeles Unified School District counselor, in an interview with a local radio station. "There's a belief that if you don't get into these twenty-five schools—or maybe even fifty—you're doomed, and your diploma is worth nothing."

Some consultants and tutors bluff, pretending to know more than they do. Before hiring consultants, make them agree to specific outcomes before signing the contract. The best consultants insist there's no way to buy certainty, but they have little financial interest in discouraging dreams. The more college applications submitted, the more money they make. Beware of consultants that encourage students to submit too many applications to hedge bets, and to use one-size-fits-all approaches.

Apart from high-priced, often impersonal, and frequently inadequate corporate chains, few consultants integrate services. There's one industry for tutors, one industry for test prep, one industry for essay prep, one industry for application prep, one industry for financial aid prep and appeals. Brian Taylor owns Ivy Coach, the one-stop shop that caters to families able to pay as much as $1 million for him to create a road map for their children. Even Taylor admits he mostly dispenses practical advice.

Taylor begins working with clients in middle school and maps out classes and standardized tests they should take. He finds what they feel passionate about and places them in those activities. He keeps them on schedule and makes them meet deadlines. The advice he gives is just "common sense," he told a *Nightline* interviewer. "Don't do three sports and play a musical instrument. Get involved in something interesting. National Honor Society is not going to impress anybody if everybody does National Honor Society."

Myth No. 2: Because I never did a service trip to [*insert name of foreign country here*], played sports, joined a dozen clubs, and didn't serve on student council, I don't have the kind of extracurriculars colleges want. Even elite colleges don't want students to overload themselves with Advanced Placement classes, sports, clubs, societies, and foreign community service. They want applicants to do well in a few areas. To start, pursue three extracurricular passions in three different areas that include an intellectual activity. (Part-time jobs to earn money to pay for college count.) For example, one student might follow this track: soccer, Latin American history, and local government volunteer work or internship or part-time job to save for college. Another student might follow this track: theater, neuroscience, and Model United Nations or part-time job to save for college.

Myth No. 3: I can get into an elite college without help on my application from a counselor and teacher. The best counselors develop strong relationships and build trust with people at colleges making admissions decisions. Those counselors then recommend students whom colleges are more inclined to accept. Private schools have teams of counselors devoted to prepping their students for college and building relationships with admissions officers. Many affluent public high schools do the same.

But most high schools, due to ongoing budget cuts, have made it impossible for public school counselors to provide the intense guidance students need to compete in the Hunger Games of higher ed. More than half of Los Angeles Unified School District counselors say they don't have enough time to properly assist students with college applications. Lynda McGee is a rare exception, but even she lacks the funds private prep schools allocate to get their students into the nation's best colleges.

McGee pays her way—or raises money through GoFundMe—to network at an annual national conference. The National Association for College Admission Counseling's annual blowout is "Las Vegas . . . on steroids. It's food and drink and just one big party," one attendee said, the place where vendors showcase their state-of-the-art admissions goods and services. "If you were ever under the illusion that college is a separate entity from business and moneymaking, all you have to do is go to a national conference. They have a huge room of vendors, every sort. Big booths, expensive giveaways. It's thriving, it's booming," McGee said. The conference is "really where you see the disparities. This is where you see the have and have-nots."

Myth No. 4: If I apply only to test-optional colleges, I'll get into a really great school and I won't have to worry about studying for the ACT or SAT. Beware the test-optional trap. Many selective private colleges allow students to apply without submitting standardized test scores. Like early decision, test optional lowers admissions barriers. This can be a great advantage for students with low scores applying to public universities and need-blind colleges that promise to charge only what families can afford to pay without loans. But test optional can also be a ruse colleges use to attract as many applicants as possible, sorting them by family income as a way to build a class that best meets their financial goals.

The pandemic forced testing companies to cancel hundreds of thousands of SAT and ACT tests in 2020, prompting even elite colleges to adopt test-optional admissions. That didn't stop wealthy parents from taking extreme measures to make sure their children sat for the tests. Privileged families interpret "optional" to mean required, especially if others in their tribe are risking their children's health to compete for higher scores. Even during a life-threatening pandemic, they jetted their children around the country to find open testing centers, a testament to the continuing power the testing companies hold.

Before you apply to test-optional private colleges, look carefully at their financial aid policies. Does the college promise to meet your family's full financial need and charge only what you can afford to pay? Does the aid package include loans? Those colleges—many are not need blind and put loans in financial aid packages—included Bowdoin, Northwestern, the University of Chicago, Vassar, Bates, Colby, Colorado College, Connecticut College, Franklin & Marshall College, Mount Holyoke College, Pitzer College, Skidmore College, Smith College, Trinity College, and Wesleyan when I checked in 2020.

Myth No. 5: If test-optional colleges accept me, I'll get enough financial aid to make attending affordable. Many test-optional colleges award merit aid, discounts frequently tied to test scores. Take, for example, Kara, a high school senior featured on the College Confidential website, a company that bills itself as the "world's largest college forum." Kara prepped for the SAT and ACT and took the tests a total of three times. Her best score was 19 out of 36 on the ACT. With a 3.9 grade point average, she applied only to public colleges and test-optional private colleges "and was accepted to all of the colleges on her list!" College Confidential gushed. "If you didn't break 20 on the test, that doesn't mean your college admission hopes are down the tubes."

That's true. But like so much about college admissions, the narrative leaves out a big part of the story: cost. Kara enrolled at Emerson College. How much is Kara paying? We don't know. College Confidential never reported her total cost. She could very well be paying full price, close to $70,000 a year. Her ACT score is well below the 29 average of students admitted to Emerson, though her grades were a little above the 3.6 average.

Emerson was need blind with a 41 percent acceptance rate when I checked in 2020. But the school wasn't promising to charge only what families can afford. Depending on how badly Emerson wanted Kara, she probably paid at least $43,400 a year—the average cost. As 2020 came to a close, financial aid directors at test-optional colleges were discussing using high school grades to award merit aid. Since admissions officers tend to more closely scrutinize applicant test scores if they're unfamiliar with a high school, they may end up taking more students from high schools they know well if they remain test optional. Policies differ at each college, so it's crucial to ask bluntly: "What are the criteria used to award merit scholarships and tuition discounts?"

Myth No. 6: Because college admissions and financial aid are so mysterious, any consultant I hire will guide me to a successful outcome. Unless consultants are working for free, they have a financial interest in touting success stories. The big players sell a variety of admissions goods and services, along with half-truths that, while not outright dishonest, are part of strategies to maximize profits for billion-dollar parent corporations.

College Confidential, for example, is a subsidiary of the company Hobsons, which owns the proprietary college-searching-and-ranking software Naviance. Hobsons is a $2 billion multinational media and information corporation owned by

Britain's Daily Mail and General Trust. The founder of College-wise, one of the nation's largest admissions counseling companies, described College Confidential on his blog as a place that can be "an online breeding ground for namebranditis, anxiety, and bad advice."

But maybe Collegewise shouldn't be so quick to criticize. A Collegewise pitch to parents for its services included an anecdote about a client with a 2.8 GPA and an 18 on the ACT getting a $6,000-a-year merit scholarship at Westminster College in Salt Lake City, Utah. The company left out crucial details: Westminster accepted 93 percent of its applicants when I checked in 2020. And the 13 percent discount Westminster gave the student meant his family had to pay the remaining $40,000-plus a year with savings or loans.

Myth No. 7: I have a 4.6 GPA and it's not good enough to get into a great college. Every high-achieving student has heard about kids with 4.6 grade point averages and 1400 out of 1600 on the SAT who weren't accepted to UCLA, Stanford, Harvard, Princeton, or Yale. These are the same kids who played on the tennis team, served as school ambassadors, were elected to student council, and joined a dozen clubs. Take comfort in knowing that even if those kids can't get into luxury-brand colleges, *anyone* with a 4.6 GPA and 1400 on the SAT will get into a great college with enough merit aid to probably make it more affordable than UCLA.

Myth No. 8: If I play club sports in elementary and middle school, and compete at the highest levels in high school, colleges will be more inclined to accept me and give me a scholarship. Dumping money into precollege club sports rarely pays off in the college admissions and financial aid sweepstakes.

Roughly 2 percent of high school athletes win athletics scholarships, and those awards range from a pittance to a full ride. "I've seen parents spend a couple of hundred thousand dollars pursuing a college scholarship," said the founding director of the Families in Sport Lab at Utah State University. "They could have set it aside for the damn college." Colleges give athletics directors tremendous power to sway admissions decisions. Some coaches take full advantage, profiting from pricey summer camps they assemble on elite college campuses. They identify the athletes they want, then hand lists of preferred candidates to admissions officials who rubber-stamp acceptances.

If you think you're among the nation's top high school athletes, contact coaches at the schools you want to attend. Submit the online recruiting form available on college websites, then email and call coaches directly to introduce yourself and find out what you have to do to get noticed and win a scholarship. Organize game film, skills and workout videos that highlight athletic abilities. Create a website using WordPress or Wix with embedded links to videos, transcripts, and test scores. Using social media to connect with coaches is an excellent first step.

Myth No. 9: It's harder than ever to get into college. False. Just about anyone who wants to can go to college. But very few families can pay for it. Nearly all colleges accept two-thirds of their applicants, although the majority don't award enough financial aid to make earning degrees affordable. Competition for affordable colleges has intensified since the end of the Bush administration in 2008, when UCLA received 55,000 applications. That number had more than doubled to nearly 112,000 in 2019. In 2005, California State University, Los Angeles, accepted 76 percent of its applicants; a decade later it accepted 41 percent.

Private schools whine about decreasing enrollment, but that's a distraction. Those numbers hide the fact that qualified students are forced to either forego college or drop out because of skyrocketing costs. More students than ever are college ready. While the number of high school graduates is decreasing, students are earning diplomas at record rates. High school graduation climbed to 85 percent in 2018, the highest ever, according to the National Center for Education Statistics.

Myth No. 10: I can't do anything about rising college costs. I have to accept that it's my fault that I can't afford to send my kids to college. This is perhaps the most dangerous disinformation campaign the government has foisted on the American people. To fix what is so clearly a systemic failure, families and the country's colleges and universities have to demand that state and federal lawmakers provide adequate tuition subsidies or free public college to all college-ready students.

Over the past forty years, laissez-faire lawmakers have cut tuition subsidies and dismantled regulations that once protected average Americans from the worst abuses of the free market. After making it easy for students to borrow far more for tuition than they could afford to repay, lawmakers looked the other way as private industry and colleges formed what the New York attorney general called "an unholy alliance" to defraud families. That pay-to-play con left millions of families— mine included—collectively holding trillions of dollars in student debt. It's the price we pay for admission.

9

Buyer Beware

The Danger Zone of Loans

By the time our third child was starting high school in 2007, my husband and I owed $120,000 in student loans, money we'd borrowed so our sons could attend the University of California. We drove aging Hondas, clipped coupons, rarely ate at restaurants, took only working vacations, and drank a lot of Two-Buck Chuck. We borrowed against our house for cash to make ends meet and struggled to save a few hundred dollars each month. We both worked full-time, managing elderly parents, maintaining an old house with DIY repairs, and sending checks larger than our mortgage payment to a student loan billing company.

We shopped for better terms and lower rates, constantly shifting loans from one lender to another. We had no idea if the loans came from the federal government or private lenders. We were too distracted to notice how paying for college and financing degrees had changed since we'd graduated. I paid attention to the news, but generally ignored stories about furious competition to get into the Ivy League and the student-loan wars. We accepted the loans, hoped for the best, and counted on the gods of government and the guardians of the ivory tower to protect us.

In time we discovered how wrong we were, how complex and competitive financial aid had become, and how student debt was a problem not just for us, but for the nation. Like so many parents, we felt powerless to do anything about it. We were trapped inside a financial aid maze built by lawmakers, their pals on Wall Street, and their allies in higher education,

Once an easy calculation parents could do at kitchen tables, financial aid had become opaque, clouded in mystery and obscured by the public obsession with competing to get into elite colleges. The real rat race wasn't about getting into Stanford, Harvard, and Yale. It wasn't even about getting into college—nearly all colleges accept more than two-thirds of their applicants. It was about getting into schools that gave grants, merit scholarships, and discounts large enough so parents could send their children to college without borrowing more money than it costs to buy a vacation home.

Nowadays nearly everyone needs loans to pay for college. And virtually no one realizes why that's so, or how laissez-faire lawmakers have turned college into a growing profit center. After destroying low-cost and free public education over the past forty years, they passed laws enabling private lenders to make enormous profits by loaning money to students and parents.

First they cut tuition subsidies at public universities where the vast majority of Americans attend college. Then they made it easy for families to borrow, and even easier for private lenders to generate excessive profits from selling them loans. Finally they convinced families to depend on private industry, not government, to help pay for increasingly expensive degrees. The changes created conditions that led to corruption, fraud, and $1.5 trillion in student debt in the United States.

Even when tuition reached record highs, families willing to pay any price for status stoked heated competition to get into exclusive colleges. Competition for elite degrees launched commercial markets for the rankings, testing, and consulting industries—the multibillion-dollar admissions industrial complex. Pretty soon all colleges were adopting free-market pricing, charging what the market would bear. Inflating sticker prices, they discounted tuition for the students who could boost their rankings—the highly prepped and usually affluent—charging them prices low enough to entice them to enroll but high enough to meet revenue goals.

Colleges gave the least-valued students they accepted financial aid packages stuffed with loans and a list of "preferred lenders"—companies the colleges recommended. The cruelest twist came at the end of a grueling eighteen-month application ordeal. After investing thousands of dollars in precollege goods and services, families received, along with acceptance letters, bait-and-switch financial aid packages. Only then did parents discover that affording dream schools meant going deeply into debt.

Most families did, oblivious to dozens of colleges getting kickbacks from loan companies they had recommended to students as preferred lenders. As schools grew fat and the campaign coffers of free-market lawmakers filled with private-lender money, families paid larger and larger shares of college costs. And those costs just kept rising, more than 500 percent between 1985 and 2012, from $1,320 to $8,280.

Passing laws forbidding families from declaring bankruptcy to free them from student debt, lawmakers rewarded the lending industry and doomed some families to generations of loan repayments. Pay-to-play financial aid—higher tuition, fewer grants, more loans—has been thoroughly normalized and accepted.

Submitting the loan forms took us a few minutes and a postage stamp. By the time our sons had graduated in 2004, we were so deep in debt that we believed we would never recover. While lawmakers battled for supremacy on Capitol Hill, people like us wrote checks to loan servicers and struggled to survive the financial havoc they created. The best we could do is what parents have always done. We blamed ourselves and tried to fix the problem.

I read dozens of books and countless articles about college loans, trying to understand the contradictory, confusing, and disorienting rules, hoping to get the best deal on what is euphemistically called "financial aid." Looking for clues, I rifled through my desk and found a copy of the document that opened the gateway to our financial aid hell: FAFSA, the government's Free Application for Federal Student Aid.

I dug deeper into the drawer and pulled out an old copy of another federal tome: the Department of Education's Student Loan Program Data Book. Scanning both, I remembered why I'd thrown them in my desk and forgotten about them years earlier.

The fifty-plus-page report is a turgid chronicle of the future foretold: PLUS Loan (FDLP or FFEL); refinancing of PLUS/SLS; Federal Direct Loan Program (FDLP); Federal Family Education Loan (FFEL); repayment period; repayment schedule; secondary market; accrued interest; Administrative Cost Allowance (ACA); alternative repayment; booked disbursements; booked loans; capitalizing interest; cohort default rates; consolidation loans; cross program participation; default, deferment, delinquency, discharge; expected family contribution; extended repayment plan; forbearance; grace period; graduated repayment plan; Guarantee Agency (GA); HEAF; income contingent repayment plan; loan limits; origination fee; Stafford Subsidized Loan (FDLP and FFEL); Stafford Unsubsidized Loan (FDLP and FFEL); Supplemental Loan for Students (SLS); USAF; variable interest; trigger rate.

I flipped to page 1, hoping that if I started at the beginning something might make sense. The fifth listing—Bankruptcy—caught my attention. Bankruptcy, defined as "legal proceedings that relieve borrowers from their creditors," ended with a kicker. Bankruptcy isn't an option for student loan borrowers. What had we done? How would we repay these loans and have enough money left to send two more kids to college?

Free-market lawmakers from Reagan forward had completely transformed America's attitudes toward higher education. Ronald Ehrenberg, the director of the Cornell Higher Education Research Institute, recognized the transformation a decade ago. "There has been a shift from the belief that we as a nation benefit from higher education, to a belief that it's the people receiving the education who primarily benefit and so they should foot the bill."

The George H. W. Bush administration amended laws so that graduate students and parents could borrow as much as was needed to pay for degrees and living expenses. To force elite colleges to let the free market drive financial aid, Bush officials sued the Ivy League in an "unprecedented action," the *New York Times* said, that "was viewed as an extreme example of a growing mistrust between government and the academic world."

Using antitrust laws intended to stop commercial price-fixing, the Justice Department sued to stop the Ivy League from cooperatively discussing financial aid awards for needy students. The lawsuit cited a decades-old agreement between the colleges to admit students based on merit and to distribute their scholarship money based solely on need. All but MIT signed consent decrees with the Bush administration to avoid costly legal battles.

MIT fought back. Rather than reduce competition, MIT's financial aid policies helped needy students and prevented bidding wars between colleges, it argued in the Justice Department's civil suit against the universities. Two years later, after continued and costly litigation, MIT settled. MIT president Charles Vest predicted free-market forces would lead to what we now have: free-for-all pay-to-play financial aid that advantages the already advantaged. Under the new rules, Vest said, colleges would begin "wheeling and dealing and bargaining student by student, shifting funds from those who need it most to paying for kids who frankly do not need it."

Today's student debt crisis has roots in the Clinton and George W. Bush administrations. Before Clinton, student lending was a financial backwater. The market was controlled by a few banks, private lenders, and Sallie Mae, the Student Loan Marketing Association, a nonprofit created to service low-cost federal loans. The backwater became a tidal bore as tuition and housing costs climbed, and families amassed more and larger loans. Everyone qualified. Bad credit, no credit, it didn't matter. Lenders handed out money like cookies at Christmas, knowing the government would repay them if families defaulted.

With billions of dollars at stake, private lenders competed viciously to grab market share during what veteran financial aid administrators still call the decade-long "Loan War" of the 1990s. The lending industry came up with "one scheme after another to gut the taxpayer-friendly government loan programs," U.S. News reported in the 2003 exposé "Big Money on Campus." "Like political ward bosses, private lenders used money and favors, along with their friends in Congress and the Department of Education, to get what they wanted. They wanted those checks made out to them."

Adopting free-market principles, colleges charged what the market would bear, doubling and tripling tuition. Tuition and fees grew nearly six times from 1985 to 2012, according to the Bureau of Labor Statistics. But few paid the sticker price. Depending on one student's worth to the college over another's, some families got massive discounts and small loans and others got tiny discounts and massive loans.

The more loans students accepted, the more colleges raised tuition and housing prices. For every dollar students and their families borrowed, schools raised tuition 58 cents, according to a study by the Federal Reserve Bank of New York. Tuition and housing costs climbed so high even affluent families couldn't afford private college without loans.

The affluent started flocking to affordable public universities, intensifying competition and making it harder for everyone else to get into low-cost flagship state schools. To win them back, some elite colleges in the early 2000s promised to charge students only what their families could afford to pay without loans. Since colleges define affordability differently, the prices those colleges charged families varied wildly. A few, like Harvard, covered housing and food in their financial aid awards and didn't consider home equity as family income. Others, like New York University and USC, considered home equity and discounted only tuition, not food and housing.

Forced to compete with selective colleges for students, small regional private colleges with small endowments were woefully outmatched. As numbers of high school students in their regions dwindled, they struggled to boost their rankings so they could attract foreign and out-of-state students to maintain enrollment. To find new revenue streams, most did what they had to do.

If they had to go overseas or lower standards to find full-paying students, they did. If they had to admit less-qualified children of the college's wealthy friends and family members, they rubber-stamped. If they had to field competitive teams to boost popularity, they let coaches make admissions decisions. If they had to stuff student award packages with five-figure loans to pay for luxury housing, celebrity hires, merit scholarships, and presidents demanding million-dollar-plus salaries, then degree-buyers beware.

Colleges raised tuition, collected more money, and used the windfall to build spas and lazy-river water parks. So many colleges have water parks that the website College Consensus ranks them: the University of Colorado's is No. 1, followed by similar parks at the University of

Alabama, Louisiana State University, the University of Missouri, Iowa State University, Colorado State University, and Texas Tech.

In exchange for millions of dollars in kickbacks and lured by the promise of a quick buck, colleges steered students to preferred private lenders, according to a *U.S. News & World Report* 2013 exposé. Student debt kept "enrollment up and tuition flowing." While lenders flooded the market with cheap money, schools got millions in kickbacks. Demand for degrees grew. Free-market lawmakers increased loan limits. Private lenders earned unprecedented profits. A few officials saw danger signs. "People will see we make more money by making more loans," University of Florida financial aid director Karen Fooks told a *U.S. News* reporter. "The linkage is so obvious it ruins our credibility."

Cortney Munna was a casualty of those loan wars, one of millions of students encouraged to borrow far more than she could afford, then blamed for her financial recklessness. Cortney's dad, a welder by trade, worked his way into management at United Airlines. He died suddenly of a brain hemorrhage just before Cortney started high school. The family moved from Indiana to rural New York near the Canadian border, where her mother, Cathryn, ran a bed-and-breakfast. Cathryn promised to do whatever she could to help Cortney—a top-ranked, straight-A student—graduate from the best possible college.

"All we needed to do was get this education and get the good job. This is the thing that eats away at me," Cathryn Munna told *New York Times* financial columnist Ron Lieber, "the naïveté on my part."

On the day Cortney received an acceptance letter and financial aid package from New York University, "all I could see was college, and a good college," Cathryn Munna said, "and how proud I was of her."

Cortney Munna was seventeen when she borrowed $20,000. Cathryn cosigned the loan from NYU's preferred lender, Sallie Mae.

By the time Cortney took the loan, Sallie Mae was no longer a non-profit. It was a private lender with a government contract, a fact the Munnas didn't know.

"When we looked at the financial aid package, we didn't understand the difference between grants and federal and private loans. It wasn't clear to me how much I was borrowing," Cortney said. NYU's dazzling brand with its high rank, status, and prestige led her and her mom to believe the degree was worth owing nearly $100,000 in loans.

Thrilled to be a part of NYU, Munna found a part-time job and worked hard to pay for college. But it was never enough. Over the next four years, NYU raised its sticker price 25 percent. Overwhelmed by the school's regular demands for payment, Munna asked the financial aid office to increase her subsidized loans. NYU referred her to Citibank, another of its preferred private lenders. Munna borrowed more money.

By the time she graduated in 2005, Munna had paid $100,000 to NYU with borrowed money. Six months later, repayments began. Neither she nor her mom could keep up with the monthly bills. "My mother has tried her best, and I don't blame her for anything in this," Cortney told Lieber. "I don't want to spend the rest of my life slaving away to pay for an education I got for four years and would give back. It feels wrong to me."

In the column he wrote for the *New York Times*, Lieber framed Cortney's story as a "shared failure." Lieber gave the private lender Sallie Mae a pass because the company eventually refused to loan the family more money. Though he faulted Citibank, he blamed the Munna family for overborrowing. "A responsible grownup cosigned for its loans." With a patronizing scold, Lieber advised Cortney Munna to find a flexible second job to pay down her debt, even while noting that she was already working nights and weekends.

Responding to hundreds of comments on Lieber's article, Cortney posted her reply on the *Times* website. She acknowledged her responsibility but strongly disagreed with Lieber's conclusions. "I accept that this was negligent on my part, but unfortunately, I was too young to know better. I am responsible for repaying the money I borrowed. I have been doing this and have every intention of continuing to do so. . . . [W]hat I really want isn't to call a 'do-over' so much as it is to re-write the rules of the student loan game. . . . I'm not alone, and I shared my story not to ask for sympathy or assign blame (that was a direction Ron took on his own) but to encourage change."

Lieber's attitude, now mainstream, is the problem. Americans have come to view student debt through a distorted lens as an individual failing, rather than what it is, a systemic breakdown. Cortney trusted that NYU's preferred lender had her best interests at heart. "I was seventeen, I thought NYU would look out for me not make money off me. They made it very easy for me to sign the papers so I could stay in school." Nobody—not NYU, Sallie Mae, or Citibank—ever made it clear "that I was signing up to owe this money for the rest of my adult life. It's been a devastating life experience honestly."

It took Cortney a decade—and literally winning a lottery to get into a low-cost nursing program at a community college—to find a decent-paying career. Now thirty-five, she became a registered nurse in 2019 and accepts with resignation that the student debt she continues to pay will prevent her from owning a home and saving for retirement.

Even a decade later, Lieber's article still stings. "It was a pretty traumatic and painful experience," she said. "I thought the article was going to be about the whole system needing changing." Instead it was "an overly critical portrayal of a single mom who wanted her daughter to get the best possible education, who wasn't able to see through the obtuse language of the 'financial aid package,' and believed what she heard about student loans being 'cheap money for college.'"

Scores of middle-class families I interviewed nationwide agreed with Munna, a finding shared by New York University social scientist Caitlin Zaloom. In her study *Indebted: How Parents Make College Work at Any Cost*, Zaloom illuminates the profound moral conflicts parents face when sending their children to college using borrowed money. "Parents try to honor what they see as their highest parental duty—providing their children with opportunity—and gamble on an investment that might not pay off."

Families are trapped in a bewildering maze of acronyms and funding formulas, confused by terms like "financial aid" that sound like help but often mean debt servitude. Colleges keep aid formulas locked in black boxes, making it impossible for parents to know how much to save or how much colleges will charge until financial aid award letters arrive. Most Americans don't save much for college. Fewer than 5 percent invest in 529 plans, federally funded college savings incentives used almost exclusively by the wealthy and upper-middle classes. The 95 percent without those savings plans, Zaloom found, "wind up feeling like they're failing."

Trying to beat the financial aid game is like expecting to win a giant panda at a carnival. The game is rigged. That's how Cortney Munna felt. While Munna struggled to repay her debts, corruption was rampant among private lenders, financial aid officers at scores of colleges, and senior officials in the George W. Bush White House. New York University was among the worst academic offenders, accepting millions in kickbacks from private lenders to refer unsuspecting students like Munna to them for business.

Executives at the publicly traded lenders Sallie Mae and Citibank were skimming billions from families and the government while Bush administration officials looked the other way. Private lending to students soared from less than $2 billion to $25.5 billion in a decade. Hundreds of companies wanted those lucrative student loans. Even the College Board teamed up with Citibank to grow "its market position as an education loan provider," a press release announced.

As lawmakers cut funding to community colleges, decimating free and low-cost jobs-training programs, Congress made it easy for publicly traded colleges to exploit moderate- and low-income students. Many urged students shut out of free community colleges to borrow to pay for expensive, often shoddy, and sometimes worthless degrees. Arguing they provide last-chance opportunities for the least advantaged, executives at for-profit colleges rarely publicly acknowledged they donated heavily to the very lawmakers who were making it possible for them to exploit the poor.

Thanks to deregulation in the late 1990s, for-profit colleges collected 90 percent of their tuition dollars from government-backed loans. If they enrolled veterans and service members, they hit the jackpot, guaranteeing even more government revenue through GI Bill tuition subsidies.

Appointing executives from for-profit colleges to run the Department of Education, George W. Bush handed for-profit colleges a license to print money. Lenders and schools gorged on student loans, collecting billions in tuition and interest payments. When students defaulted, the government garnished their wages, seized their Social Security income and even their tax refunds—$4.3 billion in 2015, the latest data available. When a borrower's resources ran dry, the government stuck taxpayers with the bill—long after colleges and lenders had been paid in full.

Private lenders thrived. Profits soared. The number of borrowers grew. Wall Street swooned. Investment bankers smelled "an easy path to big bucks," federal student aid policy analyst Barmak Nassirian said. The smartest people on Wall Street "figured out how easy it was going to be to grow geometrically."

By George W. Bush's second inauguration, the eight largest publicly traded for-profit chains had a combined market value of $26 billion, according to the *N.Y.U. Journal of Legislation & Public Policy.* For-profit colleges enrolled hundreds of thousands of students online and on scores of campuses nationwide. One of the largest, the publicly traded Apollo Education Group, increased its revenues from $12 million in 1994 to $1.34 billion by 2003, its stock price rising 9,000 percent, from 72 cents a share to $63.36, a Century Foundation analysis found.

The lending and for-profit college industries rewarded Bush and his allies with generous donations. Sallie Mae gave $250,000 to Bush's second inaugural party. For-profit colleges and student loan companies fueled Republican congressman John Boehner's bid to become Speaker of the House, donating more than a quarter million dollars to him in 2004 alone, the Century Foundation reported. The largest for-profit contribution to Boehner came from Corinthian Colleges, a publicly traded chain that collapsed in bankruptcy a decade later amid thousands of fraud claims.

The government forced defrauded students to repay their loans but let the executives who perpetrated the fraud declare bankruptcy and keep their personal fortunes intact.

The corruption outraged Jon Oberg. A Nebraska native, former navy officer, and career public servant, Oberg stumbled on the worst financial aid fraud in modern history. In decades working in public finance and government, "I'd seen fraud," he said. "But this was the most audacious. I hadn't seen anything like this one before."

Oberg was a research analyst in George W. Bush's Education Department when he discovered documents that made no sense. "I thought, hmmm. This language is a masterpiece of obfuscation."

He dug in and discovered that "this was all illegal."

While Bush administration officials abetted graft or ignored it, the federal government was illegally paying student lenders hundreds of millions of dollars in excessive fees. Big lenders "were gaming the system," Oberg said, "ruining the lives of families, damaging the foundation of our economy and our society." Oberg was determined to do something about it. He launched a crusade to right the wrongs inflicted on American families.

"Too many personal futures have been ruined simply because financially needy students sought to better themselves through higher education," he said. "No wicked social engineer could have devised a better way to hurt students, families, and the U.S. economy."

Oberg reported the abuses and remedies to Bush officials. His boss, Grover Whitehurst, told Oberg to work on another project until his planned retirement a year later. "In the 18 months you have remaining," Whitehurst told Oberg in an email, "I will expect your time and talents to be directed to our business of conceptualizing and monitoring research grants."

But Oberg was dogged. He sent his findings to the inspector general, the department staff, and Bush's education secretary, Margaret Spellings. He warned that the government's refusal to stop illegal payments could cost taxpayers billions of dollars.

Whitehurst was unhappy. Senior Department of Education officials seemed to consider Oberg an annoyance, "like a dog on a bone, agitating on this issue," Whitehurst told a *New York Times* reporter. "Plus, I didn't understand the issues. It was Greek to me— preferential interest rates on bonds? I didn't know what he was doing, except that he wasn't supposed to be doing it." (Whitehurst later agreed Oberg was right.)

Even after he retired, Oberg persisted. He uncovered more fraud and illegal payments. Senior Bush officials had given private lenders access to confidential databases so they could compile customer lists with detailed information about student borrowers. One told the giant lender Nelnet to keep $124 million in ill-gotten gains. Though the Department of Education "would never put the approval in writing," the official said, he urged the billion-dollar company to "take its chances. The department will never ask for the money back." Nelnet kept the money and awarded more than $20 million in bonuses to executives.

Over time, Oberg's fight became a war to reform pay-to-play financial aid. He filed ten lawsuits against lenders, talked to reporters, testified in the Senate. He won millions of dollars in settlements, donating the money to various charities, including Veterans Education Success, a bipartisan nonprofit that protects service members from being exploited by financial aid programs. The organization's bill to stop predatory lending landed on President Trump's desk to sign in May 2020. Trump promptly vetoed it.

The Trump administration protected unscrupulous colleges as they deceived veterans, swiped their GI Bill benefits, saddled them with predatory loans, and left them with no degree, no jobs, and massive debt. But that is likely to change during the administration of President Joe Biden and Vice President Kamala Harris, who aggressively prosecuted Corinthian Colleges as California's attorney general. The Biden administration has promised debt relief and to stop schools and lenders from forcing swindled students to repay loans and interest year after year.

America's secretive pay-to-play financial aid system is "a national disgrace," Oberg told a Senate hearing. "If students and families knew how their aid packages were put together, they would march on Washington. The reason they don't march is that the information is not available to them."

Oberg was not the only crusader trying to reform what he calls "Big Education." A couple of college buddies running the upstart lender MyRichUncle publicly attacked corrupt banks controlling student debt. Exposing pay-to-play kickbacks, they published ads in the *New York Times* warning, "Know the truth about financial aid offices. They're supposed to help you choose the best lenders, but in reality, they may steer you towards lenders that benefit them, not you."

Lenders, bribing colleges to put their companies on preferred lists, guaranteed them hundreds of millions of dollars in loan business. Some colleges didn't just recommend but required students to use the very lending companies showering financial aid officers with payola.

The magnitude of the ongoing scam caught the attention of prosecutors in the offices of Andrew Cuomo, then attorney general of New York State. In 2007, Cuomo and his staff recalled their amazement at the unfolding scandal to Inside Higher Ed's Doug Lederman.

One of Cuomo's lieutenants sat, stunned, listening to colleagues describe corruption and kickbacks among private lenders and college financial aid officers.

"Wait—they give schools a cut of the profits in exchange for preferential treatment?" prosecutor Benjamin Lawsky asked. "How many schools are we talking about?"

"About 100."

"At that moment," Lawsky told Lederman, "we knew we were on to something big."

Cuomo's team uncovered what the attorney general called "an unholy alliance" between financial aid officers and private lenders. Fraud, misconduct, and widespread conflicts of interest between colleges and the $85 billion lending industry were infecting the entire system. Lenders paid financial aid officers to market directly to students at dozens of elite colleges, including Columbia University, the University of Southern California, the University of Texas at Austin, Johns Hopkins, the University of Pennsylvania, and New York University.

Throughout the industry, colleges and lenders were conspiring against students. Financial aid officers at one school were allowing lenders to install company sales teams in their offices in return for kickbacks. Colleges were authorizing lenders to link directly to student loan applications on their websites. In return for student referrals, lenders printed and distributed course catalogs. They provided free legal services. They hired support staff and put them to work in financial aid offices. They paid college officials excessive compensation for joining lender advisory boards, for referral fees, for consulting services. They gave them expensive gifts: tickets to concerts and sporting and entertainment events, computers, electronic devices, elaborate fruit baskets, cruises, vacations to exotic locales, steakhouse dinners, and ice cream carts.

To solicit loans, companies operated marketing call centers at one of the schools and identified themselves as college employees. At others, they cut side deals with athletics directors, sponsored golf tournaments, and gave college officials financial stakes in their companies. They marketed their loans on campus in sales events they called "financial aid counseling sessions," workshops that students incorrectly assumed were unbiased and informational.

They hired students to persuade their friends to borrow from them. They gave students gift cards and preloaded debit cards and handed out swag campuswide: T-shirts, sweatshirts, flash drives, yo-yos, booze, catered lunches. Sales teams made deceptive direct appeals to potential borrowers: fake checks and rebates and promotional materials with the word "federal" and eagle insignias suggesting that the government sanctioned their loans.

Lenders lured borrowers with hidden prepayment penalties and low teaser rates, then sold the loans to other lenders at a profit. They paid off financial aid officers with cash and stock, hired them to lobby Congress and to convince colleagues at other colleges to bring them new business. They even bribed a former Sallie Mae executive in the George W. Bush administration.

That executive, Matteo Fontana, collected nearly $220,000 in cash and Student Loan Xpress stock while private lenders illegally accessed a confidential database that he supervised to retrieve personal data about student borrowers. Lenders then used the Social Security numbers, email addresses, phone numbers, and birth dates of students to build marketing databases.

"You can't dismiss it as just the bad apple in the barrel. You couldn't just say it was one financial aid officer, well, it's just one college. It affected so many people, on such a precious commodity. It was such a betrayal for so many people," Cuomo told Inside Higher Ed. "It's not like you're going to a used-car dealer, and you get surprised when you get defrauded. This was your college."

The investigation was never about corrupt individuals. It was about a deeply corrupted system, Cuomo said. "What was endemic, systemic, was the relationship between the [lender and the] school. . . . Our whole point is it's not about individuals, it's about the system, and it's about the relationships."

As part of a settlement agreement with the attorney general's office, colleges and lenders refunded millions of dollars to student borrowers. They paid millions more to educate families about borrowing. The National Association of Student Financial Aid Administrators agreed to allow Cuomo to monitor its offices. Colleges promised to end payola schemes and fired the worst-offending executives. Others were allowed to quietly resign or retire.

Congress and dozens of states passed reforms in 2008, forcing colleges to adopt strict codes of conduct. Fontana went on paid leave, collecting his $142,227 annual salary for seventeen months until he resigned. He pled guilty in a plea agreement to two misdemeanors and paid $85,000 in fines, a pittance compared to the $362,000 he earned from the stock sale and the government salary he took while on leave. He served no prison time. Today he owns a Web.design company in Reston, Virginia, according to his LinkedIn page.

By the end of the George W. Bush administration, it's no wonder the nation's financial system had collapsed. Though Cortney Munna couldn't declare bankruptcy to discharge her student loans, dozens of private lenders did, walking away with fortunes and leaving behind their debts for the government to repay. "Watching the banks get bailed out and knowing that I had no recourse to free myself from the burden of my private student loans was a hard pill to swallow," Munna said.

After a lull, student lending roared back in the past decade. Even if students default, the government repays lenders. For America's captains of industry, student lending and for-profit colleges are still sure-bet Wall Street investments. The University of Phoenix, ITT Tech, and Corinthian Colleges were Wall Street darlings throughout the 1990s and 2000s. Expanding furiously, they lured risky borrowers by promising them better futures.

Corinthian recruited nearly impoverished single parents and isolated loners with low self-esteem. They then enrolled them in schools that later were revealed to have fabricated graduation and job-placement rates, according to California's then attorney general Kamala Harris. Urging students to borrow money to pay tuition, for-profit colleges charged six times the cost of community colleges. Two-thirds of the students at for-profit colleges left with no degrees and enormous debt.

Lenders loved it. Student debt "is the most collectible kind of debt there is. They will garnish your wages. They will intercept your tax refund. They will sue you in court," said Nassirian on *Last Week Tonight* in an exposé of fraud and loan-sharking rife within the industry.

"Student debt is like HPV," host John Oliver said. "If you go to college, you're almost certainly going to get it. And if you do, it will follow you for the rest of your life. They'll steal your wallet, pawn your baby shoes. They will shrink themselves down into two inches high, hide into your pocket, and take that money back one dime at a time."

Four decades of reverse Robin Hood policies and crony capitalism have produced an inequality gap, now a gaping divide that continues to grow. The Obama administration attempted to change the system, but free-market lawmakers in Congress defeated every proposed reform. "Bankers make student loans at no risk because they know the federal government will bail them out in case of default," said Arne Duncan, President Obama's education secretary. "We cannot in good conscience let $87 billion in subsidies go to banks when our students desperately need financial help to realize the dream of getting a college education."

The Obama administration tried but never went far enough to eliminate the worst practices of pay-to-play financial aid. It required colleges to provide families with net price calculators to figure out their actual costs after grants, scholarships, and other discounts. It demanded schools advertise the average debt their graduates hold and how much income they earn. Obama signed laws to replace all private lending with direct lending from the government, a blueprint George H. W. Bush had proposed but free-market lawmakers had blocked for two decades.

Lenders attacked Obama for "nationalizing the banking industry," as one wrote in the *Wall Street Journal*. Another accused him of laying the groundwork to transfer "taxpayer money to the bottomless and unaccountable pit of the education lobby, the community 'early childhood' education proponents and probably other 'community' groups."

At a congressional hearing on student debt, Representative Barry Loudermilk, a Republican from Georgia, agreed with the lenders. He lambasted the federal government for having allowed student loans to become what they were supposed to be: "an entitlement available to anyone. Government, not private lenders, is the fundamental problem."

Free-market lawmakers like Loudermilk have ingeniously shifted the student loan burden to parents. That shift began in 1986 when

Ronald Reagan amended the Higher Education Act to make it easier for parents to borrow to pay for college expenses. George H. W. Bush went further, ending lending limits for parents in 1992, just as tuition began its relentless rise.

The loan wars of the 1990s, the financial aid corruption and kickback scandals of the 2000s, and the financial collapse of 2008 prompted lawmakers to limit subsidized undergraduate borrowing. But they placed no limits on parent borrowing. Students can borrow a maximum of $19,000 in government-subsidized loans over four years of college, nowhere near the average of $88,000 it costs to graduate from a public university, or the $200,000 families usually pay private colleges over four years.

To make up the difference, the government and colleges encourage parents to borrow as much as their children need to pay for college using unsubsidized PLUS loans—few questions asked. More than 70 percent of borrowers older than sixty are paying student loans they took to help children or grandchildren. As parents go deeper into debt, they jeopardize any hope of a comfortable retirement. "We're taught that sacrificing for our children is what we're supposed to do," Persis Yu, student loan expert with the nonprofit National Consumer Law Center, he told the *New York Times*. "What parent would say, 'No, I'm not going to provide this opportunity for my child to go to college, even if it's to my own financial detriment'?"

That's how my husband and I came to borrow $120,000 to send our sons to college. We made the last payment in 2017, around the same time the news media was discovering other hoodwinked middle-class parents struggling to retire while repaying student loans for their children. One of those parents, Patrick Donohue, was infuriated by how expensive college had become and how easy it was to borrow so much. "The cost of college has become a nightmare and a scandal," he told the *New York Times* in 2020.

Facing retirement, he and his wife, Kay, owed nearly $100,000 they had borrowed a decade ago to help their children pay for degrees at public universities. Like many middle-class parents, they borrowed without fully realizing how punishing the loans would become. "They give out money too easily, and you backslide," said Donohue, sixty-five, a customer service executive. Donohue had graduated from a small private college in 1978 with the help of a California state scholarship and a $3,000 loan that he repaid before he married.

Now that he has retired, his $1,000 monthly pension is roughly equal to the amount he owes to student lenders. To make ends meet, he took a job at a local grocery store. Like the Donohues, people age sixty and older are the fastest-growing group borrowing for college, according to the Consumer Financial Protection Bureau, with Black parents shouldering a disproportionate share of the student loan burden. Their children enroll in college as a way out of poverty far more than whites, according to the Department of Education.

Nearly 35 percent of poor Black parents borrow to help their children pay for college, compared to 10 percent of poor white parents. When they can't repay, the government confiscates the money from their wages, Social Security payments, and tax refunds. A total of $2.8 billion was taken from America's poorest families in 2017, according to the Brookings Institution.

Michael Arceneaux recounts in heartbreaking detail the hardship he and his mother faced as he struggled to repay loans he had taken to earn a journalism degree from Howard University in 2007. Despite his mom's reluctance, Arceneaux persuaded her to cosign for a $100,000 loan so he could chase a dream of upward social mobility, he writes in his startling and frequently hilarious 2020 essay collection, *I Don't Want to Die Poor.*

Student debt and economic anxiety permeate every part of his life in a way affluent media and entertainment industry gatekeepers have no way of understanding, he told National Public Radio.

People love to talk about economic anxiety, he said. "What's missing is the working-class perspective . . . and yet we don't really hear from people [with] my background's perspective."

His mother's reluctance to cosign came from "a real, genuine concern for her child, knowing how difficult this country makes it for people like us," he said. "She has supported me along the way. It's my guilt and my shame that I carry, because to me, my struggles with that debt—which impacts her credit—I don't want to be another Black man letting my mama down."

Though wealthy students feel aggrieved when they can't get into elite colleges, the sting is lessened knowing their parents can afford the excellent colleges that accepted them. That's not the case for a growing number of middle-class students accepted to dream colleges they can't afford.

Jennifer Cone, a Connecticut high school senior, voiced her bitterness in an essay for her local newspaper in 2018 about turning down her dream college. Jennifer declined "the No. 1 college of my dreams," she said, because her family didn't have the money to pay for it. After reducing tuition 35 percent, the college expected her parents to cover the remaining $40,000 a year with loans. The paltry discount riled Jennifer.

"These 'discounts' come from money that is taken from the tuition checks of students who come from middle- to high-income families and is given to low-income students who can't afford the price of the college. So, how is that fair?"

Both her parents worked, she wrote. "We don't live extravagantly, we don't spend our money traveling the world, and we don't waste our money on fancy cars or diamond rings." But, she wrote, she had no idea college would cost so much, and hadn't saved enough.

"The issue is not how much it costs to go to college, but why some students are expected to pay top dollar to attend and others don't pay anything at all," she wrote. "It's not right that the cost of a college education is so steep that very few families can afford to pay the full tuition bill . . . It's the middle-income families that don't have the wealth or are not given enough money to fund their college education." And that, she said, is unacceptable. "I want to be able to go to my dream college, too."

The pay-to-play financial aid crisis is a national catastrophe, what policy planners call a "wicked problem." Back when college was an entitlement, parents didn't need consultants, accountants, and attorneys to figure out how to pay tuition. Today, trying to figure out which loans to buy is like being lost in a bustling street market packed with vendors chattering in baffling foreign languages as you search for something you desperately need but can't quite figure out how to get.

Private lending to pay for college has grown 400 percent, to $125 billion in the past decade. Confusing lending websites like Edvisors, ELMSelect, and NitroScore blur the lines between sales pitches and unbiased information. Sallie Mae, once a nonprofit created to service low-cost federal loans, has transformed into a multibillion-dollar publicly traded corporation that earns billions from consumer lending. Companies and consultants promising to guide families safely through the markets often can't be trusted to prioritize clients over profits.

Sallie Mae aggressively markets loans to students while its $5.1 billion spin-off debt collection company, Navient, harasses financially strapped borrowers like Cortney Munna to repay. Navient services $300 billion in student loans and "has consistently been the most hated federal student loan servicers for quite some time," according to Student Loan Planner. Navient ranked worst among the nation's nine largest student loan servicers.

"When it comes to screwing over borrowers, Navient is legendary. If you can think of an evil thing, Navient has probably been accused of doing it. Fucking over military members? They settled a lawsuit after being sued for overcharging troops. Ripping off disabled people? They were accused of damaging the credit of disabled borrowers. In some cases, they've actually double charged them," comedian Hasan Minhaj reported in a student loan satire for Netflix. "Student loan debt affects pretty much everyone I know," he said, "and if you're one of the ten people it doesn't affect, congratulations on being a Kennedy."

Navient has been a defendant in lawsuits for fraud, abuse, and deceit going back decades, including the original suit Oberg filed in 2007. A few years ago, the Consumer Financial Protection Bureau sued the company "for failing borrowers at every stage of repayment," a federal case still being litigated in 2020.

Another student lender, Citibank, hounded author Michael Arceneaux to repay loans for more than a decade, he told NPR. "Sometimes I've gotten calls as early as 7 or 8 a.m. . . . . They call you whenever. They don't care. . . . They'll call me and say, 'You owe such and such and such.' But if I don't have $3,000 to give you that day, or even $1,800, I don't have it. And then they say, 'Maybe I'll have some options' . . . But the reality is you don't really have any options—either pay or your credit is going to go to hell." The worst demand to know, " 'Well, why don't you have it?' And then start giving you career advice. And what annoys me about that is, 'OK. With all due respect, you're working at a call center. So you are speaking down to me based on the presumption that because I can't pay my bills, I'm broke or poor, and so by virtue, I should be treated less than?' "

Such ultra-aggressive debt-collection practices spawned what's become the billion-dollar student debt–settlement industry, filled with con artists bilking millions from desperate borrowers. They "promise the impossible—fast loan forgiveness. But instead of re-negotiated payment plans, the scammers pocket fees collected for their bogus services," financial adviser Michelle Singletary wrote in the *Washington Post*. Addressing borrowers directly, she said, "I know you need a break from your crushing student loans. But if you sign up with a sham company, you'll get more pain than relief."

Donald Trump consistently sided with debt collectors, for-profit colleges, and lenders, supporting new rules to give them even more power. He appointed Betsy DeVos, a billionaire heiress with financial ties to debt collection, loan servicing, and for-profit colleges, to lead the Department of Education. After hiring industry insiders to staff the Department of Education, DeVos ended investigations into fraud, making it harder for students to get promised debt forgiveness. She dismantled regulations designed to protect families from predatory lenders and for-profit colleges, and killed reforms Obama had enacted to help student borrowers.

DeVos even assigned a former dean from DeVry University—ranked the No. 1 worst college in America by Money Inc in 2019—to investigate DeVry University's recruitment practices and job-placement claims. He shut down the probe and reassigned the investigators. "At the very same time that people had less money to pay for college, they had to pay more for it," higher education public policy analyst Ben Miller told MarketWatch two years ago. "The thing that scares me the most is this is where we are years after this recession. What's going to happen the next time we have a recession?"

That time is now, and the nation stands bitterly divided. On the free-market side, Americans deplore government handouts to college students: "the welfare of the twenty-first century," as former Montana Republican congressman, Tea Party member, and Trump supporter Denny Rehberg called them. On the other side are President Joe Biden, Elizabeth Warren, and Bernie Sanders, committed to reforming a broken system and bringing back free college, a position 58 percent of registered voters support, according to a 2019 Harris poll, the same percentage favoring student debt elimination.

Handout? Hand up? The stakes in the debate have never been higher. "We can either continue going down the road to oligarchy, the road we've been on since the Reagan years, or we can choose to go on the road to a more pluralistic society with working class people able to make it into the middle class. We can't have both," reformer Thom Hartmann presciently observed. "And if we want to go down the road to letting working people back into the middle class, it all starts with taxing the rich."

London School of Economics professor David Graeber has predicted how the "wicked problem" of student debt will resolve itself. And it doesn't end well for lenders. "For thousands of years, the struggle between rich and poor has largely taken the form of conflicts between creditors and debtors," he wrote in *Debt: The First 5,000 Years*. Likewise, he said, "for the past five thousand years, with remarkable regularity, popular insurrections have begun the same way: with the ritual destruction of debt records."

Until then, we just keep writing checks to loan companies. After repaying the money to send our sons to college, we're left with $20,000 in parent loans for our daughters. For as long as the debt wars rage, families who can't afford sticker prices will need to solve the problem of paying for college on their own. The solutions are out there. You just need to know where to look.

10

What They Don't Tell You
on the College Tour

The Secret to Admissions Success

Being trapped inside the college admissions industrial complex can feel like you've been dropped into a sequel to *Jumanji*, a landscape rife with quicksand, scary creatures, booby traps, and death-defying tests of strength, intelligence, and courage. To win the game and return to the real world without getting stuck forever in debt requires puzzle-solving, persistence, confidence, and nerves of steel.

What you hear and see makes no sense. How is it possible that Harvard is more affordable for 90 percent of American families than their local state universities? Or that anywhere from 20 percent to half of the students eligible for financial aid never receive it? Or that public universities are rejecting their own state's middle- and working-class applicants to enroll 25 to 50 percent of their classes with wealthy out-of-state students?

For anyone outside the nation's richest families, getting into college—and paying for it—has become a terrifying roll of the dice. It doesn't have to be. Before you cross into the admissions Maze of Doom, figure out where you want to go and how to get there.

Having a plan forces families to proceed with logic instead of emotion, relieving stress and anxiety as they parse the contradictory messages along the way.

Don't start the search with vague goals. Wanting to get into the highest-ranked, best-brand college that will accept you often leads to unmanageable loans. To spare yourself disappointment or decades of debt, be far more deliberate. Unless your teenager is paying for it or you can afford full tuition, choosing a college has become—for better or worse—a family decision. A financially responsible adult has to lead the way.

If you're blessed with a remarkable child who understands the intricacies of admissions strategizing, financial aid optimization, and preferential pricing, put her in charge. If not, you'll need to do it yourself or pay someone else. If you hire help, think of yourself as the mission leader and the consultants as allies. Before you begin, use this GPS to get you to your destination.

Step 1: Narrow the choices to great schools you can afford. A stunning lack of transparency makes winning the admissions game seem impossible. It doesn't have to be. Use the right resources and you'll find great colleges that fit your family's budget. Start with the rankings. Focus on finding instruments that prioritize quality and affordability over status and prestige.

Search for statistics that show what percent of enrolled students receive financial aid and the average debt each carries. To stay in or rise beyond the middle class requires graduating debt-free. Debt prevents graduates from acquiring middle-class markers: a home, paid vacations, health security, retirement, and savings to send their own children to college.

Among industrialized nations, the United States provides the least economic opportunity and mobility for its citizens. Competition to get into the highest-quality, most affordable public universities is more intense than ever. Affluent students unable to afford private colleges are taking seats at public universities that once went to middle- and moderate-income students. It's now harder to get accepted to the University of California, Santa Barbara, than it was to get into Stanford in the late 1970s.

To find great colleges at affordable prices, start with these rankings:

- *Washington Monthly*'s **National University Rankings** identifies the most affordable elite colleges and the "Best Bang for the Buck." It also ranks the contribution each school makes to the public good in three categories: social mobility, research, and providing opportunities for public service.
- *The Wall Street Journal / Times Higher Education* **College Rankings** allows students to create personalized rankings based on the factors that matter most. The site provides tools to customize, sort, and filter the data.
- *Forbes*'s **America's Top Colleges** reviews the top 650 undergraduate institutions—out of more than 4,000 degree-granting colleges—that deliver quality academics, career success, and the lowest debt.
- *Money*'s **Best Colleges** targets schools that successfully combine quality and affordability, and includes information about tuition, family borrowing, and career earnings.
- **Kiplinger's Best College Values** lists hundreds of colleges that deliver a quality education at an affordable price.
- **The Princeton Review's Best Value Colleges** ranks colleges using institutional and student surveys, including academic rigor, affordability, and career outcomes for graduates.
- **CollegeNET's Social Mobility Index** assesses how well colleges educate students from families with incomes below the national median. The SMI measures tuition costs, the success graduates have finding good-paying jobs, and

how well colleges promote the public interest and provide upward economic mobility for graduates.

Step 2: Identify one or two good affordable public colleges in your state. State schools usually have transparent pricing and discounts based on family need. One important caveat: Housing, food, and fees are often excluded from scholarships, tuition discounts, and need-based financial aid. Exceptions are made for the most academically qualified applicants who often get enrollment bonuses, housing stipends, and perks like admission to honors colleges, internships, and travel grants.

Those who don't qualify for bonuses are often shocked at the high price of housing and food—an average of $12,000 per year at public universities and $13,000 at private colleges. Room and board accounts for nearly half of what it costs students to attend public universities in their state, and on average a quarter of the cost to attend private colleges, according to a 2019 College Board analysis. Because housing and food are fast becoming sources of revenue, many colleges require students to live on campus their first and second years. To save money, appeal the rule and find off-campus housing.

The most valued out-of-state applicants—usually those with the highest grades and test scores—get the best discounts at public universities. High-achieving out-of-state students could find the best discounts in 2020 at the University of Alabama, the University of Colorado, Texas A&M, the University of Missouri, the University of Arkansas, Louisiana State University, the Colorado School of Mines, Louisiana's Grambling State University, the University of North Carolina at Pembroke, and Virginia's College of William & Mary.

Step 3: Ignore sticker prices at private colleges. What you'll pay at most private colleges has little to do with sticker price and everything to do with grades, test scores, family income, and each school's financial aid policies. With the exception of a handful of colleges, they all discount tuition an average of 50 percent. They call the discounts merit scholarships, but they're really used to recruit students at various price points. My university knocks 75 percent off tuition for a small percentage of the highest-achieving applicants. They give a larger number of less-qualified applicants 25 to 50 percent discounts.

Since students will never know how they rank against other applicants the year they apply, the best way to guarantee the highest discount is to look at the average test scores and grades of accepted students on each college's website. Choose colleges where your grades and test scores are better than the top 25 percent. That's how families can identify the private colleges that may end up costing less than public universities.

Step 4: Thoroughly understand each college's financial aid policy before applying. Few colleges are transparent about the baseline qualifications students need for grants, merit scholarships, and discounts. You won't get that information in marketing brochures or at public presentations. It's usually buried in jargon, an alphabet soup of muddled syntax like "need blind and meets full demonstrated need without loans." Or "need blind and meets full demonstrated need with loans." Or "need aware, need sensitive, meets full demonstrated need." Or "need blind, does not meet full demonstrated need." Or "need aware, does not meet full demonstrated need." Or "early decision, early binding decision, early action, single choice early action, restrictive early action."

Definitions are imprecise and meaning is subjective. Take, for example, the essential-to-understand phrase "need blind." It means, in theory, that colleges judge applicants on their merits without regard to their ability to pay tuition. Sounds good. In reality, admissions officers see just fine. By applying—or not—for financial aid, students tip off colleges to their family's social status and income. Committees see income markers on applications—parents' level of education, professions, neighborhoods, prep and high schools attended—and use that information to inform admissions decisions.

Colleges impose various prices and discounts on individual families without ever having to justify how they calculated the final cost. In other words, colleges can say they're need blind. But when it comes to deciding which students they want to admit, they can do whatever they want. Consultant and former admissions officer Eric Dobler saw this firsthand while visiting colleges in eastern Pennsylvania. "Several of them indicated that they are need blind until they get to the last 15 to 20 percent of their decisions," he wrote on his blog. "At that point, an applicant who has a greater ability to pay would get the nod over a student who was going to need significant financial aid in order to attend."

Step 5: Translate the jargon of financial aid. The way colleges dole out financial aid seems deliberately constructed to keep families confused and befuddled for as long as possible. Start your journey into the financial aid inferno by preparing the necessary documents—the FAFSA and CSS Profile. (See Step 7 for a more complete explanation of the CSS Profile.)

The FAFSA is the Free Application for Federal Student Aid. Private colleges supplement the FAFSA with the CSS Profile (the College Scholarship Service) to make financial aid decisions. The College Board administers the CSS Profile, charging families $25 to apply, and $16 for each subsequent form sent to colleges.

The government returns the FAFSA with the Expected Family Contribution, or EFC. The EFC ranges from $0 to the full cost of attendance. The updated FAFSA is released annually, usually in the fall. It takes about an hour to complete and doesn't require parents to include home equity as an asset. Apply as early as possible. Several states have first come, first served financial aid and run out of money quickly. Practically that means as soon as the budgeted money is gone, so is the aid—even for students who are eligible to receive it. (The Trump administration renamed the EFC the "Student Aid Index" in late 2020 but changed nothing else about it.)

The CSS, a far more complicated picture of family finances, can take three to four hours to complete. It includes all assets—home equity, small businesses, investments, real estate, second homes—that aren't part of retirement funds. Though most public colleges and universities use the FAFSA to determine financial aid, a few in 2020 also required the CSS, including the University of Michigan and the University of North Carolina at Chapel Hill.

Step 6: Know your family's EFC / Student Aid Index and use it to choose colleges. What the government thinks a family can afford is often far less than what colleges expect them to pay. The EFC versus the real cost of attending can be confusing. Final prices and expected parent contributions vary widely from college to college, depending on family income and how badly the school wants the applicant. My neighbor's son was accepted to Harvard and Vanderbilt with a $124,609 EFC. That means the family was wealthy enough to pay $124,609 in costs his first year. Harvard gave him no financial aid. Vanderbilt gave him a 50 percent discount. He chose Harvard.

Vanderbilt is one of forty private colleges that promise to admit students solely on their merits without regard to their ability to pay *and* to charge only what families can afford. But Vanderbilt, like many other selective colleges, puts hefty loans in financial aid packages. Harvard is one of a dozen elite colleges that promises enough aid to cover each student's tuition and room and board with no loans. But even that promise can be misleading. Some students attending colleges that officially exclude loans from financial aid packages wind up with debt anyway. Take the University of Pennsylvania.

Despite a no-loan promise, 32 percent of the class of 2015 graduated with debt, the *Daily Pennsylvanian* discovered. Penn students needed loans to cover costs beyond their family's means or to defray study abroad, summer classes, personal emergencies, and decreasing grants relative to rising costs. Other colleges hide behind the fine print of their policies.

In 2020, Williams College, for example, restricted no-loan packages to students from families with incomes less than $75,000; Dartmouth limited no-loan packages to students from families earning $100,000 or less; Rice didn't include loans in aid packages for students from families earning $130,000 or less, according to *U.S. News*. Some no-loan schools like Colby College promised to meet a family's full need but with a caveat: the college is not need blind. They sometimes reject qualified students because they're too poor.

Knowing your EFC / Student Aid Index can help you estimate how much you'll pay and how much you'll get in grants and loans, as well as focus your search on colleges your family can afford. The difference between the aid colleges offer and your family's financial need is called "gapping," the difference between grants and subsidized loans and what schools expect you to pay out of pocket and with private loans.

Especially for accepted students with academic credentials that put them in the middle or at the bottom of their class, a growing number of public and private colleges aren't meeting the financial needs of families. Colleges will suggest families bridge the gap with unsubsidized parent PLUS loans, traps masked as financial aid. Unsubsidized parent PLUS loans cost far more than the subsidized loans the government gives students. To avoid being one of the many parents facing retirement with burdensome PLUS loans used to pay their children's college costs, parents should avoid borrowing altogether. Or borrow only what students can comfortably repay within a year of graduation. Knowing the minimum your family will be expected to contribute early in the search—and how much you reasonably can afford to borrow—can prevent the common heartbreak students face when they're accepted to "dream schools" they can't afford.

File the FASFA as soon as it is available—usually October 1. Several states have first-come-first-served financial aid programs that run out of money quickly. Complete the form ASAP to maximize the amount of aid you are eligible to receive.

Step 7: Use the CSS Profile to lower costs. You can't beat death or taxes, and you can't appeal your EFC to lower it. But your EFC / Student Aid Index isn't your destiny at private colleges. There's another way to lower your expected family contribution. It's the CSS Profile.

The CSS Profile allows families to include special circumstances that may lower what private colleges charge. These include job losses, unforeseen medical expenses, credit card debt, private school tuition for younger siblings, college tuition payments for older siblings, loans to repair a leaky roof or plumbing disasters, and lost wages from time off to care for elderly family members. Parents with small or no retirement funds can explain they need to channel any extra cash into savings for old age.

The CSS Profile is why colleges tell families to ignore sticker prices when applying. That's good advice. But it doesn't go far enough. Schools almost always neglect to warn families about the specific terms and restrictions they put on financial aid. They also use different words to describe the same or similar policies. If you're confused, email or call the college to ask specific questions; they rarely volunteer information.

Colby College is a great example of why asking questions is so important. In 2020, Colby promised to meet 100 percent of a family's demonstrated need without loans. Families earning less than $65,000 with assets typical of this range will have a parent or guardian contribution of $0. Families earning up to $150,000 with assets typical of this range will contribute no more than $15,000. More than 95 percent of families earning $200,000 or less have had financial assistance in recent years. The average financial aid award is $51,000.

Great deal, right? Except for what they don't tell you. Colby also rejects qualified applicants based on their family's inability to pay. It's one of dozens of colleges that describe themselves as having "need-aware or need-sensitive" admissions policies. Harsh as it may seem, in theory the policy protects students from taking on massive loans. The alternatives are colleges like Chapman University and St. John's College. They accept all qualified students. But they don't meet a student's full demonstrated need and often don't come close to awarding grants big enough to cover costs.

With merit scholarships reserved for students recruited to boost rankings, families can never accurately predict how large a discount they'll find in award packages. Start investigating financial aid policies early as a way to decide how and where to apply. If you're having trouble finding those policies online, call or email the college and drill down on how loans—subsidized and unsubsidized—figure into aid awards. Ask about the percentage of students with loans and the average debt load each has at graduation.

Get started by reviewing how these popular colleges allocated financial aid in 2020:

Golden Ticket Colleges. What academia calls them: **"need blind, meets full demonstrated need, no loan."** These colleges separate admissions decisions from financial need. They evaluate applicants without considering their ability to pay. They promise to charge students only what their families can afford without loans. As private colleges with billion-dollar-plus endowments, they're the hardest to get into. Some won't put loans in aid packages but will offer them informally as a way to fill the gap between what they expect families to pay and what those families can afford.

- Harvard University
- MIT
- Pomona College
- Princeton University
- Stanford University
- Swarthmore College
- University of Chicago
- University of Pennsylvania
- Vanderbilt University
- Yale University

Caveat: These are the elite of the elite, with acceptance rates in the single digits and low teens. Even among these colleges, the definition of "need" is subjective. Grants can vary widely. Until 2020, for example, Stanford used home equity to calculate need, a common practice among most colleges. Offers made to our daughter ranged from paying nothing at Bowdoin to paying $40,000 a year at Pomona, with seven other colleges at various points in between. Harvard charged $18,000 for room and board and tuition, and provided one round-trip plane ticket home and a winter coat. Yale charged $30,000 and offered no travel or coat allowance. After I showed Harvard's award letter to Yale, Yale matched Harvard's offer.

Platinum Card Colleges. What academia calls them: **"need blind; meets full demonstrated need; includes loans."** These schools offer good deals that can—for the most qualified students—match in-state tuition at elite public colleges like the University of Michigan or the University of California. They promise to evaluate applicants without considering family income and to charge accepted students only what they can afford to pay. If your expected parent contribution is higher than you can afford, colleges will award loans to make up the difference. Some have no loan policies but will ask you to borrow against the equity in your home. They all have small acceptance rates.

- Amherst College
- Barnard College
- Boston College
- Bowdoin College
- Brown University
- California Institute of Technology
- Claremont McKenna College
- Columbia University
- Cornell University
- Curtis Institute of Music
- Dartmouth College
- Davidson College
- Denison University
- Duke University
- Emory University
- Georgetown University
- Grinnell College
- Hamilton College
- Harvey Mudd College
- Johns Hopkins University
- Middlebury College
- Northwestern University
- Olin College
- Rice University
- Soka University of America
- University of Notre Dame
- University of Pennsylvania
- University of Richmond
- University of Southern California
- University of Virginia
- Vanderbilt University
- Vassar College

- Wellesley College
- Williams College
- Yale University

Caveat: Having equity in your home can kill your chances for affordable discounts at most of these colleges. Yale, the University of Southern California (USC), and Williams are among scores of colleges that consider home equity a source of income. USC is a great example of how colleges manipulate tuition financing to burnish their public image while overcharging families. The university announced amid great fanfare in 2020 that it was eliminating tuition for students from families with an annual income of $80,000 or less.

But the devil is in the details. Even if moderate- and low-income students from underresourced high schools can get accepted into USC—the university rejects nearly 85 percent of its applicants—those students will borrow or pay 20 percent of their family's income to attend. Why? Free tuition is great, but they still have to pay for housing, food, books, supplies, personal expenses, and transportation, costs the university estimates will add up to about $20,000 a year. And who knows how the university figures home equity into the equation. The explanation is so vague it would take an expert to estimate how much USC charges any individual needy family.

Take, for example, Elsa, a housekeeper in Southern California whose name has been changed to protect her family's privacy. When her youngest was applying to college, she didn't even look at private schools. She and her former husband scraped together enough money to buy a house in a working-class neighborhood after the 2008 financial meltdown. After they divorced, she stayed in the house with her three daughters, raising them on about $1,000 a week, working in the gig economy. The two older daughters attended community college and had to leave to find full-time work. Her youngest applied only to state colleges and universities. In 2017, she received what Elsa thought was a free ride to the University of California.

The award letter told a different story. Even paying no tuition, the family had to accept more than $8,000 in loans for housing, food, and fees, a total the university estimated would cost more than $17,000 a year. The university expected Elsa to pay the difference—nearly $10,000 a year—out of pocket or use private loans. Because the amount was one-quarter of her annual income, she took the loans. When her daughter graduates, the family will have nearly $70,000 in debt plus interest. In late 2020, Elsa was struggling to survive. She had lost all but two of her eight housekeeping clients during the coronavirus pandemic. She takes home $300 a week, so little she can't afford the Wi-Fi her daughter needs to complete her classes online during the pandemic.

Wild-Card Colleges. What academia calls them: **"need aware; need sensitive; meets full demonstrated need."** Most private colleges (and public universities evaluating out-of-state applicants) have wild-card, or unpredictable, pricing. These selective colleges reject applicants based on their ability to pay, but also promise to charge accepted students only what their families can afford. They tend to use confusing definitions of what it means to "meet full demonstrated need." The definition of "need" is highly subjective, varies from college to college, and always includes subsidized and unsubsidized loans. Some offer merit scholarship tuition discounts to students with the highest test scores and grades.

- Bates College
- Boston University
- Bryn Mawr College
- Carleton College
- Case Western Reserve University

- Colgate University
- Colorado College
- Connecticut College
- Franklin & Marshall College
- Haverford College
- Kenyon College
- Lafayette College
- Lehigh University
- Macalester College
- Mount Holyoke College
- Oberlin College
- Occidental College
- Reed College
- Scripps College
- Skidmore College
- Smith College
- Trinity College
- Tufts University
- Union College
- Washington University in St. Louis
- Wesleyan University

Merit Aid Colleges. What academia calls them: **"need blind; does not meet full demonstrated need."** These colleges tend to be less selective and practice some form of Robin Hood pricing—taking more tuition from the less-qualified rich to give to the highest-qualified middle-, moderate-, and low-income students. They flatter all qualified students with acceptances, then leave some low-, moderate-, and middle-income students without the subsidies needed to pay the cost of attending. A few low- and middle-income students with the highest test scores and grades stand a good chance of getting deep discounts. But they don't know the full cost of attending until the award letter arrives.

These schools tend to offer the highest discounts to applicants in the top 1 to 5 percent of the pool and good discounts to students with the highest test scores and grades relative to the college's top 25 percent. For students ranked average or below, they don't provide enough aid to make degrees affordable. New York University, for example, admits applicants regardless of financial need but often doesn't give discounts high enough to allow students to attend without private loans. That means students they accept but desire least might pay half their annual earnings to the college. Financially needy students who qualify for admission at NYU may actually be better at "need-aware" schools that meet the full demonstrated need of the middle- and low-income students they enroll.

To maximize merit aid, consult databases that help customize the search:

- **DIY College Rankings** created "Best Bets for College Merit Aid," a list of colleges and universities built using newly available federal data. The schools and the methodology are available at www.diycollegerankings.com/35-best-bets-college-merit-aid/.
- **CollegeVine** also lists colleges with competitive merit aid: https://blog.collegevine.com/which-colleges-give-out-the-most-merit-aid-a-list-of-the-top-50/.
- **MeritMore** simplifies the merit aid search with a database that allows students to enter GPA and SAT or ACT scores along with the region (New England or the Rocky Mountains, for example) where they'd like to attend college to identify schools most likely to award individual applicants merit scholarships.

These colleges usually offer generous merit discounts to the most desired applicants:

- Babson College
- Bard College
- Baylor University
- Bucknell University
- Carnegie Mellon University
- Chapman University
- Cooper Union
- DePauw University
- George Washington University
- Hampshire College
- Ithaca College
- New York University
- Saint Louis University
- Santa Clara University
- Southern Methodist University
- St. John's College (Annapolis/Santa Fe)
- St. John's University
- St. Lawrence University
- Syracuse University
- Texas Christian University
- University of San Diego
- Whitman College

Rich-Kid Colleges. What academia calls them: "**need aware; does not meet full demonstrated need.**" These colleges evaluate applicants based on financial need and don't promise accepted students enough aid to make attending affordable. They might reject highly qualified applicants with incomes too low to pay full tuition and accept less-qualified wealthy applicants to meet revenue goals. If racial and income diversity are goals, they may practice a limited form of Robin Hood pricing, depending on their financial health. Rich-Kid Colleges seeking to boost rank may offer merit aid to students with high grades and scores. For students with need, they rarely offer high discounts—unless their grades and scores are so exceptional, they help boost the college's *U.S. News* ranking. Some offer great financial aid in the first year, then gradually reduce it over subsequent years by increasing tuition and leaving grant awards unchanged.

- Abilene Christian University
- Agnes Scott College
- American University
- Auburn University
- Beloit College
- Bennington College
- Berklee College of Music
- Berry College
- Bradley University
- Brandeis University
- Catholic University of America
- Centre College
- Clark University
- Clemson University
- College of Wooster
- Creighton University
- DePaul University
- Dickinson College
- Drexel University
- Fairfield University
- Furman University

- Gettysburg College
- Hampton University
- Hofstra University
- Howard University
- Johnson & Wales University
- Loma Linda University
- Loyola Marymount University
- Loyola University Chicago
- Loyola University New Orleans
- Marquette University
- The New School
- Pepperdine University
- Quinnipiac University
- Rensselaer Polytechnic Institute
- Rhode Island School of Design
- Rhodes College
- Rochester Institute of Technology
- Rollins College
- Sarah Lawrence College
- Seton Hall University
- Southwestern University
- Spelman College
- University of Dayton
- University of Denver
- University of Rochester
- University of San Francisco
- University of St. Thomas
- University of Tulsa
- Wabash College
- Wheaton College
- Willamette University
- Worcester Polytechnic Institute

Step 8: Build a list. At the start of junior year, applicants should assess their qualifications, then look at the average grades and test scores at colleges they want to attend. Group the schools into three categories: target, safety, and reach, or dream, colleges. You'll get the best discounts from safety schools, average discounts from target schools, and loans from stretch schools—unless you're accepted at a Golden Ticket College.

Kudos to Muhlenberg College in Allentown, Pennsylvania, for being more transparent about financial aid than any school I've seen. Financial aid isn't just to overcome financial barriers. It's also an important part of recruitment, Muhlenberg explains on its website. "The Real Deal on Financial Aid" accurately describes how most colleges assemble aid packages. Like many private colleges, Muhlenberg makes aid decisions based on "preferential pricing." That means the most desired students will receive the best aid packages.

With that in mind, carefully build your list understanding that the price you pay will depend on your comparative worth to the college. Compass Education Group publishes a table showing ACT and SAT score ranges for accepted students at more than four hundred colleges, and notes which of those require or have optional testing: https://www.compassprep.com/college-profiles/.

Target schools: If your qualifications put you in the 50 percent or above range of accepted students, those are your target schools. Competing for the best discounts at target schools will require boosting high school grades and test scores to the top 10 percent of accepted students.

Safety schools: If your qualifications far exceed the average of those accepted, these are "safety schools," colleges that will most likely accept you and give you the best discounts.

Dream, reach, and stretch schools: Only one hundred colleges—

out of more than three thousand nonprofits offering undergraduate degrees—accept fewer than 25 percent of their applicants. They represent the "dream" of status and prestige, but also frequently leave low- and middle-income families in debt. Applying to schools where your qualifications fall below the average of those accepted likely means you'll get puny discounts and financial aid packages stuffed with loans if you're accepted.

Step 9: High school prep. Highly competitive public and private colleges give students with the highest scores and grades in challenging courses the best discounts.

"Challenging coursework" means taking one or two Advanced Placement courses beginning sophomore year *and doing well in them.* As someone who spent years on admissions committees, I can say with certainty that most colleges outside the elites want to see appropriate but not excessive challenge. They want to see hard work that pays off with As and occasional Bs.

Students with weak grades in the first few semesters of high school are frequently rewarded if they demonstrate that they reversed the trend with steady improvement. I've been on committees that admit students based on essays explaining why their grades slipped and how they recovered. Nearly all students struggle in challenging courses. But the struggle is especially difficult for students attending underresourced public high schools.

Getting significant tuition discounts requires investing time and money in tutors to help struggling students through difficult classes. How to do that economically? Many high schools offer free peer tutoring. Khan Academy has free online assistance, though the site can be difficult to navigate without someone to guide students through confusing sessions. Check with schools in your area, especially expensive private preps that offer peer tutoring as part of community service requirements. Boys & Girls Clubs, the Y, and municipal governments provide free and low-cost tutoring to high school students.

To find quality SAT and ACT coaches, bypass high-priced tutors and expensive chains with large classes. Look for neighborhood kids with high scores who were admitted to elite colleges. Ask high school counselors for referrals and advertise on neighborhood sites like NextDoor.

Take the ACT and SAT once. Request copies of the corrected tests. Focus on studying for one of the two, either the ACT *or* SAT, the one that seems easiest to master. Ask tutors to build sessions around reviewing wrong answers and reinforcing those sections with practice. Taking a timed practice test every two weeks all summer long—and reviewing and mastering wrong answers—is the best prep students can do.

High school is overwhelming for the vast majority of teenagers. Structure, kindness, and empathy usually yield the best results—and the highest tuition discounts.

Step 10: Use tools to calculate costs at individual colleges. Narrow the college list, then search each using at least three crucial tools: CollegeCalc, College Scorecard, and net price calculators. Used together, the websites will lead you to great affordable colleges. At the least, you'll have a good sense of what to expect when the financial aid package arrives.

- **CollegeCalc** had the best information, was the easiest to access, and seemed most accurate. Unlike net price calculators, there's no need to input personal financial data. CollegeCalc lists sticker prices and net prices, along with comparisons to similar private colleges in the region. For each college, it estimates the average net price parents will pay at various income levels. It predicts debt, interest payments, and how

long it will take to pay off expected loans. It frames important questions students should ask themselves, like "Can I
afford to attend [*insert name of college*]?" Then it helps sort
factors that go into making the decision, with tools to estimate future costs and expected tuition increases based on
past increases. See https://www.collegecalc.org/colleges.

- **College Scorecard** is another excellent tool to access information about how much any particular college will cost, the
  debt students will have when they graduate, and expected
  return on investment. The federal government created College Scorecard in 2013 so families can compare costs among
  various colleges. The data covers five areas: cost, graduation
  rates, employment rates, average amount students borrow,
  and graduate loan default rate. See https://collegescorecard
  .ed.gov/school/.

- **Net price calculators**, found on each college's website,
  estimate what families will pay after subtracting grants,
  discounts, and loans based on financial information that
  parents input. Net price calculators are notoriously inaccurate, according to a study done by Laura Perna at the University of Pennsylvania. If you have questions about your
  family's individual financial circumstances, call the college
  financial aid office.

- **GradReports** looks at the returns on investments graduates
  can expect. Search by school name and major, and find
  out what sorts of jobs graduates have and how much, on
  average, they earn. The site publishes median alumni salary
  and debt one year out of school. It organizes information
  according to majors and ranks the top 25 schools for each
  area of study. GradReports was one of the first to synthesize
  and publish recently released data from the Department of
  Education. See https://www.gradreports.com.

- **College Factual** allows families to see the cost of obtaining a degree from one college as compared to other colleges of similar quality nationwide. When the site worked, which was rarely, it was buggy and littered with annoying ads. The results struck me as off the mark. For example, it compared Chapman to Oberlin College. Oberlin is ranked No. 33 among national liberal arts colleges and Chapman is ranked No. 125 among national universities—an odd equivalence. To quickly access College Factual information about cost and value at any particular school, the easiest way is to google "What is the value of a degree from [*insert name of college here*]?" Or try your luck on the landing page: https://www.collegefactual .com/colleges/.

Step 11: Jargon Alert: How to decide when and where to apply. Colleges use various ploys to lure students into applying early. Most benefit colleges and wealthy applicants at the expense of students of lesser means. Colleges lump early application programs into baffling categories using various names that sometimes mean the same thing: early decision, binding early decision, early decision 2, early action, nonbinding early action, early action 2, single choice early action, restrictive early action.

Some schools combine early application jargon with financial aid jargon, creating more opportunities to confuse and obfuscate. Not only is financial aid insufficient for most students, but award letters are filled with confusing terms that make offers difficult to decode, according to a 2018 study by the think tank New America and nonprofit uAspire. Colleges offering a common federal loan program used more than one hundred different terms to describe it, "including two dozen that didn't even mention the word 'loan,'" researchers reported, "making it exceedingly difficult for students and families to make a financially informed college decision."

Here's how the worst get you. They combine need blind (they accept all qualified students regardless of income) with early decision (if accepted you promise to enroll) but leave out the crucial detail that they won't meet your full financial need.

Once accepted early decision, students usually receive financial aid awards with small discounts and lots of loans that they're obligated to accept. How do they trick you?

- You applied early to take advantage of the better odds of getting accepted.
- Then you agreed to accept whatever aid they offered.
- But you never checked the fine print.

Most colleges usually charge more than families can afford to pay. Baylor, Bucknell, New York University, Syracuse University, and the University of Miami were among those in 2020 combining early decision, need-blind admissions, and little warning that they don't meet a family's full demonstrated financial need. To avoid these and other traps, here's a primer:

- **Early decision and early decision 2 are always binding.** That means if you're accepted, you have to attend. You can apply to only one college in the first round of early decision. If you're rejected, you can apply to one more college in the second round. You'll double and triple your odds of admission to selective colleges using early decision. But unless you can pay near-full or full tuition, the pain you'll suffer after taking out loans is far worse than attending a just-as-good lower-ranked school that costs less. Colleges offer various schemes, so plan accordingly.

- **Early action** is much better. Early action means you can apply to as many of the dozens of colleges that have early action as you want, with no commitment to attend. The trade-off? Early action rarely gives students better admissions odds. On the plus side, early action is a no-risk way to find out that you've been accepted by at least one college on your list. It also gives middle- and moderate-income students the chance to compare aid offers and make informed financial decisions.

- **Single choice early action (aka restrictive early action)** permits students to choose one of six elite colleges to apply to early. In 2020, Harvard, Princeton, Stanford, Yale, Georgetown, and the University of Notre Dame, all with acceptance rates in the single digits or low teens, were accepting applications in November and prohibiting students from applying early to any other colleges until they'd rendered decisions in December. They were, however, allowing students to apply to as many colleges as they liked in the regular decision round. And if one elite college rejects you in December, you can apply to another college that offers early decision 2—if you can afford to take a lowball or no financial aid offer.

Before wading into the early application morass, do some research. Figure out how the admission rates for each college on your list change under various early application programs: early action, early decision, and regular decision. About fifty colleges with early decision promise to meet a family's full financial need. But colleges can—and will—define your financial need any way they please. If their definition is not the same as yours, you must appeal and negotiate for more grants. If they won't budge, you can reject early decision due to financial hardship, and hope for the best in regular decision.

College Transitions and PrepScholar have easy-to-use websites that allow you to quickly compare colleges using specific search terms like:

- Need blind and meets full need without loans.
- Early decision and early decision 2 that promises to meet full need.
- Early action or single choice early action.
- Accepts the highest percentage of students receiving Pell Grants.

Step 12: Open a 529 account. Fewer than 5 percent of all Americans invest in 529 plans, federally funded college savings incentives. Used almost exclusively by the wealthy and affluent, 529 plan contributions grow tax-free. When the money is spent to pay for college, the federal government won't tax withdrawals. Anyone can start a 529 with any amount up to $300,000 per child. The accounts have little impact on a student's eligibility for financial aid. If used for education, families pay no taxes on earnings.

When financial advisers set up a 529 account, they usually charge sales fees for their services. Since fees relating to 529 plans must be disclosed, look for 529 plans that charge less than others. The website Saving for College (https://savingforcollege.com) has tips for finding the best 529 plans for individual family needs. A few states offer income tax benefits for 529 contributions to *any* 529 plan (not just the home state's plan), including, as of 2020, Arizona, Arkansas, Kansas, Minnesota, Missouri, Montana, and Pennsylvania.

Step 13: Beware hidden costs that force overborrowing. Revenue-hungry schools now have backdoor tuition, hidden fees they collect for parking permits, books, transportation, computers, and other mandatory charges unique to each campus. USC charges up to $1,000 for a two-semester parking permit. Chapman charges a loan fee, and wellness-center and associated student-body fees that add $450 to the bill, plus an additional $300 for parking. Add personal expenses—toiletries, the occasional dinner in town, drinks or movies with friends—and it's reasonable to conclude students will need as much as $2,000 extra each year to keep up with their wealthier peers.

Students should never borrow more than they expect to earn their first year out of college. If the total cost for college—including subsidized loans—is beyond your means, colleges will expect you to borrow from private lenders to pay the difference. Private lenders may entice you with great introductory offers, but those can be bait-and-switch schemes. Lenders want to make as much money as possible from families, not help them pay for college. Bottom line: Accept only low-interest subsidized loans that defer payments until six months after the student graduates. Families would be wise to agree to borrow only the maximum the federal government awards in subsidized student loans—currently $3,500 per year or $14,000 over four years—and the subsidized parent loans a few colleges offer.

Putting it together. Junior year should mark the beginning of the end of the college search. Your family will have to choose a path. Are you Ivy bound, headed for a top 50 college? Or are you still confused and need help applying to state universities and private colleges with acceptance rates above 25 percent?

If you're headed to Ivy-plus colleges, you'll need the strongest possible test scores; extracurricular passions that indicate committed intellectual pursuits; accomplishments that show character-building leadership, service, and dedication to a cause; the highest grades in the most difficult classes available; a strong record of demonstrating interest with college visits, emails to faculty, research projects, and connections to individual colleges.

You'll also need help prepping applications, staying on deadline, writing and revising essays, researching colleges to match your interests to the programs they offer, preparing for admission interviews, then doing at least one or two mock sessions to practice. You'll have to assemble athletics or arts supplements, a website, and résumés. For arts colleges—only 0.2 percent of high school applicants enroll in a handful of degree-granting art and design colleges—contact individual schools you want to attend for audition and academic requirements. The most reputable are members of the Association of Independent Colleges of Art and Design.

If you're unsure if you're competitive, answer the following questions to figure it out.

Are you willing to assemble an application that shows you're seriously interested in each elite college you want to attend? If so, you'll have to:

- Visit and email colleges; attend courses; talk to admissions officers, students, and professors; and reflect what you've learned and how it impacted you in unique essays for each college.
- Research and write about the courses you want to take and why those programs are important to your intellectual growth.
- Apply early action (or early decision if you're wealthy).
- For art and design colleges, assemble award-winning portfolios and pay to travel the country for auditions and interviews.

Are you willing to take the hardest classes your high school offers and find tutors or teachers to help you master difficult subjects? If so, you'll have to:

- Choose the most advanced option for a subject. Colleges will lump grades and standardized test scores into one Academic Index Score and scrutinize transcripts closely.

- Take four years of math, lab science, and a foreign language.
- Supplement high school classes with community college or online college courses.

Are you willing to pursue three extracurricular passions in three different areas? If so, you'll have to:

- Follow the *Is*: pursuits should be interesting, interdisciplinary, and include internships.
- Make sure at least one passion is academic or intellectual.
- Seek professional training in at least one of your passions.

Are you willing to develop the character traits of a good student? If so, you'll have to:

- Be motivated by intellectual interest rather than grades.
- Be open to people different from you.
- Develop a track record of leadership at school or in your community, motivated by a desire to give back or help others.
- Show success in college-level research and classwork.
- Demonstrate dedication, focus, and commitment.

Are you willing to assemble time-consuming supplements? If so, you'll have to:

- Create athletics or arts supplements and résumés—including one with photos—and a website.
- Individualize supplements for each college.
- Write cover letters or artist statements.
- Make performance videos highlighting artistic or athletic achievements.

At the end of your junior year, do you have strong numbers? If so, you'll have:

- ACT or SAT scores that put you in the top 5 percent nationwide.
- High scores on Advanced Placement tests.
- A high unweighted and weighted grade point average.
- A rank in the top 2 percent of your high school class.

If applying to elite colleges and arts schools seems like too much work, shoot for universities and colleges with acceptance rates higher than 25 percent. If you tend to procrastinate, you'll need help to assemble applications that include:

- Transcripts.
- Letters of recommendation from teachers and a counselor.
- A personal statement for the Common App.
- Essays specific to each school or state college you want to attend.
- Supplemental essays and short answers to multiple prompts for private colleges.
- ACT or SAT scores, except for schools that are "test blind." Test-blind colleges will refuse to consider the SAT or ACT when making admissions and financial aid decisions. FairTest's list of test-blind schools as of late 2020 includes:
  - California Institute of Technology (two-year trial)
  - California State University system (twenty-three campuses, one-year pilot)
  - Catholic University of America
  - City University of New York system (eleven campuses, one-year pilot)

- Cornell University (programs in agriculture, architecture, finance, and hotel administration)
- Dickinson College (one-year pilot)
- Hampshire College
- Idaho public universities (four campuses, one-year pilot)
- Loyola University New Orleans
- Northern Illinois University
- Northern Michigan University
- Reed College (two-year pilot)
- Saint Xavier University (one-year pilot, except for nursing program)
- University of California system (nine campuses test blind for 2023 and 2024; Berkeley, Davis, Irvine, Santa Barbara, and Santa Cruz have stated they will begin test blind)
- University of Minnesota Crookston (one-year pilot)
- University of New England
- Washington State University (one-year pilot)

Meeting deadlines is crucial to getting into desirable, affordable colleges. To stay on track, here's a high school timeline to follow:

- **Freshman and sophomore years:** Develop extracurricular passions; take the PSAT; get good grades in college-prep classes; research colleges; take the ACT and SAT once and begin studying over the summer for the test that best suits you.
- **Junior year:** Pursue leadership, internship, and/or extracurricular passions; take the PSAT for the National Merit competition; get good grades in tough classes; visit or email colleges to meet professors and students; study for the ACT or SAT and take the March/April test.

- **Senior summer:** Finalize your college list and visit or email officials whenever possible to build relationships; complete applications, keeping in mind some essay prompts are released August 1; write cover letters to teachers and your counselor requesting letters of recommendation; keep trying to boost ACT or SAT scores until you reach the high range of the colleges you want to award you merit scholarships.
- **Senior fall:** Continue pursuing passions, getting good grades in tough classes, interviewing or auditioning; connect with local alumni interviewers or admissions officers; take the last ACT or SAT test if you need to boost scores; make final applications revisions; submit applications, FAFSA, and CSS Profile by deadlines noted.

Don't fall prey to self-sabotaging:

Myth No. 1: I'm not Ivy League material. If you've done the research, have competitive test scores and grades, and will work hard on applications, never be discouraged from applying, especially if you think you don't have the money to pay tuition or the background of an elite college student. You're exactly the sort of applicant these colleges want.

Myth No. 2: I'll apply to as many colleges as possible, then research and visit them after I've been accepted. This works at state colleges that don't require campus-specific essays, but not with private schools. Selective colleges want proof that you want them.

Myth No. 3: As long as I get straight As, it doesn't matter what classes I take. For some state colleges, good grades tend to matter more than rigor. To improve admissions chances, and for higher tuition discounts, aim to take a few honors and Advanced Placement classes to boost your grades above 4.0. For the University of

California, for example, freshman grades don't count, but difficult first-year high school classes can prepare you for doing well in competitive courses sophomore, junior, and senior year. For selective private colleges, the rigor of classes taken over four years, and grades earned, is most important. It's better to earn one or two Bs in the hardest possible classes than straight As in easy classes.

Myth No. 4: I can send more or less the same application to all the colleges on my list as long as I remember to change the names. That's true if you're applying to more than one of the public universities in California, for example, but not true for other colleges. Too many students wrongly assume applying for college is like playing the lottery: I'll send my Common App to Stanford just to see if I can get in! Don't waste time and money. Do the research and apply smartly. Each private college has a personality; find the parts of your personality that mesh with the colleges you want to attend. Build connections on campus. Closely review websites and application questions; talk to alumni, students, professors, and admissions officers. Pay attention to the kind of students each college wants to recruit.

Myth No. 5: I can't get into a highly selective college unless I take every Advanced Placement class offered. Selective colleges accept students with a few As in Advanced Placement classes all the time. The trick is how you tell your story. Don't be afraid to explain extra courses you've taken, what you did after school—part-time work is valued—and how much money your club raised and who you helped. It may feel like bragging, but it's crucial information so the committee knows you better. Tell your story clearly, consistently, and boldly. A strong narrative of who you are—what you value, how you envision your life in five years—can overcome perceived flaws and missteps. In telling your story, connect the past (what you've done) to the present (who you are) to the future (where you're going).

Myth No. 6: Saving for college will harm my family's chances of getting the maximum amount of financial aid. Though saving for college can feel like a moving target, it's important to start. Set a goal and stick to it. Saving as little as $27 a month—the cost of a McDonald's family meal—will add up to thousands of dollars over eighteen years.

Myth No. 7: Don't worry about taking out student loans—it's good debt. Taking loans doesn't guarantee you'll graduate. Family income not only strongly correlates with the chances students have of being admitted to college but also with the likelihood of earning degrees, according to a Pell Institute study. Nationally, colleges graduate only 60 percent of enrolled applicants and only 16 percent of their low-income students. In other words, colleges take the money you borrow, spend it, then refuse to refund anything if you're forced to leave before graduating. Higher student debt means young households have lower incomes and fewer assets than previous generations. To avoid debt, focus on attending lesser-known but more affordable colleges rather than borrowing $100,000 or more to attend high-status high-ranked colleges with stingy grants and discounts.

Myth No. 8: College is so expensive it just isn't worth it. False. College graduates will earn 66 percent more than those with high school diplomas. At least 65 percent of new job openings in the coming decade will require degrees beyond high school, according to a Georgetown University study. Even as the need for a degree becomes more crucial, uncontrolled costs and free-market lawmakers are pushing families into the arms of rapacious lenders. Pell Grants, once reserved for low-income students, now go largely to the middle class, according to the National Center for Education Statistics. In 1975, a Pell Grant paid 80 percent of the cost of college. Today, the average grant is $4,000, and pays 30 percent. Graduating—with little or no debt—is crucial if you want to get ahead financially.

Myth No. 9: My family should use retirement funds, deplete grandparent savings, and borrow whatever it takes so I can attend the most exclusive college that accepts me, because elite brands open doors after graduation. Absolutely not. The federal government defines middle-class not by income but by aspirations: homeownership, a car for each adult, health security, retirement security, an annual family vacation, a college education for each child. Parents should hold on to their achievements and help their children aspire to the same.

No one nearing retirement should work seven days a week, morning to night, so his kids can attend expensive, prestigious universities and graduate schools, a plight award-winning nonfiction writer Neal Gabler described in his nightmarish tale of affluent debt and discouragement, "Many Middle-Class Americans Are Living Paycheck to Paycheck." Let his woe serve as a caution. "Lack of money ruins everything," he wrote. "It keeps you up at night and makes you not want to get up in the morning. To fail may constitute our great secret national pain, one that is deep and abiding. We are impotent. While the affliction is individual and hidden from view, it has begun to diminish our national spirit."

Statistics, surveys, and stories of successful Americans have busted this myth over and over. For most students, the salary boost from going to a superselective school is "generally indistinguishable from zero," concluded a landmark study published by economists Stacy Dale and Alan Krueger. Subsequent studies have shown that selective college degrees help two groups most—women and low-income students.

Women earn more not because they have an elite degree but because they delay marriage, kids, and stay in the workforce longer than similar women who graduate from less selective schools, the data show. Low-income students at elite schools have a good shot of reaching the top 1 percent of income earners, but few get the chance.

Children whose parents are in the top 1 percent of the income distribution are seventy-seven times more likely to attend an Ivy League college than those whose parents are at the bottom, according to a study led by the economist Raj Chetty.

Given that so many colleges outside the top tier springboard students into great careers, why do families accept debt servitude to buy status degrees? Blame social-climbing universities that sell exclusivity like Birkin bags. "We get a lot of ego gratification every time our deans stand up in front of the faculty and say, 'This year, we didn't reject 85 percent of applicants; we rejected 87 percent!' and there's a huge round of applause," New York University professor Scott Galloway told *New York* magazine. "That is tantamount to the head of a homeless shelter bragging about turning away nine of ten people who showed up last night." Though academia pretends to be a meritocracy, it's really a caste system. Galloway predicted "a four-year liberal-arts-campus experience is going to become something that's largely relegated and positioned to the children of rich people."

Myth No. 10: Free college is a terrible idea. In practice it will be another boondoggle for the rich. College admissions is rigged to favor the wealthy, but it doesn't have to be. France, Germany, and many Scandinavian and eastern European countries offer free or nearly free degrees. In the United Kingdom, graduates make no payments on loans until they're earning at least $33,000 a year. Payments are then tied to income; after thirty years balances are forgiven.

Countries with subsidized degrees give students formulas for success. Applicants follow the instructions and off they go, graduating with little or no debt. No tricks. No secrets. Not so in the US. In three generations, free-market lawmakers have taken away free public college as an American right and replaced it with massive student loans to benefit themselves and their corporate cronies. Restoring free public college will give Americans a fighting chance to reach or stay in the middle class. Long-term investment in the American people will do more to support economic growth than subsidizing corporations as they shovel more money into the pockets of a very small number of affluent, highly educated shareholders.

Without free college, student indenture will only worsen. Even the few schools promising to charge only what families can afford to pay without loans are sometimes suggesting students borrow to cover costs, as Harvard did to us in the fall of 2020.

Wealthy Americans have hoarded resources and opportunity long enough. It's time for those who benefited most from government largesse to return the favor. It's time for them to give others the same opportunities they had. It's time again for free public college. Rewriting the rules will require tremendous public courage. As with Social Security and Medicare, a plurality will support free public college only if it's an entitlement available to everyone. US representative Alexandria Ocasio-Cortez put it best when she said: "Universal public systems are designed to benefit *everybody*! Everyone contributes and everyone enjoys. We don't ban the rich from public schools or libraries because they are public goods."

For a brief time, higher education was a public good that lit a path to the middle class. Government taxed elites to make it possible for the rest of America to earn subsidized degrees. Millions— mostly white men—benefited from free college after World War II, using those opportunities to become wealthy enough to send their children and grandchildren to college. But those opportunities were never equally divided. Today higher education reflects the country's rigid class system far more than it works to equalize it.

Delivering the 1965 commencement address at historically Black Howard University, President Lyndon Johnson spoke of equality as an ongoing struggle that started at the nation's birth and would continue long after. "We seek not just freedom but opportunity," he told graduates. "Not just equality as a right and a theory, but equality as a fact and as a result." Two decades later, free-market lawmakers were slashing taxes and redefining free public college as a government handout. They embraced Milton Friedman's exhortations to deregulate corporations and get out of the way of executives who he said had no social responsibility except to make money.

Starting with Ronald Reagan, free-market lawmakers steadily replaced grants to students with loans, working to erode public support for tuition subsidies. Over time, Americans of both parties opposed free public college as a regressive boon for the affluent, even as lawmakers enacted policies that resegregated public high schools and blocked funding to help the less advantaged adequately prepare to compete for higher education. In the past four decades, "greed-driven extremes of inequality, insecurity and immobility" have put Americans on "a path that looks crazily self-destructive," political analyst Kurt Andersen concluded in the *New York Times* in late 2020.

Not long after Andersen's essay appeared, a team of research economists from MIT and Harvard released the results of a study that illuminated how crucial tuition subsidies are. Nearly three-quarters of students in the study who received full or near-full scholarships for the cost of college earned degrees in six years, 10 percent more than those who didn't receive scholarships. "The returns to [graduating] college are so large," one of the study's authors told the *New York Times*, noting that students of color whose parents never attended college gained the most. Not only do college graduates earn more than other Americans, they live longer and report higher levels of happiness, myriad studies have shown.

But even as the economy—and our lifelong well-being—demands degrees, voters refuse to fund them. Why? The myth of meritocracy deludes us into believing successful Americans use brilliance and diligence to get ahead, rather than benefiting from luck, inheritance, and a rigged system. When scarce opportunities are allocated in anticompetitive ways, no amount of individual hard work and sacrifice will make an unequal system fair. British expatriate Richard Reeves, an Oxford-educated historian who became a US citizen, despised English snobbery and class consciousness. He preferred the way Americans regard social divisions as "quaint, something to observe in wonder through imported TV shows like *Downton Abbey* or *The Crown*.

"Imagine my horror at discovering that the United States is more calcified by class than Britain, especially toward the top. The big difference is that most of the people on the highest rung in America are in denial about their privilege. Some of my most progressive friends send their children to $30,000-a-year high schools. The surprise is not that they do it. It is that they do it without so much as a murmur of moral disquiet. For Americans to solve the problem of their deepening class divisions, we will have to start by admitting their existence and our complicity in maintaining them. We need to raise our consciousness about class. And yes, I am looking at you."

Scholarly pundits like Reeves and NYU professor Scott Galloway agree that higher education is rigged. But they scorn free public college as a transfer of wealth from rich to poor. To fix growing inequality, Reeves advocates that government allocate more resources to vocational programs. Galloway suggests big tech could subsidize higher education. He says so few Americans earn degrees that voters should "resist populist proposals like free college."

Galloway's pro-business ahistorical analysis is just wrong. The New Deal and GI Bill enabled unparalleled prosperity and increasing equality in the United States. In 1947, fewer than 5 percent of Americans had degrees, compared to 45 percent in 2018. That's a lot of opportunity for a lot of people, most of them white and not nearly as rich as Galloway. Ironically, Galloway opposes a system that allowed him, raised in an apartment by a single mom who worked ten-hour days as a secretary, to benefit from government subsidies. He graduated from once-free UCLA when tuition was $1,200 a year, nearly ten times less than today's cost.

While on the faculty of New York University, Galloway started a digital marketing company that he sold for $155 million in 2017. In 2020, *New York* magazine reported that Galloway had founded a virtual classroom startup and predicted that should his market-driven tech takeover of higher education come to pass, "it will make a handful of people very, very rich."

Corporations can't fix the systemic sickness infecting higher education, one Galloway readily admits he sustains. Just one of his courses produces $1.2 million in revenue for NYU, $100,000 a night. Higher education's corporate partnerships will ultimately benefit corporations and privileged Americans like Galloway and do nothing to end the outrage that a college can collect $1.2 million from students—a lot of it from government-subsidized loans—for a single course.

To fuel the country's economic recovery, we need more publicly funded degrees, not fewer. Funding those degrees requires a long slog through leagues of political minefields that pit states and the federal government against each other. As President Biden wrangles with Congress, university executives will likely try to recoup losses sustained during the COVID-19 pandemic by moving more instruction online, enriching big tech and impoverishing real learning. That would be a mistake free public college can fix. But convincing the entitled to pay to educate others won't be easy.

There has to be something in it for them. Yes, some rich parents will send their children to free public college. And why shouldn't they? Their taxes support it. But most will continue to send their kids to Ivy-plus, elite, and highly selective schools. On the plus side, free public universities will siphon students away from incompetent private colleges, forcing prices to fall and the worst to adapt or fail. And few students will overborrow to attend expensive for-profit colleges if they can go for free to state universities, community colleges, and trade schools. Academic standards may fall as students from underfunded and poorly resourced public high schools flood free colleges. But public colleges will be filled with great professors attracted to government benefits and pay, even as affluent and wealthy students choose exclusive and expensive brand-name private colleges like NYU.

We can start to pay for public higher education by taxing Wall Street speculators 10 cents on every $100 they trade. That small tax would raise tens of billions of dollars each year, nearly $800 billion in a decade. We can also demand that lawmakers restore the Internal Revenue Service to its full vigor, with the mandate to force tax scofflaws like Donald Trump to pay their fair share. That could swell public coffers with an additional $7.5 trillion in the next decade, the *New York Times* estimated.

Finally, we can change the tax code to eliminate loopholes and raise taxes on the top 1 percent of Americans holding 40 percent of the nation's net worth, roughly one million families with an average of $25 million each. It's time for them to give back to the country that has so handsomely rewarded them. Donald Trump sold himself as a lavishly spending Horatio Alger billionaire. In fact, he's a huckster who paid no income tax in ten of the fifteen years that preceded his 2016 election, and only $750 in both 2016 and 2017. In 2020, the United States had the highest level of unemployment in nearly ninety years. While millions lost their jobs and incomes, Trump measured his administration's success with a surging stock market, an indicator that means nothing to 50 percent of Americans who have no equities, no college degrees, and little hope of bettering their diminishing financial circumstances.

After forty years of unfair economic policies that have restricted social mobility, Americans elected Joe Biden to move the country in a new direction. With a few changes, the nation can fund high-quality public degrees and have money left for health care and climate change. Fewer than 4 percent of Americans have individual incomes of $200,000 or more. That means the rest of us—the 96 percent—wield significant political power. Why has no one harnessed the clout of the 96 percent to force the 4 percent to stop hoarding wealth and start sharing resources?

The outsize profits of oligarchs and corporate America can't come at the expense of the common good. The rules must change. And the government—we the people—must change them. If the nation commits to making public college free, we can, with small sacrifice, begin to realize America's long-standing promise of equal opportunity for all. Ignorance remains, but so does opportunity. President Johnson's battle is far from over. Change begins at the ballot box.

11

Biden and Beyond

How the Game Is Changing

When parents ask, "What should worry us most?" my response is always the same: "Debt." As degrees become more important and more expensive, student debt will continue to rise, threatening the financial health of the next generation.

To afford rising college costs, many families will have no choice but to borrow more from private lenders in coming years. With no government oversight or regulation, and interest rates as high as 14 percent, "the private student loan market is the wild, wild west of consumer finance," financial aid expert Seth Frotman told the Hechinger Report.

Having a degree will continue to be a partisan dividing line. In 2016, Donald Trump told supporters at a Nevada rally, "I love the poorly educated," then spent the next four years as president attacking science and higher education. Higher education became a scapegoat for white voters unable to afford degrees or find jobs that pay living wages. By the end of 2020, jobs were scarcer than ever.

Unemployment was nearly 8 percent, more than twice what it was at the same time the previous year.

As long as wage inequality continues to grow, so, too, will inequity in college admissions and degree financing, giving greater advantages to the wealthy and well connected. Private and elite colleges will revert to propping up wealth and privilege to generate revenues, "and that will be increasingly acceptable to wealthy families familiar with the model from private K-12 education," Inside Higher Ed predicted.

In a sharp reversal of Trump administration policies, Joe Biden campaigned on a promise to "strengthen college as a reliable pathway to the middle class." He pledged to double the maximum Pell Grant to $12,690 for moderate- and low-income students, to eliminate community college tuition, and to make public colleges and universities free for families with incomes below $125,000. Until he does, though, families will have to navigate an even more convoluted path to college. The admissions landscape will continue to shift in the next decade, leaving families off balance, worried, and unable to figure out how to find the answers they need to make informed choices.

Colleges and universities will hike tuition and fees to recover pandemic losses even as many have said they would allow students to defer tuition payments for up to a year. State lawmakers will reduce budgets at public colleges, which will likely halt free tuition programs, as the University of Connecticut did in late 2020. With continued state cuts and no federal relief, the fifteen million students enrolled in public colleges and universities will be forced to make up the shortfall.

"If one were to invent a crisis uniquely and diabolically designed to undermine the foundations of traditional colleges and universities, it might look very much like the current global pandemic," Brian Rosenberg, recently retired president of Macalester College, wrote in the *Chronicle of Higher Education*. In other words, plan for change.

In a time of evolving admissions standards, families can stay ahead by anticipating coming disruptions.

Admissions barriers will fall but costs will rise.

Colleges vowed not to penalize applicants for changes in their academic circumstances, or for their inability to take standardized tests or visit campuses, according to a survey of three hundred admissions deans in 2020. The deans encouraged applicants to explain their social and financial situation in essays, including details about taking care of relatives or providing family income to "positively impact the review of their application."

Even after recovering from the most recent economic crisis, colleges can expect enrollment to fall 15 percent starting in 2025, experts predict. The good news: it will be easier to get into a great college. The bad news? It will be harder to pay for it. Most schools, fearing unfilled beds, will do whatever they can to encourage more applications, enroll students, and charge them what the market will bear.

Admissions barriers will come down. Applicants who would have been accepted to selective second-tier schools have a good shot at the Ivy League, Stanford, and Little Ivies, especially if they can pay full tuition. Colleges will recoup losses by filling classes with wealthy students or middle-, moderate-, and low-income students willing to accept loans. As the economy continues a downward slide, more and better prepared students will seek low-cost degrees at nearby public colleges and universities, creating a domino effect.

Students from the best suburban and private schools will take seats away from students trapped in low-quality, underresourced public high schools. Students who attend mediocre secondary schools and don't have the money to pay for college prep will lose scholarships to wealthier, better-prepped peers.

Colleges will hard-sell binding early decision to lock in early as much certainty as they can. More students than ever will take the bait and the loans that come with binding early decision, worsening the student debt crisis.

College admissions will become a buyer's market for the rich. Colleges that lost full-paying international students during the Trump years will recruit wealthy full payers wherever they can after Biden reverses policies that restricted foreign students from entering the country. During the Obama years, selective colleges were boosting revenues by enrolling 25 percent or more foreign students, some as much as 70 percent. Northeastern enrolled 54 percent from overseas in 2018; Columbia University, 45 percent; the University of Southern California, 33 percent; New York University, 31 percent.

In late 2020, the investor service Moody's predicted a widespread drop in net tuition revenue, the money colleges use to operate. To make up lost revenue, colleges will give preference to children of alumni and donors. "If you're a rich kid you can probably buy your way into any school you want," said Ben Miller, higher education policy analyst at the Center for American Progress. "You'll see mediocre kids buying their way into college because colleges are so desperate for full payers. If you're willing to pay full freight, I can see people making bigger jumps getting accepted to colleges they couldn't have gotten into before. So many colleges are going way down the wait-list. It's a buyer's market for the rich."

In spring 2020, top colleges were taking applicants off wait-lists even before the traditional May 1 deadline, said Bruce Poch, a veteran admissions dean at Pomona College who now directs college counseling at the Chadwick School, an elite private prep school in Palos Verdes, California. Students from families able to pay full tuition—"not necessarily the stars"—were plucked off wait-lists and asked to join first-year classes at colleges "way up in the universe of desired schools at the most-and-almost-elite colleges."

As they wait for word from wait-lists, wealthy families will hedge bets by putting down deposits at multiple colleges. That way they'll dodge traditional spring commitment deadlines and select the school with the best option of price, prestige, and location. Schools will offer bigger discounts to students threatening to accept offers from rival colleges. More colleges will reject students with substantial financial need, or offer aid packages with large loans.

Like airline fares, the cost for college will continue to vary widely from family to family.

Colleges nationwide increased tuition prices while mandating online learning for most students during the 2020–21 academic year. Texas Christian University raised tuition 5 percent; Yale, and Wake Forest in North Carolina, 4 percent; Northwestern, and the University of Southern California, 3.5 percent.

Even if colleges promise sticker-price reductions, look carefully at the bottom line. Chances are they'll reduce sticker price while reducing tuition discounts. That means no net savings for families—and likely increased costs. "If they freeze the sticker price and decrease the discount, then they've raised the price," higher education policy analyst Ben Miller said. "Right now, colleges are so desperate—it's about minimizing losses. Colleges are doing all they can to keep as many students as possible as at high a price as they can get."

Small liberal arts colleges face the bleakest financial future, especially if they depend on tuition payments to operate. Colleges will rely even more heavily on algorithms to predict how many students will enroll, how much revenue they'll collect, and how much to discount tuition to convince the most desired to attend. At the end of the process, some schools will ditch admitted students with high financial need "because they can't afford them," Angel B. Perez, CEO of the National Association for College Admission Counseling, told a *U.S. News* reporter in late 2020. Colleges will replace those students "with students with ability to pay. Every institution has a financial bottom line."

Many colleges will go out of business, merge with larger universities, or reduce sticker prices to attract more applicants. "Everyone's stuck," Miller said. "The education isn't as good as what students get in person, but it's not like colleges are realizing cost savings that will make it any cheaper to deliver. They're not saving money because professors are doing Zoom lectures. It's the same cost."

In 1978, federal Pell Grants paid half the cost for moderate- and middle-income students to attend private liberal arts colleges, and almost the entire cost of a public university, an average of $3,120 each year. In 2018, the average Pell Grant award was below $4,000, even though private colleges cost, on average, $60,000 to attend, and public universities almost $30,000. If free-market lawmakers prevent President Biden from fulfilling his promise to double Pell Grants, the financial outlook for families will worsen. "I'm afraid a lot of kids with financial need will get left in the dust," said Chadwick's Poch, largely students from moderate- and middle-income families. "That problem has never gone away. They're always the most neglected."

Test scores will continue to play a key role in financial aid awards at selective test-optional colleges both public and private.
Nearly all elite and selective colleges announced test-optional policies during the COVID-19 pandemic. How long those colleges

remain test optional depends on how quickly the economy recovers from the economic devastation the pandemic has caused.

Fewer than sixty colleges are "test blind"—meaning they refuse to consider test scores for admissions and financial aid decisions. The rest will continue to advantage high-scoring applicants. That's why students from private and wealthy suburban high schools will continue to prep for and take the SAT and ACT. Those with the highest scores will go to the front of the line for admissions advantages and tuition discounts.

"We've always said test optional is not a silver bullet. Offering a seat without money is a meaningless offer," said Robert Schaeffer of FairTest, the National Center for Fair & Open Testing. Separating high-stakes admissions test scores from financial aid "is the next frontier." Many state colleges and universities still base financial aid on test scores. The State University System of Florida's Board of Governors, for example, required applicants to Florida's public universities to take the ACT or SAT during the pandemic, stating publicly that the decision stemmed from concern about eligibility requirements for Florida's Bright Futures merit scholarship.

"It's pernicious," Schaeffer said. Especially in high-poverty states with notoriously bad public schools like Mississippi and Alabama, public universities use test scores to award grants. "Florida takes money out of lotteries that poor people support and gives it to upper-income kids who score high on the SAT," said Schaeffer. "It's reverse Robin Hood."

Ask colleges to explain the precise metrics used to award merit aid and discounts. Is it test scores? Grades? Both? If they withhold the particulars, be suspicious. And remember: only test-blind colleges flatly refuse to consider the SAT or ACT when making admissions and financial aid decisions.

Colleges will admit students using evidence easily massaged by paid consultants.

The power of paid consultants will grow. High grades in the toughest classes offered, personal essays, and letters of recommendation will become essential to get into selective colleges.

With standardized testing off the table for those who don't need merit aid, selective colleges will favor applicants from families that are wealthy enough to pay to send their children to expensive prep schools with professional college counseling staffs, and those able to hire private tutors and admissions consultants to massage their application portfolios. At some selective colleges, grades will replace the SAT and ACT as the highest barrier to admission. That means competitive applicants will need to earn the highest grades in the hardest classes their high schools offer. Parents will pay premium prices for enrichment, tutors, and private consultants to boost grades and to brand applicants.

More parents at wealthy high schools will pressure teachers to inflate their children's grade point averages. "Grade inflation is out of control," Poch said, and is fast becoming a litmus test for wealth. "The wealthier the school, the higher the grade inflation." Prep schools and public schools in wealthy suburban neighborhoods have grade inflation so severe that "basically the average grade is an A minus."

Highly selective colleges will place more emphasis on social and emotional intelligence. Those values will supersede test scores—slowly at first, but with more strength as more colleges remain test optional. "If a family is going to future-proof against admission changes they need to make sure their kids are truly engaged with academics, and not in classes just to get a good grade. They have to be learning the material, engaging with ideas, with teachers and classmates," said Arun Ponnusamy, chief academic officer for admissions consultants Collegewise. Colleges will want to know how an applicant is growing emotionally and intellectually.

"How are you impacting the community around you? It's not about raising a lot of money for charity. It's about character, integrity, resilience," Ponnusamy said. "These are the kinds of students who will be incredibly valued by the process. The ones who want to be learners and valuable citizens in the community they'll join. Colleges will place more value on finding kids with empathy that moves them to action. They'll value those kids more than just another kid with 800 on the SAT." To find out how selective colleges will choose applicants for admission, he suggests families parse the Common App's teacher and counselor recommendation checklist.

Using the Common App, the nation's most widely used application form, to its best advantage requires maximizing every section. Too many students leave empty "Additional Information," for example. "Additional Information" gives applicants the chance to provide crucial details about themselves that they're unable to showcase in other parts of the Common App. Other tips to follow when filling out the Common App include:

- Take time to thoughtfully complete all the information you provide to colleges.
- Start as early as possible. The most successful students start writing the personal statement months before the Common App launches on August 1.
- Create a Common App account as soon as it opens and start to fill out each section.
- Complete the tedious personal information section first to get it out of the way.
- Fill out the Activities section strategically. Focus on quality, not quantity.
  - Put most impactful and meaningful activities first.

- Provide detailed descriptions of your leadership, initiatives, and how you made a positive impact.
- Leave off activities that you did once or for a year and stopped.
- Carefully consider the personal statement.
  - The prompts are broad, so choose the one that best fits your personality.
  - Ask a counselor or teacher for help choosing the right prompt.
  - Write to the prompt. If you don't want to write to the prompt, choose another.
  - Tell schools something about yourself that they can't find in other parts of the Common App.

Funding cuts at public colleges will lead to overcrowded classes and increased debt for families unless lawmakers make radical changes.

Postpandemic economic structural changes will prevent even more Americans without degrees from finding jobs that pay living wages. As students search for affordable degrees at state colleges and universities, government subsidies will dry up, tuition will rise, and cash-starved schools and private lenders will entice families to borrow more money than they can afford to repay.

Public colleges in California, New Jersey, Texas, and Alaska that enroll 90 percent or more resident students will weather the disruptions better than those schools that depend on out-of-state and international students to make up the losses. Public universities that enroll 40 percent or more from out of state—North Dakota, Rhode Island, Vermont, New Hampshire, Alabama, and Mississippi, for example—will suffer most. Colleges were shuttering programs and laying off staff and faculty in late 2020. Consolidation and cutbacks will continue in the coming years.

Students looking for low-cost options will flock to community colleges, Moody's predicted, because they have few alternatives. High demand at community colleges will lead to overcrowded or closed classes. Shut-out students will borrow money to enroll at for-profit colleges. Loan volume at for-profit colleges was booming well before the pandemic, said Barmak Nassirian, director of federal relations and policy analysis at the American Association of State Colleges and Universities. Lenders and for-profit executives will continue to victimize moderate- and low-income Americans while free-market lawmakers ignore rampant fraud throughout the industry.

"The government should stop allowing the loans, but they won't do it. It's not part of their policy discourse," he said. The fraud is perpetual. "It's like buying a mattress. As soon as you think about buying a mattress, you notice there's a big sale. But because you never really thought about buying a mattress, you never realized that there's always a big sale. At that point the pitch is fresh, but it's really just the same old song."

That's how for-profit colleges stay in business. "They target low-income first-generation kids whose families have never navigated the system and don't know how it works. Rip-off joints are hiring admissions consultants which are really just boiler room operators." They succeed because they claim to give low-income students opportunity that the government refuses to provide. "To deny their students access to loans is to deny their students opportunity, they say. Opportunity for what? To be ripped off?"

Colleges and universities will rely more on distance learning, widening the gap between high-income residential learners and everyone else.
Only wealthy and high-achieving students will be able to afford traditional residential education in the coming decades, experts predict, especially if the federal government refuses to pass GI Bill–like

tuition subsidies for all Americans. Without tuition reform, the vast majority of Americans will be relegated to weaker online or partially online programs, many part-time.

Graduates of traditional residential colleges will have major advantages in employment markets, fueling increased income inequality. Even before the pandemic, Moody's Investors Service downgraded the higher education sector from stable to negative and reported that roughly 30 percent of American universities were carrying operating deficits.

Private industry will disrupt higher education even more, pressuring colleges to award students credit for work experience and expanding funding to private credential programs that serve a market niche: coding boot camps and apprenticeships in the trades and white-collar industries. Tech companies will push schools to adopt the untested distance-learning products they're peddling. Elite schools will survive, but at least one hundred small private colleges will die in the coming decade, Inside Higher Ed predicted.

More than a dozen private and public colleges announced they would close by summer 2021, including Marlboro College in Vermont, Wesley College in Delaware, Holy Family College in Wisconsin, Urbana University in Ohio, and MacMurray College in Illinois. Others announced draconian cuts to faculty. Ohio's state University of Akron fired 97 full-time professors, 17 percent of its total faculty of roughly 570, adding to an attrition that included nearly two dozen full-time teachers who had resigned or retired. Illinois Wesleyan University, a small college historically known for its liberal arts programs, announced in 2020 that it would no longer offer degrees in religion, anthropology, French, and Italian.

Before choosing a college, look for warning signs that indicate a school may shut down. At-risk colleges have fewer than one thousand students, attract a dwindling number of applicants, and report a growing number of first-year students who drop out. Any college with less than an 81 percent retention rate is flying a red flag.

How do we balance the value of the degree and the cost of the college? Many selective colleges have become country clubs with libraries. Families should question the value of paying colleges to entertain teenagers on campuses with water parks, high-tech gyms, gourmet food, expensive social clubs, and luxury housing.

Requiring students to live on campus has made housing a source of revenue. Administrators spent billions replacing barrack-style dormitories with residential amenities most Americans can't afford. Average on-campus housing costs rose at the same rate or more than tuition at public and private colleges, according to annual surveys. Room and board, a large chunk of the cost of college, is rarely included in scholarship funding. State residents attending public universities spend, on average, 43 percent of their budgets on campus housing and food; students at private four-year colleges spend nearly a quarter of their annual expenses, according to a 2020 Inside Higher Ed report.

By enrolling more students than campuses can comfortably accommodate, colleges increased revenues but degraded the academic experience. Students and faculty circled parking lots waiting for spaces to open and jammed into classrooms where they sat cheek by jowl. To assess the academic value of the degree you're buying, look for colleges and programs that allow students to connect with faculty passionate about what they teach and willing to mentor and guide them. Studies show connecting with engaged faculty keeps students in school and makes them more likely to graduate. As one faculty member said, "The answer isn't to throw classes online but to *teach* better, to connect with our students and personalize the college experience."

Ask officials about their funding priorities. What percent of the budget is spent on capital and campus expansion? What percent is spent on scholarships? What percent is spent on academic enhancement? If the president and board are spending three times more money on buildings and amenities than they are on learning, steer clear unless there's a good explanation.

Look for colleges with strong career centers and internship opportunities that aren't cash cows. Verify how much money and resources administrators invest in helping students find right-fit first jobs. This is especially important in the coming decade as colleges and universities struggle to balance the need to survive and their commitment to educating middle-, moderate-, and low-income students.

Before applying anywhere, consult the Hechinger Report's Financial Fitness Tracker to identify the financial stability of thousands of the nation's public and four-year nonprofit colleges and universities. Experts predict 40 percent of America's colleges and universities will struggle to recover from the losses the COVID-19 pandemic caused. The fitness tracker examines enrollment, tuition revenue, public funding, and endowment health, and flags those in the worst financial shape. Because the data were collected before the pandemic worsened, the authors predicted that "with the added pressures of the pandemic, the fabric of American higher education has become even more strained. Lower revenues have already forced some schools to slash budgets and could lead to waves of closings." To locate the tracker, google "Hechinger Financial Fitness Tracker" or go to https://tuitiontracker.org/fitness/.

It will take decades for higher education to recover from the losses and disruptions the pandemic caused, wrote University of Michigan economist Susan Dynarski in the *New York Times*. Is college still worth it? Yes, she said. "The lifetime payoff to earning a college degree is so very large, in health and wealth, that it dwarfs even high tuition costs. College is an especially smart choice during a terrible job market."

Now that colleges are making the SAT and ACT optional, does that mean the end of high-stress high school? No. Competition will stiffen for top grades in the hardest high school classes. Elite and selective private colleges will still prioritize applicants with high test scores and Advanced Placement classes for admissions and merit scholarships. Public pressure forced the College Board to drop its inane decision to sell the home version of the SAT in 2020. But it is still heavily marketing at-home AP testing. The AP is a significant portion of the College Board's nearly $100 million in annual revenues. Over the past decade the College Board doubled the number of AP exams it administers, up to 5.1 million in 2019. Multiply that times $94 per exam and it comes to about $470 million.

To give families a look inside the few elite colleges that loom large in the psyche of the aspiring classes, author Jeffrey Selingo analyzed three selective schools over seven months. Examining prepandemic admissions practices at the University of Washington, Davidson College, and Emory University, Selingo told a *Forbes* reporter that elite admissions is messy, arbitrary, agenda driven, murky, convoluted, and vague. While Selingo faults the process, he sympathizes with administrators in the trenches, "people trying to do their best while being buffeted by a system that few can control."

Competition for merit aid will become more unmanageable and brutal. To qualify, applicants without ACT or SAT scores will need the highest grades in the hardest classes and error-free essays and writing samples that illuminate character and intellectual development. After academics and essays, selective colleges will prioritize applicants with a clear, demonstrated interest in their particular school, for example, "Why Yale?"

Some colleges will continue replacing need-based financial grants with merit aid and small discounts to attract the wealthier students they need to meet revenue goals. Financially desperate colleges will lure applicants with even more marketing and advertising, dropping application standards and deadlines. Families would be wise to remember that "merit aid always goes to the wealthier students," said Stephen Burd, a senior education policy analyst at the research institute New America. Even moderately affluent families can no longer afford college "without vast heaps of merit aid," he said. "The whole system is whack. The next few years are going to be a real mess."

If the college you want to attend accepts 35 percent or fewer applicants, take the SAT or ACT even if those schools are test optional. You'll stand a better chance of getting into elite colleges that promise to charge only what families can afford to pay. If you score high enough, you'll get better discounts. To maximize merit aid, submit scores at or above the school's median or midpoint scores.

How will the influence of *U.S. News* rankings change? *U.S. News* changed its ranking method once again in the spring of 2020. It now ranks test-blind colleges, schools that refuse to consider SAT or ACT scores for admission or financial aid. The company also slightly reduced the weight given to SAT and ACT scores, accepted students' high school class standing, and the amount of money alumni donate.

Editors shifted a little more weight to graduation, retention, and social mobility rates. Though ranking now includes statistics on students with subsidized federal loans, there is no information on loans students take from private lenders. Private lenders will often allow students to borrow nearly the full cost of college and begin charging interest as soon as the loan is funded. The government, on the other hand, caps the amount students can borrow and won't charge interest for six months after students graduate.

Since changing the *U.S. News* methodology invalidates comparisons to previous findings, "Best Colleges" rankings are even less useful now. In 2021, top-ranked colleges stayed in the top- and lower-ranked colleges continued to battle for supremacy. The flagship University of Florida in Gainesville, for example, gamed the rankings to climb from No. 17 to No. 6 among public universities. While its ranking improved, the percent of admitted students from low-income families fell, as did the number of Black students. In a state where 22 percent of young adults are Black, fewer than 6 percent of enrolled students are Black or African American, according to the *Chronicle of Higher Education.*

Ranking colleges numerically made no sense three decades ago, and it still makes no sense, said Gerhard Casper, president emeritus of Stanford, an early and outspoken critic of "Best Colleges." "Universities don't change one year to another the way *U.S. News* captures it. It's superficial. If there's change, that creates curiosity and news. The only reason it makes sense is because it adds to the sales of the book."

How do we appeal financial aid award letters? Most families will see rising net costs, lower discounts, fewer grants, and more loans in financial aid packages. The postpandemic years will become an unprecedented time of asking for and receiving more money.

First, apply for financial aid as quickly as possible. Submit the FAFSA as soon as it's available, usually in October, to make sure you get the maximum amount before the money runs out of some state budgets. When completing the FAFSA and the CSS Profile, remember that the tax documents you submit will reflect your family's previous year's income. Current tax year losses—from job cuts, medical bills, or the death of an income-generating family member—demand individual review. After receiving an acceptance letter, immediately contact the financial aid office and request a review, also called "professional judgment."

The officer will ask for additional documents—layoff notices, unemployment checks, pay stubs proving wage cuts, medical bills—to see a fuller picture of your family's current financial circumstances. As distasteful as haggling may seem, buying a college degree has become as odious as bartering for a new car. Getting the best price requires strategy. Once acceptances arrive, ask for a price reduction. If you have a better offer from a rival college, press the college you'd rather attend to match the price.

To coach parents on how to extract more money from colleges, yet another specialized admissions industry has emerged. High-priced consultants collect data from schools, then use algorithms and software to determine which families will have the most success leveraging more money. Prices for the service range from $6,000 to $10,000 flat fees, plus hourly rates for advice. Happily, negotiating tuition discounts doesn't require paying yet another private consultant. It's just common sense if you apply judiciously:

- Avoid binding early decision unless you can pay near-full or full tuition.
- Apply to colleges where your qualifications put you at the top of the applicant pool and in the front of the line for merit scholarships, grants, and tuition discounts.
- Apply to colleges that promise to charge only what families can afford to pay.
- Make sure everyone agrees to keep annual costs at no more than 10 percent of the family's income.
- Accept only government-subsidized loans.

How do we negotiate the best deal? Start early. Develop an email relationship with admissions or financial aid officers at a few colleges so you have a personal connection when it comes time to appeal. If you visit campus, make an appointment and introduce yourself.

- If you don't have a prior relationship and you want to appeal awards from small or medium-size private colleges, call the college's local admissions representative and ask for help. At a large private college or public university, call to ask the name of the person to receive your appeal. If you can't get anyone to help on the phone, use the appeals process listed on the financial aid office website.
- Structure your appeal strategically. Make sure officials know their college is your first choice. Attach documentation to the appeal that provides specific reasons—numbers and statistics—showing why your family needs a bigger tuition discount, merit aid, or grant. Some examples: a letter that shows a more generous aid offer from a rival college; investment losses; unemployment checks; letter of job termination; death certificate; pay stubs; support checks sent to sick or aging relatives with no health insurance; job interruptions and loss to care for sick family members; medical bills; debt from necessary home repairs (roof repair is acceptable; spas or high-end appliances are not).
- Make sure to submit appeals as soon as your award letters arrive. The few weeks between receiving awards and deposit deadlines are the sweet spot to leverage and maximize discounts.
- Appeal two top-choice colleges only. Start with one; if it doesn't work, appeal to the second. If one offers a price your family can afford, send the deposit and attend. It's only fair.
- Google "financial aid appeals letter" for samples and templates.

Should we try to save money by enrolling in online schools offered by brand-name colleges and universities? No. Even when prestige colleges are selling online degrees, they're usually "the same old garbage," a well-respected loan analyst told me. "It's like a really bad restaurant that's under new management. All they did was change the sign. The food is still garbage. The management changed, but that doesn't really matter if the food sucks. What matters is: Who's the cook?"

Peddling online degrees for selective colleges is a wildly lucrative niche. Be wary of brand-name colleges outsourcing online learning to for-profit companies. In "The Creeping Capitalist Takeover of Higher Education," Kevin Carey, an education policy analyst for the research institute New America, argues that a new industry has figured out how to gouge students in creative ways. The industry helps America's most lauded colleges provide online degrees, Carey reported—including Harvard, Yale, Georgetown, NYU, UC Berkeley, UNC Chapel Hill, Northwestern, Syracuse, Rice, and USC, to name a few. Companies typically take a 60 percent cut of tuition from the college and sometimes more, Carey reported.

These invisible online program managers, obscurely called OPMs, "have goofy, forgettable names like 2U, HotChalk and iDesign." But they rake in exceptional profits, estimated at nearly $8 billion total. The $2.51 billion, publicly traded company 2U paid its CEO, Christopher Paucek, $6.6 million in 2019, the website ExecPay reported. Paucek sold $37 million of 2U stock over the past six years and is currently worth nearly $60 million, according to financial news reports. Another OPM, Kaplan University, had $1.5 billion in revenues when Purdue University purchased it in 2018. To increase its online learning market share, Purdue rebranded and converted Kaplan into the nonprofit Purdue Global.

"An innovation that should have been used to address inequality is serving to fuel it," Carey wrote. Instead of giving students reasonably priced, quality online degrees, "universities are using them as cash cows while corporate middlemen hoover up the greater share of the profits."

Is it worth attending for-profit colleges if they offer discounts? No. For-profit colleges are worse than OPMs. Many defraud moderate- and low-income students to enrich executives of billion-dollar venture capital funds. Yet enrollment is surging. The largest for-profit universities have poor graduation rates, usually no higher than 25 percent, and some in the low single digits. They mislead students, encourage them to overborrow, take their money, and leave them in debt with no degree.

Executives want to enrich stockholders far more than help students. Grand Canyon University, the University of Arizona Global Campus, and Strategic Education, Inc., are reporting record revenues. Strategic Education, Inc., parent company for Capella and Strayer universities, saw profits rise to $46.5 million, an increase from $36.7 million the year previous to the pandemic. "I hate to call anybody a winner in this crisis," a financial analyst told the *New York Times* mid-2020. "But I think growth will increase this fall and thereafter."

Choose community colleges instead, and use subsidized loans to pay living expenses. Before starting, register for classes that will transfer to a degree-granting public university. Almost always—even now—a public college or university will cost less than a low-quality for-profit school. Avoid debt if possible. Starting college with debt is like starting a race "and the guy with the starter pistol uses the gun to shoot you in the leg." That's how comedian Hasan Minhaj explained loans in an accurate send-up of cable TV's *Paid Off with Michael Torpey*, a game show where contestants compete to win money to repay student loans. Minhaj created his own version of *Paid Off*. He called it "Debt Fucked."

I have my heart set on an elite school like Harvard or Yale. How do I get in? Go *Inside the Yale Admissions Office*, a free Apple Podcasts series, to find out. A couple of admissions officers promise to divulge "everything you need to know" about the otherwise secretive admissions process and "pull back the curtain" on how officers make decisions. The first few episodes reveal that each admissions reader is responsible for reviewing nearly 1,500 applications. Most of those get tossed in less than five minutes.

"First readers" summarize favorite applicants with "a really short quip, a pithy little remark for the next admissions officer who is reading the same application." (Tip: write that pithy quip yourself so you don't have to depend on an overworked, underpaid admissions officer to do it for you.) Applicants who make it past rounds 1 and 2 go to round 3: the committee. Each wanna-be Bulldog becomes a "printed slate" with a code that "tells us a lot. We can glance at it and understand the basics." That translates into test scores, grades, and a quip. Committee members spend anywhere from thirty seconds to thirty minutes discussing before they vote.

The *Harvard Crimson* charges $65 for a "College Insights" class. The course promises to provide secrets about getting into Harvard and other elite colleges. During six virtual, self-paced classes, Harvard students share "all we know about the admissions process at Harvard and other competitive universities." They also promise to give paying participants access to Harvard admissions files. To enroll, go to the College Insights https://www.globalprograms.the crimson.com/admissions.

Should I consider going to school in Canada or the United Kingdom? As tuition at US colleges rises, more Americans will look for less-expensive degrees in Europe, Asia, and Latin America, Inside Higher Ed predicted in late 2020. It's easier and cheaper to get a world-class education in Canada or the UK, though undergraduates can expect much less coddling. American students could pursue humanities and social science degrees in the UK for about $14,000 a year in 2020. University College London was charging students an additional $11,000 a year for room and board, which is considerably more than UK universities outside London charge. Since UK colleges award degrees after three years, Americans can save a year's worth of tuition and living costs. In Canada, annual tuition cost about $11,000 in 2020. Unlike the British and US governments, the Canadians took the pandemic seriously and, as of mid-2020, had it under control, according to the World Health Organization.

The pandemic shone a bright light on how free-market lawmakers have turned higher education into a ruthless market. The British government's decade-long campaign to cut state grants forced schools to depend on tuition fees and room rents to make up the shortfall, the *New York Times* reported. Encouraged to jam more students onto campuses, one college, Manchester Metropolitan University, imposed a draconian lockdown in the residence halls as COVID-19 "tore through chockablock student suites," the *Times* reported. "Students had to nurse roommates back to health, parents drove hours to deliver food."

The Trump administration also ignored the COVID-19 threat, causing panic, loaning trillions to keep corporations afloat, and doing nothing as executives laid off millions of workers who stood in long lines for unemployment and free food. The *New York Times* compared the United States to a pirate crew forced to hand over more and more of its booty to the ship's corporate owners. The annual sum that has shifted from workers to corporate owners now tops $1 trillion. It's comparable, the *Times* said, to every American in the bottom 90 percent of the income distribution sending an annual check for $12,000 to a richer person in the top 10 percent.

Despite a seemingly bleak future, we can change the American ending. If we want to make affordable degrees an unalienable right for everyone, we can rewrite the rules that rigged the game in the first place. Making college truly affordable for all Americans will begin to right past wrongs and put the nation on the path to a more equitable future. Joe Biden has promised student debt relief and hundreds of billions of dollars in new education spending for preschool through college. Jill Biden, an English professor, is fighting for debt-free degrees. But the new administration faces strong resistance from free-market lawmakers in Congress. American voters will decide who wins the ongoing battle for justice and equality. We can advance together or stumble backward in discord and disarray. "A house divided against itself cannot stand," Abraham Lincoln warned more than a century ago. As that divide grew wider, Lincoln implored Americans to unite and move forward or face stark consequences. "We shall nobly save, or meanly lose, the last best hope of earth," he said. That choice remains.

Acknowledgments

This book draws on the efforts, insights, and intellects of more people than I can possibly name. I owe my deepest gratitude to those generous and brave enough to tell their stories. The courageous Norman Coulter, Cortney Munna, and John and Kim Turner fought through their pain, hoping it might lead to much-needed reforms. They're among a legion of colleagues, friends, family, parents, students, and sources whom I consider to be the group of thoughtful, committed citizens that Margaret Mead said can change the world.

Game On could not have been published without Bonnie Solow at Solow Literary and Stephen Power, the last executive editor at Thomas Dunne Books. Bonnie's faith, tenacity, advice, and advocacy have continued for years. She deftly edited every draft and never stopped fighting for a project that no doubt has cost her more grief than it has earned her money. Her steadfast determination is a gift I can never repay. No editor is a greater champion of writers than the incomparable Stephen, who sharpened my focus with passionate patience. The work he did to send this book into the world even after he left Thomas Dunne has been astounding and humbling. Thanks to the wonderful St. Martin's editing team: Elizabeth Beier, Hannah Phillips, Barbara Cohen, and Jennifer Fernandez carried *Game On* across the end zone.

John Nielsen and Karin Klein were crucial *Game On* players. John, a faithful and reliable reader, reviewed multiple drafts and edited almost every chapter. Karin and I were two helpless moms commiserating about our kids' college applications when we had a light bulb moment: "Hey! Somebody ought to write a book to help parents like us." Karin's astute editing and guidance carried me forward even when our paths diverged. I also drew on the fine work of her *Los Angeles Times* colleagues Teresa Watanabe, Anh Do, and Scott Martelle.

Scores of families shared financial aid letters and their personal finances to help me understand the secretive ways colleges award admission and money to applicants. Thank you, Jon Oberg, for revealing those secrets on a national scale. Jon, along with Jack Maguire and Richard Freeland, spent considerable time illuminating the history they lived and shaped.

I'm deeply grateful to Peter Paterno, Elsie Mora, and the late Arthur Fox for their unstinting support. My unflappable mentor Myron Yeager, a consummate scholar, exceptional colleague, and faithful friend, taught me all anyone needs to know about academia, integrity, and perseverance. His encouragement, wisdom, and optimism kept me going, as did dinner parties and Zoom cocktails we shared with Brad Smith.

Many thanks to my journalism colleagues and friends. Bill Davis, Mike Stanton, and Michael Grundmann have provided indispensable advice and letters of reference for decades. I never had more fun or learned more about journalism than I did with the great Rem Rieder at the *American Journalism Review*. Chuck Tobin gave me a crash course on libel and defamation while protecting press freedom in California. Thanks to the brilliant young journalists and reporters Julie Zauzmer, Michelle Hackman, and Katherine Nagasawa, who knocked on doors for hours during the pandemic to interview neighbors of a key source.

Pico Iyer encouraged long walks to puzzle through deep

questions—some related to the book. Victoria Chang helped frame many an argument. Rebecca Skloot inspired me to persevere in the face of obstacles. Marty Dugard has shared invaluable advice going back a decade. Doug Cooney's brilliance lights up every mind he engages and every room he enters.

My academic family deserves far more recognition than I have pages to give. Thanks to Joanna Levin for her constancy and myriad letters. Dean Matt Parlow challenged me to think more deeply with thought-provoking questions over numerous lunches. I could have no better friend and ally than newshound Brig. Gen. David C. Henley (ret.). Jonathan Alexander wrote a key letter and provided insight into changes at public universities. A confederacy of committed journalists teaching at Chapman had my back: Vik Jolly, Sheila Feeney, Dennis Foley, Jerry Hicks, Hal Wells, Norberto Santana, Zoey Smith, Gary Metzker, Sonya Quick, and Jeff Pearlman.

Research assistants—Blake Huntley, Danika Hazen, Tonika Reed, Sam Risak, Kylie McGuire, Lily Taylor, Maddie Moore, Ariel Banyan, Haylee Barber, Igor Bosilkovski, Mark Luburic, Gardie Royce, Katie Malin, Jenna Linden, Xavier Leong, Morgan Pullin, Sean Stroh, Katherine Lai, Morgan Yuvienco, and Kira Weiner— proved themselves to be able reporters. Jennyfer Torres, Chris Espinoza, and Mckynzie Romer provided vital insight into elite college admissions. I've learned more from my students (you know who you are) at Occidental College, Cal State Long Beach, and Chapman than I could hope to teach them.

Heartfelt thanks go to Greg Moe and David Bustillo for restoring order to our chaotic home. I still don't understand Guy McEleney's magical powers, but I'm grateful he uses them for good. Max McEleney and the late Robin McEleney taught me the meaning of "finish strong."

It's impossible to quantify how much I owe my friends. They made me laugh when I wanted to cry, edited columns, shared college admissions intelligence, offered invaluable insights, and marched into battle whenever I needed them. Thank you, Liz Blackman; Victor Mason; Hilary Hanafin; LeaAnn Gould; Laura Forbes; the Huntley family; the Collinson family; the Olson family; Barbara Granoff; Mike and Shira Strongin; "College Kelly" Curtis; Patrick Brennan; Dave Fuller; and Liz Sayre, who introduced me to the world's greatest agent.

Perhaps most important are my parents, Rina and Pat, and the visionary founders of Brooklyn College. Without them, I wouldn't be here. Finally, I'm beholden to my Occidental College mentors and professors David Axeen, Eric Newhall, and the late Roger Boesche. They taught me life's greatest lesson: the truly educated never graduate.

Index